MARK SHAW

WALKING
ON THE
WAVES

MEETING JESUS THROUGH
STORIES & SCRIPTURE

Baker Books

A Division of Baker Book House Co
Grand Rapids, Michigan 49516

Published by Baker Books
a division of Baker Book House Company
P.O. Box 6287, Grand Rapids, MI 49516-6287

Printed in the United States of America

Library of Congress Cataloging-in-Publication Data

Shaw, Mark, 1949–
    Walking on the waves : meeting Jesus through stories and Scripture / Mark Shaw.
      p.   cm.
    Includes bibliographical references (p.).
    ISBN 0-8010-6364-7 (paper)
    1. Spiritual life—Christianity. 2. Jesus Christ—Meditations. I. Title.
BV4501.3.S53 2001
232—dc21   2001025127

For current information about all releases from Baker Book House, visit our web site: http://www.bakerbooks.com

WALKING
ON THE
WAVES

To
Anne and Jonathan,
treasured companions on the great journey

CONTENTS

PREFACE

G. K. Chesterton, author of the Father Brown mysteries, always wanted to write a book about a modern Englishman who discovered England. It would go something like this. Imagine a man standing on a sandy beach. His eyes are bright with adventure. Imagine that our bright-eyed man on the beach is determined to discover a new world, a world lying out there on the wine-dark sea, like a virgin Atlantis. The man climbs into his sturdy craft and sets sail toward the great unknown. He braves storms and wild waves. He endures hot days and freezing nights. He plunges forward in darkness and fog.

Imagine this man, without knowing it, losing his way in the darkness and the fog one night. He ends up getting turned around and heading back to his sandy beach. He lands near the very place he started but doesn't recognize it. He plants his flag in the moist sand and claims it for his sovereign. The man sees his old haunts as a new world, freshly discovered, alive with possibilities, brimming with adventure and treasure. His friends and relations would no doubt think him mad, as would the queen. But who would not envy such a madman that moment of rediscovery? Who does not want that gift of new eyes to see the worn and weary world of everyday life as though it were an exotic island of new possibilities.

The subject of this book is not G. K. Chesterton's blissful madman. *Walking on the Waves* is about spirituality, a word as misunderstood as it is overused. There are as many flavors of spirituality as there are ice cream. The kind of spirituality I want to talk about is Christian spirituality, that is, a kind of Godward living that finds its inspiration in and gleans its instructions from the life of Jesus Christ.

In many ways I feel like that bedazzled explorer imagined by Chesterton. I became a Christian when I was young, but the conversion was still dramatic. When our house burned down in the middle of a January night, our family of five escaped unharmed. My parents, who had little time for God prior to the fire, afterward began to seek him. The conversion of my father made a big impression on me. He changed overnight from someone who lived only for money and success to someone who now was focused on the kingdom of God and the satisfaction of knowing Jesus Christ. His dramatic change made the message of Jesus real to me.

Soon after my own conversion, I sensed a strong call to Christian ministry, and after graduating from high school, went to a Christian college. After college, I married a woman who shared my passion for Christian service and supported me through many years of further study. Upon completion of my graduate studies, we went to Africa to teach and train leaders for the African church. Most of the last twenty years of my life have been spent in that pursuit.

During the last few years, I realized something was missing. I felt that I had made ministry the major purpose of my life rather than knowing and enjoying God. I was growing weary in my work and needed a new injection of spiritual life. I embarked on a new quest to rediscover and deepen my delight in knowing God. One of the most significant aspects of that quest was a year of study in the Gospel of Luke. The question I kept asking as I journaled my way through Luke concerned Luke's own view of the spiritual life. The writers of the Gospels, I am convinced, were geniuses who were creative theologians and thinkers in their own right. They were men so full of dazzling insights from the Spirit of God that to get on their wavelength is to get to the heart of the great questions of life and spirituality.

I was reading for the one hundredth time things I had known as a kid, but they were coming alive for me in new ways. I began to realize how much I was like the elder brother in the parable of the prodigal son. Though the elder brother worked hard near his father's house, he never had the profound homecoming experience that the prodigal did. He never enjoyed his father's love, grace, and celebration as the younger brother did, despite the elder brother's years of faithful service. I saw what a powerful role the themes of that parable played throughout Luke. I also saw that I was living to a large degree in the state of inner exile in which the elder brother lived. I wanted out of the exile. I wanted to feel the full force of the homecoming experience again. I wanted to know God, the fatherly source of life and satisfaction in all of life, through Jesus. That quest for a homecoming spirituality led on to further exploration, and, I am happy to say, deeper experiences of God. This book is a summary of what treasures I have found so far on this journey of rediscovery.

So like Chesterton's madman, I found that the greatest of all adventures is the roundabout journey of finding your way home. If you have similar longings, I invite you to ride with me out on the waves of the stories and scriptural reflections found in the pages that follow. The spiritual journey outlined in these chapters contains, I believe, a few surprising twists and turns for those interested in either Jesus as a spiritual model or the subject of spirituality in general. Let me sketch out a rough map of the voyage ahead.

1. *The use of stories.* One of the first things you'll notice about this book is that each chapter begins with a fictional story based on one of the defining moments in the life of Jesus. Readers hungry for content and more at home with ideas may be tempted to rush through the stories to get to the meat. Avoid that temptation. Rereading the Bible with the imagination unleashed can be a very useful spiritual exercise. Spiritual writers from John Bunyan to Ignatius Loyola were convinced that the imagination was a crucial tool for spiritual transformation. We can feel the awesome power of imagination when we put ourselves into a story and join the journey in progress as though we were one of the characters in the action. I do it with novels all the time. The new trick is to learn to do it with the Bible. Slow down as you read these opening stories. Imagine you are there. See yourself as part of the action. After immersing yourself in the story, feel free to move on to the reflection part of the chapter, which analyzes the episode by bringing in theological and biblical insights. Each chapter ends with a few points of application for pilgrims in hot pursuit of a true spirituality.

2. *The clash of spiritual models.* In this book, I also examine popular models of contemporary spirituality and draw contrasts between them and the spirituality of Jesus. I talk, for example, about the New Age spirituality of Deepak Chopra as well as the humanistic spirituality of Stephen Covey. Though I have learned a number of useful things from each, I tend to "pick" on these two popular writers for a reason. Most models of spirituality emphasize mysticism or morality. Chopra emphasizes mysticism. Covey is all about morality. In both cases, spirituality is an *upward movement.*

These models of spirituality demand that we become "superhuman," to a certain degree. They call us to escape from the world of everyday life and enter into a transcendent realm where the sources of mysticism or effective moral habits are found. In contrast, I present a third alternative to these two models, something I call the *homecoming* model of spirituality learned during my year soaking in Luke.

Instead of telling us to *go up*—that is, to follow the way of ascent (mystic envisioning of God or moral imitation of God)—Jesus tells us to *go back,* to return to his story in the Gospels. In other words, Jesus' model of spirituality is different from the way of mysticism or moralism. History, not heaven, is the realm of spiritual transformation. Spiritual renewal comes through entering a certain story set in the past, not ascending to an exalted state of consciousness in the present.

3. *The problem of exile stories.* You will see in the pages that follow another thing I learned from Luke. Behind our beliefs and models lie our stories. Down as deep as you can go are the stories that shape the way we view God, the world, the self, and all of life. If these controlling stories are important in shaping the way we think, and I hope to demonstrate that they are, then the wrong story can hurt someone seeking authentic Christian spirituality. These wrong stories usually start with an alienated person who is angry at God. God is seen as the enemy of fulfillment. To find fulfillment, that person believes he or she has to seize the day and steal this particular fire from the gods. Behind the prayers and postures of submission and worship lies a strong aversion or at least ambivalence to the God of the Bible. *The great paradox of modern spirituality is that our attempts to know God actually deepen our exile from him.*

Many popular brands of spirituality are in fact imprisoned in exile stories in which God is far away and it takes a Promethean act (from the character in Greek mythology who saw the gods as the enemy and stole their fire) to storm heaven and steal the fire of spiritual reality from the indifferent hand of the deity. This Promethean approach to spirituality becomes so scripted in our psyche that we actually find ourselves pursuing spirituality and spiritual disciplines (having a life vision, pursuing God's law of behavior, prayer, quiet time, church, etc.) from within a Promethean (or elder brother) exile story. My own relationship with God as a vocational missionary was stymied by a deep elder brother mentality that kept me locked in an exile story far from the enjoyment of my Father's house. But this elder brother exile story can also lead to the opposite story of the prodigal, who is in exile in the far country. As a prodigal, I can live out a story of self-love and pain-soothing indulgence.

Because these various exile stories fight within us, we need to see within ourselves the cast of characters Christ taught about in Luke 15. We are at times the arrogant and angry Pharisee, working hard in the fields of the father. At other times we are the indulgent and selfish prodigal, wasting our father's good gifts in the far country of sin and self-love. The point is that both roles belong to an exile story in which God is far away or difficult to please and the self is an abandoned orphan required to survive on his or her own. Stories of external exile (an open lifestyle of self-indulgence outside the church) and internal exile (a more hidden lifestyle of anger, arrogance, and anxiety inside the church) are just two sides of the same coin. As I discovered the hard way, even the practice of spiritual disciplines are only of limited help until we get our stories straight and escape from the downward pull of the master narratives of exile.

4. *The spiritual significance of the life of Jesus.* The main feature of *Walking on the Waves* is its focus on the personal biography of Jesus. I'm convinced that true spirituality must be defined by the life of Jesus as presented in the Gospels. To avoid the spiritualities of exile and find the true spirituality of homecoming, we need a new encounter with the story of Jesus. Each chapter of *Walking on the Waves* deals with a defining moment in the life of Christ. We will walk through the story of Jesus as he is born, baptized, and tempted. We will follow him around as he heals, transforms, teaches, dies, rises, reigns, and prepares to return.

In each of these defining moments, Jesus was aware of the closeness of God as his Father, the presence of his kingly rule, and the fullness of life in the Spirit. Instead of a spirituality driven by an exile mentality (God is far away and is the enemy), the life of Jesus points beyond the experience of exile. The life of Christ is a master narrative of homecoming—that God has returned to earth fully and forever in the person and work of Christ. The words of the father at the end of Luke 15 are thus a summary of homecoming spirituality: "You are always with me, and everything I have is yours" (v. 31). It is only in his personal story found in the four Gospels that Christ gives us a new master narrative calculated to break the grip of the exile stories of the younger brother and the older brother that haunt me and so many others.

To live, work, go to the movies, pray, mate, and minister from out of this new master narrative is the path of life. It is a life in which God is always personally present in fullness and in favor. This is the heart of the homecoming model of spirituality displayed in the life of Jesus. A new encounter with the Jesus story thus opens up the possibility of a new breakthrough in Christian living. A homecoming and narrative approach to the life of Christ breaks through the stories that are killing us and lays out a new plot that offers life and fulfillment.

Before we embark on this quest together, let me mention a few people who helped make this voyage possible. I begin with student groups who have heard pieces of what follows at campus gatherings. My thanks to students at Nairobi Evangelical Graduate School of Theology, Amherst College, and Brown University who listened and gave feedback. Many thanks to my acquisitions editor, Bob Hosack, for believing in this book even as it took some new directions not originally planned. Thanks also to the keen eye and literary ear of Melinda Van Engen, who did the editing. I have been privileged for several years to co-teach a course on spiritual development with Dr. Suraja Raman, a colleague at NEGST, and have learned much from both her words and her life. Men who have been spiritual friends and accountability partners over the years prayed for this project at various points along the way. These include Lanny Arensen, Tom Kenney, David Kasali, Sam Ngewa, George Renner, Karl Dortzbach, Oscar Muriu, Mark Olander, and Fred Nyabera. I owe you all a great deal. To my life partner, Lois, who has walked out on the waves of life with me for over thirty years, I can only whisper a thanks too deep for words. This book is dedicated to my daughter, Anne Bradsteet Shaw, and to my son, Jonathan Edwards Shaw, fellow pilgrims on the way, with the prayer that the homecoming journey described here will increasingly be their own.

Let the voyage begin. Armed with this rough map of the way ahead, you are now ready to climb into this humble craft. Push out onto the choppy waters of the wine-dark sea of spirituality. Encounter there the one who walks on the waves. Follow him through the narratives of storm and fog and darkness. Let the journey described in this book then lead you back to your own familiar beach. Walk with him on that old ground but with new eyes. Hear with new ears the whisper of the Father as he says to you, "You are always with me, and everything I have is yours." And with those new eyes and new ears, experience all of life again for the very first time.

1

OF WATER AND WINE

EXPERIENCING
THE PROMISE OF JESUS

In the case of religion and spirituality, starvation has been building for 400 years, since the Enlightenment first challenged the traditional vision of God, paving the way for Marx, Darwin, and Freud to reduce the human being to a complex of economic, biological, or psychological vectors.

Philip Zalesky, e-mail newsletter

Therefore, there is now no condemnation for those who are in Christ Jesus, because through Christ Jesus the law of the Spirit of life set me free from the law of sin and death.

Romans 8:1–2

Story: Of Water and Wine

The wedding was a smashing success, at least until the wine ran out. The red-faced father of the bride sent his servants to the neighbors to borrow what they could. They came back empty-handed. "All we have is water—and we have lots of that, Mr. Ben," his anxious butler, Ezra, said.

"Water is not enough," Ben replied, his face growing redder and his blood pressure rising. "It's dull. Wine makes everything fun."

"Nice wedding, Ben," said a familiar voice behind him. Ben turned to see Moshe, his neighbor and business rival. Ben always seemed to play second fiddle to Moshe. Besides being his competitor in business, Moshe was also the Master of the Feast, an honorary position Ben had given to his neighbor in order to impress him and maybe mend a few fences. But his attempt to impress Moshe was now about to backfire. Moshe continued.

"Too bad about the wine. Water is great, but it's so dull. Wine is like life should be—full of color and joy. You know what I mean? I always order extra wine for an event like this. Remember when my Sarah got married . . ." and off Moshe went about the great wedding he had thrown for his daughter just months before and how much he had spent. Ben couldn't stand it. He needed to silence Moshe and come up with an idea about what to do.

"Excuse me, Moshe. I've got a private stash of real vintage stuff in my cellar. I'll be right back. You'll love it." It was a lie, but at least it bought him time.

Ben staggered toward the main house wondering what he could do. It was a holiday, and all the wine shops would be closed. Just then he spotted the Theologian. Everyone knew him as a member of the prestigious Moses Seminar, which met annually at the King David Hotel to determine what Moses actually meant by some of his laws. He was even better known for his television documentary, *When Good Things Happen to Bad People: A Short History of the Gentiles.* He was also the author of the best-selling book *Ten Habits of Highly Effective Pharisees: A Modern Guide to the Law of Moses,* which had been on the *Jerusalem Times'* nonfiction best-seller list for almost a decade.

16

The Theologian was the last word on true religion, and he knew it. Ben decided to ask for his advice.

"Nice wedding, Ben," said the Theologian as Ben approached. "But you look terrible. What's wrong?"

Ben explained the wine problem.

"We have lots of water," Ben added, hoping that this information provided a clue to a solution.

"Water is great," the Theologian responded with a weak smile, "but it's dull. Wine makes people celebrate life."

"Yes, I've heard that," Ben said, his face now turning a plum-like purple.

"I've got just the solution," said the Theologian. "You know the law of Moses covers all the issues of life. One of the ways I cope with a crisis like this is to remind myself of some of the habits of highly effective Pharisees. I like to be proactive rather than reactive. Reactive people would just run around red-faced in the face of a problem like this. Proactive people pray and act."

The Theologian then put on his prayer shawl, lifted up his face, and prayed. As soon as he finished, he turned to Ben.

"Do you have any water jars?"

"Yes, I've got about six thirty-gallon jars."

"Perfect," said the Theologian. "Fill them with water, and I'll bless them. Then you can serve your guests holy water. You might want to pass the word that I was the one who blessed the water," he said with a wink.

"But water is dull. You said so yourself," Ben protested.

"Now, now, Ben. Ineffective people are negative and reactive. Who says we are supposed to enjoy life? Obedience to the ten habits is what's important. Holy water is the perfect solution to the problem. Let's be proactive here. I can feel the synergy already."

Just as Ben was about to call Ezra, a tall thin man nearby looked his way. Ben recognized him as the Philosopher, a visiting scholar from overseas. The Philosopher cleared his throat.

"I couldn't help overhear what the two of you were talking about. Holy water is certainly an option, but have you considered other possibilities?"

"Like what?" Ben and the Theologian asked at the same time.

"Don't you think some of the problem is really in your head? We think we need wine in order to feel happy and to celebrate life. I have discovered that I can feel happiness and the joy of life simply by altering my consciousness. You don't need either wine or water. You need to sense a higher reality than the conflict or anxiety experienced on this level of reality. I have found the wisdom of the East far superior to your law of Moses as the path of satisfaction. Why worry about water or wine when you can drink in the ocean of infinite spirit?"

Ben was speechless. The Theologian was livid. He and the Philosopher exchanged words. The Theologian was particularly loud in advocating the way of the law.

At that point Ben noticed an attractive girl, probably in her first few years of university, standing nearby. He smiled. She smiled back and gave him a look that spoke of boredom mingled with intelligence. When there was a lull in the conversation, she spoke up.

"Sorry to interrupt, gentlemen. I'm not really into weddings very much, but if you want this one to be a good time, then I think we should try both approaches. When it comes to the world of spiritual reality, I'm all for a little bit of this and a little bit of that. You know what I mean?"

Both the Philosopher and the Theologian looked disapprovingly at the Girl. Ben looked more bewildered than ever. Before anyone could speak, an African Woman who had stopped to listen to the discussion moved closer to the small circle of agitated people.

"Pardon my intrusion. Your search for spiritual solutions to this problem is not going to help this man or his wedding guests. I think a more pragmatic solution is needed. Where I come from water is enough. When you struggle simply to survive, wine is a luxury few can afford. If you've run out of wine, let them drink water. Let them be reminded how the rest of the world lives. Water may be dull, but it's better than wine that doesn't exist."

This brought the conversation to an abrupt end. Mumbling their apologies, each one drifted off to another part of the gathering. Ben hurried up the path toward the house. He was looking behind him, dazed by the conflicting advice, when he bumped into a woman on the path and almost knocked her down.

"Mary Joseph, pardon my clumsiness," Ben said to her, now pale from worry. "I'm so distracted by the wine crisis and the contrary advice I've received that I don't even know where I'm going."

"What crisis?" she asked.

He explained about the wine and the advice he had received from the Theologian, the Philosopher, the Girl, and the African Woman.

"What would you do in my situation?" he asked, and then regretted it. The last thing he needed was another opinion.

"Let me ask my son about this," Mary said. She trotted off, and Ben went onto the verandah of his house and sat down to think.

Five minutes later, Mary was back. Ezra was beside her accompanied by a dozen servants carrying the six water jars. Slightly behind them both and surrounded by a crowd of people was her son, or so Ben presumed. He saw that the Theologian, the Philosopher, the Girl, and the African Woman were part of the group of spectators.

"Do whatever he tells you to do," Mary said to Ezra. The servant glanced up at Ben. Ben nodded in agreement, too exhausted to do anything else.

The crowd waited for Jesus to do something.

"Fill the jars with water," he commanded.

Both the African and the Theologian smiled. They suspected that their advice was about to be followed. After the jars had been filled with water, Jesus spoke again.

"Now take some out and give it to the father of the bride." Ezra scooped out a goblet full and then gasped. The water was bloodred. He steadied himself. He looked up. Jesus spoke.

"Wine is like life should be—full of color and joy."

Ezra smiled, took the cup to the porch, and handed it to Ben.

The weary host was as puzzled as everyone else. He sniffed the goblet. It smelled good. He looked deep into its purple contents. It looked good. He put the edge of the cup to his lips. The taste was sensational.

Ben noticed Moshe slowly chugging up the hill to the house. He had an inspiration.

"Ladies and gentlemen, Moshe, the honorary Master of the Feast has arrived just in time to give us his expert opinion on the new supply of wine. Moshe, my good friend, come and take a sip."

The crowd waited while Moshe, eyes squinted in skepticism, gingerly lifted the goblet to his lips. They all watched as he swished the wine around in his mouth. Then he spoke.

"Ben, you've pulled it off. I thought you'd run out of wine. In fact, you simply got rid of the average stuff so that you could pull out the best vintage I've ever tasted. This must have cost a fortune." Moshe looked at his neighbor and rival with new admiration. Ben beamed with pride. But all eyes were on the young man from Nazareth. (Based on John 2:1–11.)

The Spiritual Quest

The letter caught me by surprise. Jeremy (I'll call him), one of my best friends back in high school, contacted me out of the blue after we had lost touch for several decades. Our paths had separated dramatically after graduation. I had gone off to Africa as a career missionary. Jeremy had pursued a career in art, eventually becoming an artist for the movie industry in Hollywood and living the lifestyle traditionally associated with Hollywood types. We lived worlds apart, and not just in miles. "Religion" was never an option for Jeremy, I had concluded. But then his letter came. He had returned to God, he informed me, reclaiming his Catholic heritage with a splash of Eastern religion tossed into the mix. He was the last person I imagined bumping into on the freeway of spiritual questers. Yet there we were, bumper to bumper, together with other baby boomers and their kids, looking for signs of God in the American landscape. Like the characters in our opening story, Jeremy had found his way into the wedding feast and was looking for a new life in a world grown boring and unsatisfying. His search for new wine led him to eavesdrop on the approaches to life represented by the various characters in the story.

Millions of people have joined Jeremy in the journey inward. This journey is in many ways a search for new wine. One doesn't have to listen long to hear the growl of spiritual hunger pains in the midst of our bored and dissatisfied culture. Consider the words of generation-X novelist Douglas Coupland. At the end of his novel *Life after God*, one of his characters offers a final diagnosis about what ails the world:

> Now here is my secret; I tell it to you with an openness of heart that I doubt I shall ever achieve again, so I pray that you are in a quiet room as you hear these words. My secret is that I need God—that I am sick and can no longer make it alone. I need God to help me give, because I no longer seem capable of giving; to help me be kind, as I no longer seem capable of kindness; to help me love, as I seem beyond being able to love.[1]

This sense of dullness in the soul that Coupland describes is fueling much of the modern interest in spirituality. And modern resurgence there undoubtedly is. As Philip Zalesky reminds us, "Religion is riding high in the American saddle: 90 percent of us pray regularly; 50 percent of us attend weekly church. As sociologist and priest Andrew Greeley puts it, we are 'a nation of mystics.'" Spiritual writing regularly tops the best-seller lists and fills the briefcases of corporate kingpins and the backpacks of college students.[2]

This new quest inward has been called a revolution of sorts. It began in the 1960s, when "people turned to drugs, sex, gurus of every stripe, whatever breached the walls of the mechanistic box in which they had been caged." Now at the beginning of the new millennium, things are calming down. "The period of free-form experimentation has passed into one of more disciplined searching. New approaches to religion abound, exemplified by such diverse movements as the New Age, the post-Vatican II Catholic Church, and the importation of Eastern practices to Western shores. At the same time, vast numbers of people have returned to traditional faiths with renewed vitality."[3]

A casual critic might dismiss this resurgence as just another fad, like hoola hoops in the 1950s or pet rocks in the 1980s. Zalesky thinks otherwise. This current revolution is a revolt against reductionism. As with other great movements, such a spiritual revolution

> rarely blossoms in response to immediate social problems. Rather, it answers a long-felt need, a desperate hunger grown more acute over decades or even centuries. In the case of religion and spirituality, starvation has been building for four hundred years, since the Enlightenment first challenged the traditional vision of God, paving the way for Marx, Darwin, and Freud to reduce the human being to a complex of economic, biological, or psychological vectors.[4]

The reductionism of Enlightenment ideology destroys human wholeness. Secularism produces not satisfaction but boredom. As Eugene Peterson explains:

> Our secular culture has failed precisely because it is a *secular culture*. A secular culture is a culture reduced to *thing* and function. . . . It is wonderful to have this incredible freedom to *do* so much, without bothering about relationships or meaning. But after a few years of this, our delight diminishes as we find ourselves lonely among the things and bored with our freedom.

Secularism kills off the "two essentials" of human satisfaction: intimacy and transcendence. Peterson continues:

> *Intimacy:* we want to experience human love and trust and joy. *Transcendence:* we want to experience divine love and trust and joy. For this reason "spirituality," a fusion of intimacy and transcendence, overnight becomes a passion for millions of North Americans.[5]

This "revolution against reductionism" fuels this new quest for inner wholeness and satisfaction. Some of the key questions new seekers are asking deal with the deepest and most intimate questions of life.

21

In the collage of questions being asked about spirituality today, I recognize at least nine life issues that have become central for millions:

1. The issue of dullness: How do I find life and enthusiasm in a world grown dull and bored?
2. The issue of emptiness: How do I find love in a world that has forgotten how to love?
3. The issue of loneliness: How do I find community and peace in a world of diversity and differences?
4. The issue of homelessness: How do I find a place to belong in a world of enmity and alienation?
5. The issue of fatherlessness: How do I find truth and wisdom in a world of confusing ideologies and competing theories?
6. The issue of evil: How do I find comfort and justice in a world of evil and suffering?
7. The issue of powerlessness: How do I find the power to love and live in a world that overwhelms me and saps my strength and energy?
8. The issue of hopelessness: How do I find hope and vision in a world that is uncertain about the future?
9. The issue of aimlessness: How do I find direction and purpose in a world that has no direction?

These are some of the most important issues of life. Human beings in their quest for happiness need to find satisfying answers to such critical questions. I am personally concerned about each of these life issues. I remember as a college student greedily devouring the novels of Herman Hesse with their Eastern vision of an earthy spirituality. Ultimately, my quest led me back to my Christian roots and to a fresh look at how the story of Jesus provides pertinent answers to these great questions.

In our opening story about the wedding at Cana, the first life issue is addressed. Ben, the harried father of the bride, has a problem. He's got lots of water but no wine. And as everyone reminds him, water is nice, but it is dull. Wine, however, gives color and gladness to life. In the story, Ben is given all kinds of advice about what to do about the wine issue. These views represent popular models of spirituality today and how they deal with the first life question: How do I find life and enthusiasm in a world grown dull and bored?

In this first chapter, we will look more closely at some of these popular models of spirituality and how they tackle this question. We will also look at the way the story of Jesus answers this question. By the time we wrap up our discussion, I hope one important answer is clear: *We overcome dullness through the love that changes water into wine in all of life.* Before we can make sense of this statement, though, I'd like you to follow me on a quick tour of the models offered by two popular writers on spirituality, Deepak Chopra and Stephen Covey. We'll end up coming back to our story and to the unique third model championed by Jesus.

Popular Models of Spirituality: Deepak Chopra and Stephen Covey

When *Newsweek* magazine ran the cover story "The Search for the Sacred: America's Quest for Spiritual Meaning," one important trend was clear: America's taste in spirituality is decidedly post-Christian. The two most dominant forms of spirituality, the new mystic model represented by writers such as Deepak Chopra and the moral model represented by Stephen Covey, marginalize traditional Christian theology in their quest for meaning.

The new mysticism is most clearly seen in the New Age movement. For well over a millennium, Western spirituality has been shaped by the story of Jesus and the cadences of the biblical narrative. In a song she wrote for Woodstock in 1968, Joni Mitchell sang that she wanted "to get back to the Garden," describing her spiritual quest in biblical terms. My guess is that few twenty-year-old songwriters today, searching for a metaphor of the spiritual journey, would use such terminology. Today the dominant imagery of the spiritual life does not come from the stories of the Christian West but rather from the mystic East. Since the 1960s, global spirituality has seen a new "Easternization" of spirituality. Consider these postcards from the spiritual front:

- In a recent best-seller, *The Art of Happiness: Handbook for Living,* the Dalai Lama and Howard Cutler, M.D., write about the importance of "reclaiming our innate state of happiness."[6] They observe what most of us have observed: Our outer world produces a great deal of suffering and throws up a host of obstacles to this inner happiness. Their key is "training the mind for happiness." How does one do this? Through developing positive thinking that makes one's inner mental state more real than the outer world of suffering. This positive mental state is called *dharma*, derived from a Sanskrit word meaning "to hold back." Dharma techniques enable the practitioner to mentally block out external reality, thus creating a garden of peace and wholeness within.

- In another popular study, *Awakening to the Sacred: Creating a Spiritual Life from Scratch*, Lama Surya Das promotes the disciplines of *dharma*, which leads to "recognizing and realizing who we are."[7] This is done through a series of meditations that internalizes the concept of infinity. One technique is "sky-gazing meditation." Another method is "oceanic goddess meditation." The purpose is to fill your mind with any meditation that releases you from your imprisonment to the particular (time, space, body, history) and lifts your inner self to union with pure spirit—the impersonal and infinite oneness that lies behind all things. For Lama Surya Das, spirituality is an inner escape from creation and its suffocating limits.

- In Leslie Kenton's *Journey to Freedom: Thirteen Quantum Leaps for the Soul*, the author addresses the "post freedom hangover" that many people are feeling after a decade or two of too many drugs, too much sex, and unrestrained hedonism. "Like the proverbial iceberg," Kenton writes, "most of us live with the lion's share of our potential for freedom, joy, creativity, and power submerged beneath a sea of unknowing."[8] The key to tapping this hidden potential for happiness within us is to follow the advice of Joseph Campbell: "If you realize the problem is losing yourself to some higher end or to another—you realize that this itself is the ultimate trial. When we quit thinking primarily about ourselves . . . we undergo a truly heroic transformation of consciousness."[9] We must become a new Greek hero, one like Prometheus, who stole fire from the gods in order to promote the betterment of life on earth. London's *Sunday Times* called Kenton's message "life transforming."

Deepak Chopra and the Mystic Model of Spirituality

While these recent publications bear witness to the Eastern element in the new spirituality, more conclusive proof comes from the pen of one of the most successful contemporary writers on spirituality. Deepak Chopra is the author of *How to Know God, The Path to Love: Spiritual Lessons for Creating the Love You Need,* and a host of other popular publications on the inner life.[10] Chopra believes he knows the way home to God for this generation. The way home calls for a journey of seven stages. The final stage, however, is not exactly coming home to God but rather discovering that you are God. Our true spiritual home is the place where we completely identify and equate ourselves with the infinite. History and daily life are only marginal to this seventh stage in the spiritual journey. Chopra's model of spirituality can be diagrammed as follows.

FIGURE 1

Deepak Chopra's Mystic Model of Spirituality: Up and Away

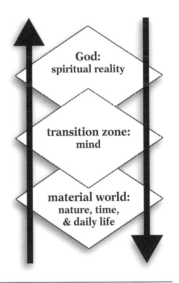

Stage 7: Infinity—I am one with God.
Stage 6: Identity—I am a servant of God.
Stage 5: Fantasy—Power of God to make things come true.
Stage 4: Self-deception—Strong intuition guides me but can be wrong.
Stage 3: Fatalism—I have inner peace, but a greater force controls my life.
Stage 2: Control—I am in charge.
Stage 1: Fear—I will fight or flee all opposition.

God: spiritual reality

transition zone: mind

material world: nature, time, & daily life

Once we have achieved the higher levels of consciousness, we can return to the issues of everyday life with this new consciousness, which opens up the way for new fulfillment, power, success, and happiness.

Basic to his model is the idea that reality is a "sandwich" of three layers. The crude crust of the reality sandwich is the material layer, depicted by the bottom diamond in the figure. This is the world of nature, culture, and daily life. It is also the world of frustration and despair. In order to escape from the frustrations of the bottom diamond, we need to explore the higher levels of reality. The second level of reality is the transition zone. This is the realm of the mind and the laws of science, such as quantum physics. Chopra believes that quantum laws, with their laws of unpredictability, show that reality is not just material; we live in a world in which anything can happen. The transition zone is a place of wonder where our view of the world is transformed. The highest level of reality is the virtual zone where the primal energy of the universe dwells. When our minds move through the lower levels and finally arrive at this level, we can experience unprecedented peace and power.

This model of spirituality advocates the way of ascent: We need to escape from the material world of everyday life, time, space, and issues in order to develop a new consciousness that will help us better cope with all the challenges of the material plane of existence. Chopra uses Jesus throughout his book to show the various stages of ascent into the new consciousness. He thereby implies that the true significance of Jesus for spirituality is that Jesus himself went through these stages and developed this new consciousness. We might call Chopra's model the mystical model because it emphasizes inner states of consciousness as opposed to behavior and action.

How does it address the problem of boredom? Like the Philosopher in our opening story, dullness is overcome not by changing water into wine but by a new consciousness, the ascent of the mind into virtual reality. Dullness is built into creation itself. We must escape from the world of dullness, the water world, into the infinite ocean of ultimate spirit. Wine is a state of mind not a commodity of the material world.

Stephen Covey and the Moral Model of Spirituality

Stephen Covey presents another popular but dramatically different model of spirituality. Covey's book, *Seven Habits of Highly Effective People*, impressed millions. It offers practical guidelines or "habits" that can add quality to our lives. In a series of follow-up volumes, Covey applies his moral vision to families, leaders, and other specific groups. At the heart of his practical spirituality of everyday living is the cultivation of seven habits that include being proactive, being personally visionary, managing the vision, seeking to listen first, thinking win-win, seeking synergy with others, and sharpening the saw through regular renewal activities.

Like Chopra, Covey also implies that reality is multilayered. In figure 2, the three levels of reality assumed in Covey's writings are depicted. Above the material world is the world of mind and conscience where the laws or habits of effective living can be comprehended. At the uppermost level of reality, God the lawgiver dwells. He is the source of effective living not because he forgives and transforms by his grace (as classic Christianity claims) but because he gives

FIGURE 2

Stephen Covey's Moral Model of Spirituality: Up and at 'Em

We tap the law of God and unleash its power by practicing seven habits:

1. Being proactive
2. Being personally visionary
3. Managing the vision
4. Seeking to listen first
5. Thinking win-win
6. Seeking synergy with others (many people working together with surprising results)
7. Sharpening the saw

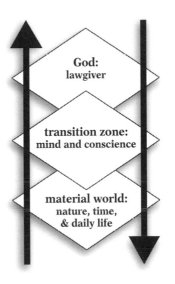

Unlike Chopra, Covey emphasizes success in earthly life through the application of moral laws. Covey believes that these laws come from God and are built into the nature of the universe. Obedience to laws, not altered states of consciousness, is the path to fulfillment and the way to solve the major life issues. Like Chopra's model, mastering these seven laws and making habits out of them is also a spirituality of ascent in that it is within our power to become God-like in these practices. We may receive supernatural assistance, but Covey is clear that we have all the natural powers within us to achieve this true spirituality of law. For Covey, Jesus is an example of someone who personified these seven habits in his life.

---

us the natural abilities to think and behave in a way consistent with the seven habits. In contrast to Chopra's model, Covey's model can be called a "moral" model of spirituality because it emphasizes practical behavior in the visible world rather than the achievement of altered states of consciousness. Covey would address most of the life issues mentioned earlier by affirming our natural powers to tackle such challenges. Through developing proper habits, we can solve these problems.

Like the Theologian in our opening story, Covey sees moral laws, what he calls habits, as the real key to transforming our lives. As we make ourselves a slave to these good habits, we find our attitudes changing. Instead of being reactive and negative about life, we become proactive and positive. Water isn't changed into wine, but we can make "holy water," that is, we can treasure what we do have as a sacred gift with value and meaning. This approach is an attractive and accessible model for millions of people who grew up without the "character ethic" Covey has so lovingly rediscovered and republished. "Do right and you will feel right" might be the motto that followers of Covey would put on their bumper stickers.

Jesus and the Problem of Boredom

In contrast to the mystic model and the moral model, the spirituality of Jesus stands out as a radical alternative. Jesus, as our opening story suggests, wants to change more than the way we think or behave. He wants to change life itself. Unlike the mystic who seeks to escape creation, Jesus wants to renew it. Unlike the moralist who emphasizes the role of the human being in adding a sense of the sacred to daily life, Jesus emphasizes the divine role in changing not only the individual but all of life as well. Karl Marx once complained that all philosophers wanted to do was interpret the world when they should be out changing it. Jesus couldn't agree more. His purpose and his promise is to change the world as it is and us along with it. Jesus comes to us as the embodiment of a love that changes water into wine in all of life. How do I know that? I've been thumbing through the snapshots he left behind, pictures that capture his true intentions. Consider the following snapshots.

Snapshot #1: Jesus pictured his work as the restoration of joy to life. The episode at the Cana wedding points to Jesus' intention to restore gladness and richness to daily life and to the whole of creation. The biblical basis of our opening story is found in John 2:1–11. You won't find the Theologian, the Philosopher, the Girl, or the African Woman in John's account, but you will find Jesus turning water into wine. What was he trying to say to his audience then and now? John himself, who was an eyewitness of the miracle, offers his own clue in verse 11 to the meaning of the episode. John calls this miracle a "sign" that would "reveal his glory." What John is driving at here is that the action of changing water into wine tells us something significant about the purposes of Jesus. He is sending a message to the world about who he is and what he is up to. What might that message be?

28

Jesus' arrival in the first-century world, as I shall develop in later chapters, is a completion of two stories, both begun in the Old Testament. The first story is the story of Israel. The miracle says something about the Jewish story and its expectations as found in the law and the prophets. We can be more precise about this because the miracle of the wine is a direct link to a prophecy found in Isaiah 25:6–9. The words of Isaiah speak about the last days of history when the God of Israel will put on a massive feast for his people to celebrate his victory over the whole earth:

> On this mountain the LORD Almighty will prepare
>   a feast of rich food for all peoples,
> a banquet of aged wine—
>   the best of meats and the finest of wines.
> On this mountain he will destroy
>   the shroud that enfolds all peoples,
> the sheet that covers all nations;
>   he will swallow up death forever.
> The Sovereign LORD will wipe away the tears
>   from all faces;
> he will remove the disgrace of his people
>   from all the earth.
>   The LORD has spoken.
>   In that day they will say,
> "Surely this is our God;
>   we trusted in him, and he saved us.
> This is the LORD, we trusted in him;
>   let us rejoice and be glad in his salvation."

The wine of Cana is the wine of the last days, the wine of joy and gladness that indicates that the day of salvation—the day of the restoration of paradise and the end of death and tears—has arrived. Jesus is claiming by his miracle not only to be able to lift boredom from Jewish lives (and others through Israel's witness) but in fact to restore the paradise experience of the Garden of Eden, before death and tears entered human history. Thus, Jesus announces that he has come to complete the story of Israel by inaugurating the restoration of paradise.

This reference to the restoration of paradise points to the second Old Testament story that Jesus came to complete. That is the story of us all. Jesus is signifying by his miracle that he has come to restore not just the promised world of Isaiah 25 but also the original world

The kingdom of God now/but not yet

is this restoration after we die or now?

of Genesis 1 and 2. This is the world of the original creation, before Israel existed. Jesus is holding out the promise, then, that he intends to turn everyone's world, not just Israel's, into a paradise where boredom, dullness, death, and tears are banished and where joy and restoration dominate. The kingdom is not just a new reality in history. It is the renewal of the reign of God over his world as it had been in the beginning before the fall of humanity.

Snapshot #2: Jesus promised that his work would restore joy and fullness to life. If one has any doubts about what Jesus' sign at the marriage feast of Cana means, matters should be cleared up by the stated promise of Jesus in John 10:10. Unlike the thief who robs, says Jesus, "I have come that they may have life, and have it to the full." The context of the verse is Jesus' discussion of Israel's "shepherds," which in the Old Testament was almost always a reference to the political leaders of the nation. The King Herods of Jesus' day were interested only in squeezing what they could out of the people. Unlike greedy and corrupt leaders, Jesus is promising that when his rule is inaugurated, he will make it the priority of his administration to fill everyone with life to the full. Accordingly, "under his protection and by his gift they can experience the best life can offer. In the context of John's emphasis on eternal life, this statement takes on new significance. Jesus can give a whole new meaning to living because he provides full satisfaction and perfect guidance."[11]

when does this take place?

Snapshot #3: Jesus preached the restoration of creation. Even more to the point, Jesus preached a spirituality that would restore earthly life completely. This preaching of the restoration of creation is found in Luke 4:18–19. The setting is the return of Jesus to his hometown of Nazareth. He has been asked to preach to the hometown crowd at the Saturday service, and the synagogue is teeming with anticipation. Everybody seems interested in what this promising young rabbi will say. He stands up and preaches one of the shortest messages the audience has ever heard. He begins by reading the powerful words of Isaiah 61:1–2: "The Spirit of the Sovereign LORD is on me, because the LORD has anointed me to preach good news to the poor. He has sent me to bind up the brokenhearted, to proclaim freedom for the captives and release from darkness for the prisoners, to proclaim the year of the LORD's favor." Jesus' simple one-point message captures everyone's attention: "Today this scripture is fulfilled in your hearing" (Luke 4:21). The Isaiah passage, as his audience knew, goes on to state that this renewal movement will be for the benefit of those who have lost their joy in life. The agent of Israel's God would come and "bestow on them a crown of beauty instead of ashes, the oil of gladness instead of mourning, and a garment of praise instead of a spirit of despair" (Isa. 61:3). Though his sermon ended in a riot, his point was unmistakable. Jesus saw himself as the agent who would give beauty instead of ashes, gladness instead of mourning, and joy instead of despair. His model of spirituality was committed to the restoration of joy in daily life, not to the abandonment of daily life to dullness, boredom, and nihilism.

Snapshot #4: Jesus predicted the restoration of creation. In Matthew 19:28–29, Jesus made one of the boldest statements of his career. Speaking about the end of history, he described the climax of the human journey not in apocalyptic or gloomy terms but rather in the most hopeful terms imaginable. Answering Peter's implicit complaint ("We have left everything to follow you"), Jesus grants the cost-conscious disciples a glimpse of the real bargain they have received. "I tell you the truth," he explains, "at the *renewal of all things,* when the Son of Man sits on his glorious throne . . . everyone who has left houses or brothers or sisters or father or mother or children or fields for my sake will receive a hundred times as much and will inherit eternal life" (emphasis added). Note Jesus' positive view of the future: Everything will be made new. The word used here, *palingenesis,* is a rare one in the New Testament, literally meaning a new beginning or a new genesis. The world of creation and culture will be completely renewed. Earthly life will be restored. Material blessings will be passed around. Life on earth will be made shiny and new again.

At this point someone might raise an objection. Isn't the death of Christ the major focus of Christianity? If Christian spirituality is obsessed with the death of its founder, how can one pretend that Jesus is all about life and renewal? Such an objection takes note of an important truth—the central act of the life of Jesus is his death. It is further true that some Christians focus on his death in such a way that there is little emphasis on the life-giving intentions of Jesus. Dallas Willard complains about just such a life-denying focus by the theologians of the religious right and left.

When we examine the broad spectrum of Christian proclamation and practice, we see that the only thing made essential on the right wing of theology is the forgiveness of the individual's sins. On the left it is removal of social and structural evils. The current gospel then becomes a gospel of "sin management." Transformation of life and character is no part of the redemptive message. Moment-to-moment human reality in its depths is not the arena of faith and eternal living.[12]

If much of contemporary Christianity focuses on the death of Jesus largely as the way to get one's sins forgiven, how then can we say Jesus came to give abundant life? Wouldn't it be truer to say that he came to perform a difficult legal transaction to take care of certain punishments and penalties we incurred? This hardly addresses the whole of life.

At first blush these objections to the Christian emphasis on the death of Jesus have an element of truth. Some Christians do restrict the value of the death of Jesus solely to the removal of sins. We will see in the pages that follow how necessary this forgiveness is in order to experience the fullness of life. But it does so much more. The death of Christ makes possible the renewal of life in all areas and in every way. The cross is a tree of life that removes all the forces of death and dullness. It will transform the waters of our doomed existence into the wine of joy and gladness.

One of the most fascinating stories of world Christianity is taking place in the African nation of Sudan. Most of us know Sudan as a place of poverty and violence, where nearly forty years of civil war have produced atrocities on an epic scale, such as the return of slavery and the systematic genocide of non-Muslim tribes by the Muslim government. But Sudan has another story to tell the world. Christianity has existed in that ancient land for over sixteen hundred years. Recently, however, Sudan has been experiencing large-scale revival. It now has one of the fastest-growing Christian movements in the world. Sudanese Christianity emphasizes the cross of Christ, which dominates their songs and prayers. I recently saw a picture of a medieval Sudanese cross. It was remarkable in its exquisite shape and intricate design. What captured my attention, however, were the roots and branches sprouting from the cross. The meaning was clear. The cross is not just a symbol of death. It is a symbol of a life-giving death. The cross of Christ is a tree of life not just a place of execution. Through that execution all of heaven has now opened and the showers of new wine drop on our weary lives and lift us up.

To those who discount Jesus' life-giving powers due to the centrality of his death in Christian thinking, we respond that the death of Jesus is a death that gives life. Jesus comes to us as a scarecrow

not only personal forgiveness but reconciliation

God who drives away all the forces that threaten the harvest of life. The purpose of his death, like the purpose of the scarecrow, is to maximize the fruits of the farm, not to abandon them. We will look more closely at this idea in chapter 6.

So how would Jesus respond to our first life question? How can we restore life and joy to a world that has become dull and bored? Mysticism is not his answer. Morality is not his answer. Jesus doesn't wait for people like the Philosopher to change people's level of consciousness or for the Theologian to renew their sense of the sacredness of the ordinary. Jesus will change life itself by his touch and his power. When Jesus enters a life, just as when he attends a wedding, he has one purpose—to maximize joy and gladness by restoring the beauty and the bounty of life. The goal of Jesus is to unleash the love that changes water into wine in all of life.

Experiencing the Promise of Jesus

Like my friend Jeremy, most of us want a spirituality that helps us not only *cope* with everyday life but *transform* it. Chopra and Covey have offered some useful advice about how to do that, but their transformation is one of attitude. Jesus is interested in inward transformation, but that's not all. Jesus wants to transform us in at least four ways.

First, Jesus wants to transform our view of the world. History is full of spiritualities that were either uncritical world-affirming spiritualities (whatever is, is right) or equally uncritical world-renouncing spiritualities (whatever is, is wrong). Jesus calls us to a third way between these extremes.[13] His call to new life, to the new wine of Christian spirituality, is *critical* in that it does not simply accept the world as it is. He insists that this world of death and tears must be changed, radically transformed. Beyond our dullness and boredom is a terrible fear that life is meaningless or cruel. We hide behind boredom in order to mask our fear. Jesus wants to change the world to remove the fear. At the same time, Christian spirituality is *world-affirming* in that it never gives up on creation and daily life, never advocates a mystic escape from creation.

True spirituality does not reject creation or daily life but seeks to redirect it for good. Human nature itself must be changed as part of this critical world-affirming spirituality. Alister McGrath explains why the restoration of creation is so important for Christian spirituality:

> The doctrine of creation affirms that the material world was created by God, and in some way reflects God's goodness. This has major implications for Christian spirituality. For example, it affirms that it is not necessary to withdraw from the world in order to secure salvation or to serve God properly. One of the most interesting developments in modern spirituality is the emergence of forms of spirituality which are specifically directed to those working in the marketplace, dedicated to allowing them to live the Christian life to the full while continuing to work outside specifically or explicitly religious contexts (such as monasteries or seminaries). It also affirms that caring for the world—including both the environment and human beings—is of profound spiritual importance, thus offering major motivation for environmental and welfare work.[14]

When Jesus turns water into wine, he announces his intention to restore creation to its beauty and former glory. Creation must be regained not discarded. This emphasis of Jesus, though lost during long periods of church history, has been rediscovered in movements such as the sixteenth-century Reformation, seventeenth-century Puritanism, and nineteenth-century British Evangelicalism. During such moments of rediscovery, Christianity affirmed that the water of fallen life can be turned into the wine of restored life in every area. Christians saw spirituality not as an escape from society and culture. Instead, they saw that the "present task and future goal of Christian activity within the world is the restoration of the divine ordering of humanity and society, after the image and likeness of God."[15] God does not give up on us or our world; rather, he seeks to draw near to us to heal and transform.

Second, Jesus wants to unleash our enjoyment of God in all of life. The joy that Jesus intends to restore in every area of life has as its ultimate purpose the glorifying of God. Jesus did not come just to renew our love for creation and culture. He came to renew our love for the source of creation and culture. Jesus came to give a joy that begins with a new engagement with God as the all-sufficient source of life. Jesus endorses what John Piper has called "Christian hedonism." As Piper explains:

> Christian hedonism as I use the term does not mean God becomes a means to help us get worldly pleasures. The pleasure Christian hedo-

34

nism seeks is the pleasure which is in God himself. He is the end of our search, not the means to some further end. Our exceeding joy is he, the Lord—not the streets of gold, or the reunion with relatives or any blessing of heaven.[16]

But should pleasure, even if focused on God, be so central to Christian spirituality? Piper answers with a qualified yes.

Christian hedonism does not make a god out of pleasure. It says that one has already made a god out of whatever he finds most pleasure in. The goal of Christian hedonism is to find most pleasure in the one and only God and thus avoid the sin of covetousness, that is, idolatry (Colossians 3:5).[17]

Some of the water that must be turned into the wine of gladness is our dullness about God. True spirituality transforms our relationship with the source of all things so that he becomes our highest pleasure and greatest treasure.

Third, Jesus transforms the meaning of happiness. Happiness can be defined as the feeling of well-being that comes from satisfying needs and thirsts. Larry Crabb classifies these needs and thirsts using a three-level model.[18] Casual needs are those needs that can be satisfied by things. One example is physical hunger, which can be satisfied with a good meal. Sex is another. On one level it's a physical need. But we can feel that something is missing even when level-one needs are satisfied.

We soon discover that there is a second level to our hungers, the level of critical needs. Critical needs can be satisfied only by a quality relationship with a person. To return to our example of sexual desire, most people view a lasting and loving relationship with a man or a woman as a far more satisfying way to manage sexual desire than entering into casual liaisons.

Beyond level two, however, lies an even deeper level of need, often denied by rationalists but deeply explored by writers, mystics, and artists. This is the level of crucial needs. We need to have a relationship with ultimate reality. We long to make contact with the center of the universe. We want to be in harmony with that center. This can take the shape of a commitment to an ideology such as humanism, Marxism, or selfism ("I am ultimate reality and am the only source of personal meaning and happiness").

Note the contradiction that can occur in the secular approach to happiness, as seen in figure 3. If happiness is the feeling of well-being that comes from satisfying needs and thirsts, and if there are three levels of happiness, then a person may be happy on level one (happy with things) and still be deeply unhappy because the other levels of need and thirst are unsatisfied (lack of harmony with other people and ultimate reality).

FIGURE 3

Secular View of Happiness: From the Outside In

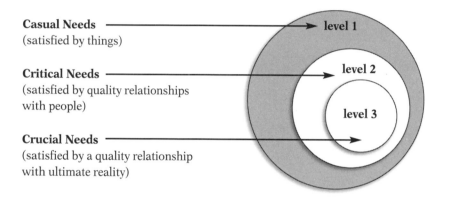

Casual Needs ——————————————→ level 1
(satisfied by things)

Critical Needs ——————————————→ level 2
(satisfied by quality relationships
with people)

level 3

Crucial Needs ——————————————→
(satisfied by a quality relationship
with ultimate reality)

In contrast to secular hedonism, however, the Jesus model of human happiness (figure 4) shows that the true path of pleasure is from the inside out. Not only does this model assume that there are different levels of need, but it also assumes that the deeper the level of need, the greater the happiness when satisfied. Secular hedonism is found wanting because its emphasis on level-one happiness misses the deeper satisfactions that come from concentrating on level-three and level-two realities. According to Jesus, only by enjoying a quality relationship with the God revealed in Jesus Christ can human beings hope to find the deepest form of satisfaction, and therefore, the highest level of happiness. Only from that satisfied innermost core comes the power to enjoy life on levels one and two.

Though the mystic model and the moral model would also support the pursuit of happiness from the inside out, their concept of what will satisfy level-three needs is radically different. The crucial difference is their conception of God. For both Covey and Chopra, God is far away. In order to steal his fire (his law for Covey, his consciousness for Chopra), I have to storm heaven. With Jesus, however, God comes to me, brimming with his gifts of grace. When Jesus turns water into wine, he gives us the best wine at the feast. That finest of wines, that greatest of satisfactions, is to give us a total relationship with the ultimate source of life, the one whom Jesus called the Father.

FIGURE 4

Spiritual View of Happiness: From the Inside Out

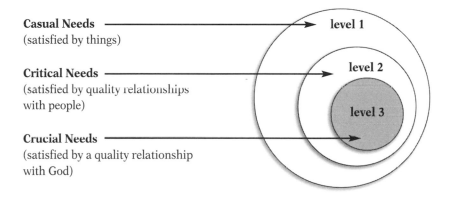

Casual Needs   level 1
(satisfied by things)

Critical Needs   level 2
(satisfied by quality relationships
with people)

             level 3

Crucial Needs
(satisfied by a quality relationship
with God)

Fourth, Jesus transforms the definition of spirituality. Spirituality, at least from a Christian perspective, must involve the enjoyment of God, through Jesus, in all of life. Such a definition rejects both *dualism* (that only parts of life, usually the higher, more intellectual, or nonmaterial aspects of life, are spiritual) and *secularism* (that things or creatures rather than God our Creator should be our highest treasure). Spirituality isn't about just achieving a certain state of consciousness. It must be relational at its heart—restoring relationship with God and others. Jesus comes to us as the one who can broker these restored relationships.

So the quest for spirituality in the story of Jesus begins. Unlike the approach of the Philosopher or the Theologian, we must not start the quest with an overconfidence in our own powers. We must resist the temptation to climb the ladders of either the mystic or the moral model of spirituality. Rather, the proper starting point is better represented by Ben. To search for wine for his wedding guests, Ben brought only his sense of need and a willingness to see what Jesus could do. We must stand alongside Douglas Coupland as he once again whispers his secret through his character Scout: "My secret is that I need God—that I am sick and can no longer make it alone. I need God to help me give, because I no longer seem capable of giving; to help me be kind, as I no longer seem capable of kindness; to help me love, as I seem beyond being able to love."[19] To those who are dull and dazed by life, a number of spiritualities offer rules for self-help. Jesus, however, offers more than manuals of self-improvement. Jesus reveals that in the midst of a world of dullness and boredom there is a love that turns water into wine in all of life.

If we accept the invitation to explore Jesus' model of spirituality, then new questions demand our attention. How does he turn water into wine? What are the dynamics that make possible this restoration of creation and daily life? We must now turn to the larger story that Jesus attempted to tell and to the implications of that larger story for the spiritual quest.

THE HAMMER
OF A HIGHER GOD

EXPERIENCING
THE POWER OF JESUS

Homer's odyssey has been taken inside. It has been interiorized. The islands, the seas, the sirens seducing us, Ithaca summoning us—nowadays they are only the voices of our interior being.

Milan Kundera, *The Book of Laughter and Forgetting*

We did not follow cleverly invented stories when we told you about the power and coming of our Lord Jesus Christ, but we were eyewitnesses of his majesty.

2 Peter 1:16

Story: The Hammer of a Higher God

Two businessmen pulled the cigars from their mouths. "Is there potential here for a few bucks or what?" said the first businessman.

"Go easy, Sol," said the second. "Let's see what happens to the sick guy before we go signing any deals." Sol nodded. The cigars went back in their mouths as they waited for Jesus' next move.

The two businessmen were watching the drama unfolding before them. Jesus had arrived in Capernaum. Word of the Cana wedding miracle had spread, and the people of Capernaum had found out where the miracle man was staying. They had crowded into the small house for an audience with Jesus until there was no room left. As Jesus began to teach, there was a noise on the roof. Plaster fell from the ceiling. Some people screamed that the roof was caving in, but Jesus commanded everyone to remain calm. Soon faces appeared through the open hole above them. Within moments a bed was lowered from the roof down to the floor in front of Jesus. A twisted body lay on the bed. Jesus looked at the paralyzed man and saw in his eyes and in the eyes of his friends gazing down from above him a silent appeal for help.

Jesus said to the paralytic, "Son, your sins are forgiven." He might as well have said, "Let there be light" or, "I am the Lord your God." His words were so outrageous that they set off a chain reaction of conversation throughout the crowd.

The Theologian had followed Jesus from Cana to Capernaum. He had been intrigued by the wine trick, but he had questions about the young miracle worker's orthodoxy. The last thing Israel needed was a charlatan. The Theologian heard Jesus' words about the forgiveness of sins. He was furious.

"Why does this fellow talk like that?" he said to himself. "He's blaspheming! Who can forgive sins but God alone? What kind of story is he trying to tell?" The Theologian knew what Jesus was doing. To announce the forgiveness of sins was more than offering a spiritual gift. He was proclaiming an entirely new chapter in the story of Israel. The Theologian knew that Jesus was announcing the end of Israel's story of exile. His mind reviewed the basic outline of the Jewish drama. Every Jewish schoolboy knew that the recent story of Israel was a story of exile. Exile meant being forsaken by God because of sin. Sure, the Jews had returned to the Promised Land five hundred years ago. The return from captivity in Babylon, however, didn't end their exile. It simply began a new stage. For most of the years since the return, foreign governments such as Syria and Rome ruled over Israel. Yahweh had left Zion, the city of God.

Yet the Theologian realized that Jesus was messing with this story of exile by announcing the forgiveness of sins. He looked at the face of the paralytic. It was etched with all the lines of exile—all the marks of being forsaken by God. He must be a sinner, thought the Theologian, for God only forsakes sinners. Then the Theologian looked at Jesus. For this young street preacher to claim that he could forgive sins was tantamount to saying that he could end Israel's exile. It was shorthand for saying that all the promises of Isaiah and Zechariah and the other prophets about the return of Yahweh and the restoration of paradise were about to come true. Only sin stood in the way of the homecoming of Yahweh to Zion and with that homecoming the restoration of creation and the glory of Israel. But the preacher was badly overstepping his bounds, the Theologian thought. Only God himself through the Messiah could remove sin, which would liberate the nation and end its state of exile. The Theologian made some notes on his legal pad. This brash young man, he thought, had crossed over the line. He would have to be watched. Eventually, he would have to be silenced.

Near the doorway someone spoke to Jesus above the general noise. "Master," said the voice, "I am but a humble philosopher who knows little about religious matters. But are you implying that this man's suffering is a result of sin and that some kind of god exists cruel enough to paralyze people for making him mad?" Some low-level laughter came from those standing around the Philosopher. Jesus recognized the Philosopher from the wedding. He said nothing in reply, however. The Philosopher continued.

"Surely you don't believe that old nonsense about sin do you? What this man needs is enlightenment not false guilt. He merely needs to realize that his illness is an illusion and that there is a cosmic love that can fill him with peace and inner harmony even though his body is paralyzed. The mind is free even if the body is imprisoned."

The room had grown silent now as people processed the Philosopher's words. Beneath his soothing and outwardly calm manner was a burning anger against Judaism in general and preachers like Jesus in particular. He rejected the idea that sin was the real story behind human misery. A false concept of God such as the one Judaism taught was the real cause of misery. The Philosopher didn't believe in the story of Israel and its hope for a Messiah who would end the period of exile. The story that made sense to the Philosopher was not the story of Israel but the story of Narcissus. Narcissus in Greek mythology had discovered the truth that nothing in life is as beautiful as the self. He had discovered the secret that the self is the center of the universe, an expression of the cosmic self. When Narcissus saw his own beautiful reflection in the water, he jumped in and drowned. While most people regarded the ending of the Narcissus story a tragedy, the Philosopher thought it was beautiful. Even death cannot keep us from union with our cosmic self. What the paralytic needed was a new and higher consciousness that each of us is God. The Jewish God concept was but a primitive and meddlesome myth that stood between the self and its liberation into the higher consciousness that one is all and all is one.

Not far from the Philosopher a group of young people huddled in a corner. They were among the growing number of Jewish youths who had stopped going to synagogue because, after all, where was God for them. They had no jobs and no job prospects. Life for them was a little music, a little sex, and a little wine. Sin was something their generation had stopped believing in—they couldn't afford the luxury of morality. A young Girl, standing at the center of the group, was annoyed by Jesus' words about the forgiveness of sins. She had seen Jesus at the wedding and had been impressed with the wine that he had produced. She was turned off, however, by his words to the paralytic.

Like the Theologian, the Girl knew that the forgiveness of sins was not just a theological concept. It was a story of the return of Israel from exile and the homecoming of Israel's God. It was a story, however, that she rejected. She thought of how her brother had died fighting for Jewish nationalism, impaled on a Roman spear. She thought of her father and his fanatical belief in the liberation of Israel from Rome. The violence and anger generated by that story had destroyed him as a man and as a father. The story of exile and the hope of the return of Yahweh was one of those oppressive master narratives that her teachers had warned against.

The Girl's controlling story was not the story of the nation. Her story was the story of herself. She believed in the master narrative of "me." Her personal story was not about Moses or the children of Israel. To a degree she was living out the self-indulgent story of Narcissus, but the real story that made much more sense of her life was the Greek myth of Prometheus. The gods were tyrants who in their jealousy of humanity withheld good things from them. Prometheus the hero was the champion of humankind against the gods. He was the universal human being who stole fire from the gods. His punishment was to suffer forever at the hand of Zeus. We are all Prometheus, the Girl mused, still staring at the paralytic and watching Jesus move around his crude bed. We are on our own. The only good we can get out of life is what we grab with our own hands. The God of Moses certainly cannot be trusted to give us what we want. We are on our own in the quest for happiness. But this battle against God has its downside. When we grab what we want, we get punished. But even with the pain, we must remain defiant against this God of wrath and rules. We must learn to live with our paralysis and not bow and scrape before a God whose only joy seems to be in robbing his creatures of their happiness and freedom. Let others salute this cosmic tyrant. The Girl for one would never bow the knee.

At first she had found living out the Promethean story quite liberating. She had made a complete break with her domineering father and had begun living on the street. She found other young people like herself and joined them. In her self-indulgence she had started living on the edge, experimenting with drugs and sex. Initially, she felt like she was in control. Now she was no longer sure. She carried around a box that contained her new addictions. It used to be that every time she opened the box it would give her a wild thrill. Now every time she opened the box she experienced less thrill and more pain. Her boyfriend had warned her that she was going too far and that she needed to throw the box away. She had told him to mind his own business. He had left. The box had become her lover. Someday, she thought, the box is going to kill me. It was, she philosophized, the price one paid for defying the gods. She was willing to accept her punishment without whining, however. She looked at the withered limbs of the man on the bed and knew how he felt.

An African Woman across the room was also thinking about forgiveness. She lived as a social outcast in this outwardly religious town. She wished she could forgive the racism that made her everyday life so bitter. But she could not. She scanned the crowd. Everyone has their story, she thought. Each has a story that gives meaning to his or her life. She had a story as well. Her father had sold her into slavery. She had made her way north through a series of masters until a Roman family living in Jerusalem bought her. Though she had earned her freedom from servitude several years ago, she still remained in exile among her oppressors, unable to return to an Africa that had rejected her. Moving to a small town in the north hadn't helped much. The south had no monopoly on prejudice. Her story, she mused, was one of homelessness and fatherlessness. She imagined that she knew the stories that controlled most of the people in the room. She doubted if those stories brought their owners any more inner liberation than her story of victimization had brought her. We are all paralytics, she thought, withered by our private stories as truly as disease had withered the legs of the man on the mat. What would it be like, she wondered, if the hammer of a higher God broke through our stories? Perhaps we would be able, unlike the man on the bed, to rise and walk. She wondered whether the young preacher, leaning over the broken man, had just such a new story. She waited and watched.

Finally, Jesus looked up at the crowd and spoke. "Why are you thinking these things?" he asked as if seeing how each person was dealing with the clash between their personal stories and the story of forgiveness and homecoming that he was about to tell. "Which is easier: to say to the paralytic, 'Your sins are forgiven,' or to say, 'Get up, take your mat, and walk'? But that you may know that the Son of Man has authority on earth to forgive sins . . ."

Jesus looked down at the paralytic on his bed. "I tell you, get up, take your mat, and go home." At first, the man on the bed didn't move. After a moment, however, a broad smile of surprise swept across his face. He stood up slowly. His legs were shaky. He leaned over, felt his legs, and then stood up again. He looked at Jesus. He muttered something that the crowd could not hear and picked up his flimsy mattress. As if in a trance, he walked out of the house in full view of them all. Everyone broke out into conversation, saying with various levels of approval or anger, "Who is this man? We have never seen anything like this." (Based on Mark 2:1–12.)

The Story of Bill

I remember the night Bill told me I was the greatest person in the world. I was a lowly student working my way through graduate school as a desk clerk at a fancy apartment building in downtown Philadelphia. The trendy tenants were from every walk of life, but what they all had in common was lots of money. Bill was an accountant. He was a friendly enough guy, always had a joke to tell, but everyone knew he was miserable. He was divorced and estranged from his kids. The few times we had talked it had been about superficial things. He reminded me of the paralytic in the opening story—a nice enough guy but in a lot of pain.

One night when I was at the front desk, Bill bounded into the lobby with more zest than he'd had in months. He came up to me and said, "You are the greatest person in the world."

Before I could answer, he added the key words that made me realize he wasn't drunk. "I know you are the greatest person in the world because I also am the greatest person in the world." He went on to explain that his accounting firm had sent him to a self-improvement seminar that was heavily into Eastern philosophy. He learned that he was a god, an expression of the cosmic self, and was therefore the greatest person in the world. But he also learned that everyone else was a god too.

I thanked him for his compliment and muttered something about wanting to talk with him about what he learned at the seminar, but I never had the opportunity. After a few months being on cloud nine with his cosmic self, Bill slowly settled back down to earth. His god story was gradually replaced by his old story of loneliness and misery.

Bill reminds me how important stories are in the search for spirituality. Spiritual breakthroughs, even if they are short-lived, come not just as a result of learning concepts. The exhilarating moments come when we discover a new story. Our mundane existence is charged with new excitement. We catch a glimpse that our lives have a plot, that we are living out a high drama with meaning and purpose. We don't have to be sailing the high seas or scaling Mount Everest to be part of this adventure story. At some point we come to the realization that the greatest adventures are internal, even spiritual, in nature.

Novelist Milan Kundera captures the truth that most of the greatest adventure stories of life are inward ones:

Since James Joyce's [novel *Ulysses*] we have known that the greatest adventure of our lives is the absence of adventure. Ulysses, who fought at Troy, returned home by crisscrossing the seas, he himself steering his ship and had a mistress on every island—no, that is not the way we lead our lives. Homer's odyssey has been taken inside. It has been interiorized. The islands, the seas, the sirens seducing us, Ithaca summoning us—nowadays they are only the voices of our interior being.[1]

Spirituality is the new Homeric journey to find our way back to our true home. Spirituality is, therefore, more than a set of beliefs or practices. At heart, spirituality is a story that we have internalized and have begun to live out.

In our opening story, Jesus heals a paralytic but in the process stirs up a beehive of clashing stories that control the lives of the characters in the story. Most of the stories have to do with spirituality. On the surface the controversy seems to be about Jesus' dramatic statement regarding the forgiveness of sins. That would have been enough to alienate the orthodox. But something deeper is going on. Jesus' words were but the first lines of a new story about God, humanity, and history that he had come to tell. This new story was about the return of God to earth in blessing, in healing, and in love. Unfortunately, most of the characters couldn't accept this new story because of some old stories that had captured their hearts. The Theologian, the Philosopher, the Girl, and the African Woman each resisted the Jesus story because it seemed to be in direct contradiction to the stories that they were carrying around in their heads. Each of these main characters had rival narratives that saw reality in terms very different from those of Jesus. If spirituality is at heart a story, then the opening narrative points to the fact that different spiritualities are built around different kinds of stories.

In this chapter I'd like to explore the issue of how our approaches to spirituality are shaped by our stories. I'd like to look at three "master narratives," or controlling stories, that help some make sense of life and shape their view of God, the self, and the world. I'd also like to show how the Jesus story provides a very different path to spirituality than the stories that underlie the mystic and moral models of spirituality so popular in our day. The important point is that stories are not all equal. Getting the right story can make all the difference in the world between staying paralyzed on our beds or being able to rise and walk.

By looking at the power of stories in general and the power of the Jesus story in particular, we will be able to answer the second life issue mentioned in the first chapter: How do I find love and the ability to love in a world that has forgotten how to love? What I want to suggest is that the stories that shape our spirituality might actually be keeping us from experiencing the love we need. Such destructive stories can be called *exile stories.* In contrast to the exile stories that lie behind much popular spirituality, Jesus provides a new master narrative, a story of homecoming. When we get his new story straight, we can experience the truth that answers life issue 2: Love's power is unleashed by a story that calls us home.

The Power of Stories

As previously mentioned, one of the features of the opening story of the paralytic is that each character's reaction to Jesus was shaped by a personal story that guided his or her life. The Theologian responded to Jesus on the basis of the Jewish story of exile, the Philosopher on the basis of a more humanistic story. The Girl interpreted Jesus in light of the story of the self. The African Woman saw Jesus through the story of the cultural resurgence of her people.

When it comes to spirituality, then, we must take such stories seriously. I hear a great deal about disciplines in spirituality. For many, spirituality is a set of actions one takes. The trouble with this approach is that while saying the Jesus prayer or practicing meditative breathing may be useful in and of themselves, their meaning is determined by a much larger reality—the stories we believe in.

We have forgotten a notion that was once well understood. One of the giants of ancient philosophy, Plato of Athens, knew the power of story in shaping belief and behavior.

> Then we must first of all, it seems, control the story tellers. Whatever noble story they compose we shall select, but a bad one we must reject. Then we shall persuade nurses and mothers to tell their children those we have selected and by those stories to fashion their minds far more than they can shape their bodies by handling them. The majority of the stories they now tell must be thrown out.[2]

Plato was convinced that fairy tales could be dangerous politically because stories shape belief.

To be human, one must have a story. Philosopher Charles Taylor has argued that "much of our self understanding and moral energy has come from frameworks provided by narratives, such as the Jewish, Christian, Marxist, and liberal humanist accounts of history."[3] Walker Percy once said, "I have learned that the most important difference between people is between those for whom life is a quest and those for whom it is not."[4] Diogenes Allen concurs: "The vision of a quest confers meaning on our lives. It enables us to see all that happens as moving us closer to or further from our goal, and to make distinctions between what helps and hinders us in our journey."[5]

Stories make sense of our world, enshrine our deepest values, and become the key to determining our behavior. We sometimes speak of "worldviews" as our basic beliefs about things. A worldview answers questions about God, the world, and the nature of persons. Beneath our worldview is a world story, a certain plot that tells us what the pattern of our life will be and what role we are to play in that plot. The question of God (whether or not he exists, and if he exists what he is like) provides the foundation and background for the story. The question of the world (whether it is purposeful or meaningless, real or illusory) provides the setting for the story. The question of the nature of persons provides the character, action, and conflict in the story. For example, the convinced communist believes his story is about an independent human being, in a materialistic world without a god, struggling against capitalism to produce a classless society. This is the story that shaped the lives of tens of millions during the cold war. The sincere Buddhist believes that the individual is a spiritual pilgrim who must escape the world of illusion in order to overcome desire and achieve happiness in a disembodied Nirvana. For traditional Africans, their story is about the struggle to live a prosperous life on earth by appeasing dead ancestors while living in a world with a remote and uninvolved deity. The struggle will end only when they join the ranks of the living dead and slowly fade away into nothingness of *zamani,* the deep past. All belief, all cultural activities, all relationships, and all behavior is affected by the stories that lie deep within our hearts.

When certain stories control millions of people and shape their worldview (including their view of spirituality), these stories become master narratives—major interpretations of life and reality. The Jesus story is one such master narrative. Stories, unlike people, are not created equal. Some master narratives lead to life. Others lead down the path of confusion or despair. I want to argue that the greatest relevance of Jesus for our day and the greatest power to transform our lives is the story that he has to tell, a story in which he is the main character. Further, we are suffering under the suffocating burden of some bad stories and need to consider the story of Jesus as a better alternative.

But I'm getting ahead of myself. This is the first point our opening story of the paralytic tried to make: Stories control our lives.

Dangerous Stories: Living in Exile

What kind of stories shaped the world of Jesus and shape our world today? In the story of the paralytic, some of the most common first-century stories were introduced. These first-century stories not only continue to dominate the modern world, but they are killing us "softly," impeding our progress toward a fulfilling spirituality.

From the crumpled paralytic to the proud Philosopher, from the stuffy Pharisee to the outcast African, from the young Girl clutching her addiction to the businessmen calculating Jesus' cash value, stories of exile abound. What do I mean?

The Theologian's Tale: The Story of a Double Exile

In the opening story, the Theologian looks at Jesus critically because Jesus' words and actions conflict with the story of Israel. "The Theologian knew, as every Jewish schoolboy knew, that the recent story of Israel was a story of exile. Israel had been forsaken by God because of sin. Sure, the Jews had returned to the Promised Land five hundred years ago. The return from Babylon, however, didn't end their exile. It simply began a new stage. For most of the years since the return, foreign governments such as Syria and Rome ruled over Israel. Yahweh had left Zion, the city of God." The experience of Jews was a kind of double exile. God was exiled from them, and they were exiled from him. The sin of Israel was the common cause of the two exiles.

The greatest need, so the national story went, was the removal of sin. Once sin was removed, the double exile would be over. Israel would return from the exile of powerlessness, and God would return to Zion from his self-imposed exile of holy protest. God's return would mean the defeat of paganism and evil, the reestablishment of the Davidic monarchy, the rebuilding of the temple, and unprecedented glory and prosperity for Israel. Israel would enjoy the double home-coming of national prosperity and the transforming presence of God. Heaven and earth would be brought back together again in the king-dom of God—a reunited heaven and earth ruled by a forgiving God and his forgiven people. This new covenant would be instituted by a new Davidic King, the Messiah or anointed one. While waiting for the Messiah, the faithful Jews were to be active—active in keeping the Torah, active in the temple, active in opposing Gentiles and the evil world around them.

This was the master narrative of Israel, the heart of Jewish spirituality in the first century—escaping from the double exile caused by sin. But how could sin be removed so that God would return to Zion and remove the internal exile? This was the Theologian's unanswered question. The story took the biblical views of God and sin seriously but could not remove the sense of alienation from God caused by sin. The story prevented one from believing that the biblical God was favorable toward his people. No matter what doctrines were proclaimed, such an inner story of exile kept pulling the people back into the sadness of alienation and distance from God. Real spiritual progress was impossible when such an exile story controlled lives.

This exile story of Israel is the story of many Christians today. Even the most ardent churchgoer can be captured by an exile story in which God is far away and we must bring him close by works of service and devotion. We become busy and active for the cause of God but do so as the elder brother in the parable of the lost son—full of anger against the father and against the world's prodigals. Our focus shifts from knowing and enjoying God to doing things for God. Writes Eugene Peterson:

> We have internalized the world's fascination with technology and its enthusiasm for activities. . . . After a few years or decades of this, we find ourselves in churches (*evangelical* churches) where there is as little intimacy and transcendence as in the world. . . . What's wrong? We are believing the right things. We are doing the right things. *Things,* that's what is wrong.[6]

I detect in the Covey model of spirituality and in many Christian models of spirituality that focus on behavioral change an exile story similar to the Theologian's. My church life becomes a mirror image of the world's desperate pursuit of inner happiness through getting the right things, believing the right things, and doing the right things. The things we collect and consume through our believing, getting, and doing do not have hands that can heal a paralytic or words that can sweep away sin and clear the way for the return of God to my life and heart. Only a person, a transcendent one, can lift us out of the addiction to things, even orthodox things, and breathe new life into us through grace.

The Girl's Story: The Exiled Self

The Girl in the story is operating from a master narrative very similar to the Theologian's. If his story comes from Moses, her story comes from Homer.

The "story that made much more sense of life was the Greek myth of Prometheus. The gods were tyrants who in their jealousy of humanity withheld good things from them. Prometheus the hero was the champion of humankind against the gods. He was the universal human being who stole fire from the gods. His punishment was to suffer forever at the hand of Zeus."

What was the importance of this old myth? The Girl saw in the Greek story the key to understanding life: "Prometheus the hero was the champion of humankind against the gods. He was the universal human being who stole fire from the gods. His punishment was to suffer forever at the hand of Zeus. We are all Prometheus, the Girl mused, still staring at the paralytic and watching Jesus move around his crude bed. We are on our own. The only good we can get out of life is what we grab with our own hands. The God of Moses certainly cannot be trusted to give us what we want. We are on our own in the quest for happiness. But this battle against God has its downside. When we grab what we want, we get punished. But even with the pain, we must remain defiant against this God of wrath and rules. We must learn to live with our paralysis and not bow and scrape before a God whose only joy seems to be in robbing his creatures of their happiness and freedom. Let others salute this cosmic tyrant. The Girl for one would never bow the knee."

If the Girl's Promethean story has a creed, it is, "I believe that God is the enemy and I am on my own." The Promethean person may believe there is a God and may further believe that he is all-powerful, but God is no friend of humankind. He is jealous of our loves, envious of our powers, cruel in his punishment. Humanity must struggle with this God—paying him halfhearted devotion all the while giving their whole hearts to the worship and service of humankind. This is the story of humanism. There are African versions and Western versions of this humanism, but they all spring from the same Promethean heart.

The Girl's particular form of Prometheanism reflects the new convictions of the postmodern world. Postmodernism believes that there is no universal reason or universal reality. We live in an inherently meaningless and unknowable world. The only meaning is that which the individual imposes on his or her private world. This profound relativism produces a deep "inwardness," which in turn creates a profound sense of alienation. As Henri Nouwen observes about the inwardness of the postmodern generation:

> It is the behavior of people who are convinced that there is nothing "out there" or "up there" on which they can get a solid grasp, which can pull them out of their uncertainty and confusion. No authority, no institution, no outer concrete reality has the power to relieve them of their anxiety and loneliness and make them free.[7]

Because of this inner exile of the retreat into the self, one of the features of postmodern life is fatherlessness. Nouwen observes that we "are facing a generation which has parents but no father, a generation in which everyone who claims authority—because he is older, more mature, more intelligent or more powerful—is suspect from the very beginning."[8] This fatherlessness is cosmic in its scope. God is no longer a resident father, living with and loving his children. He is an absent father, a rejected father. His children, even in their search for things of the spirit, are homeless and fatherless. Promethean orphans look within themselves for meaning and look at God as irrelevant or even an obstacle to getting what they want out of life.

What happens if one searches for spirituality but is controlled by a Promethean story in which the self is the savior and God is the enemy? The search is doomed from the outset. How can one pray or get close to God if something deep inside tells that person that God is the enemy? Promethean spirituality is just one more hostile assertion that a person doesn't need God. The Promethean spirit, even at prayer, shakes the fist toward the heavens as if to say that humanity is independent enough to find spiritual satisfaction without any help from God. Though it denies that sin is the problem that separates the self from God, like the Theologian's story, it sees humanity as living in exile from the Almighty. The sign of exile is often the bondage to hidden sin that frequently accompanies the Promethean story of self-reliance. The pain of that addiction was destroying the Girl, but she remained defiant in her narrative of exile.

The Philosopher's Story: The Exiled Mystic

The Philosopher in the story has a different controlling narrative than either the Theologian or the Girl. His is the story of Narcissus, the mythological character who was so self-absorbed that he drowned in a pool trying to unite with his own reflection. Many in the postmodern world have turned from Promethean stories of achievement to narcissistic stories of self-indulgence or self-adoration. Narcissists can even seek spirituality. Spiritual highs are another way "to make myself beautiful" for God.

Deepak Chopra's mystic model is an expression of this new spiritual narcissism. The search for God is really just a search for the cosmic self, the god inside us. The language is beautiful, as the language of worship should be, but it is a narcissistic beauty. We are really engaging in a spirituality of self-worship. This form of spirituality is immensely popular in the modern world and fits quite nicely with the therapeutic movement in psychology with its emphasis on selfism and self-fulfillment. But it is at heart an exile story. The god that Chopra seeks is not the God of Abraham, Isaac, and Jacob. He is a god who is merely the ultimate projection of the self. This is a "high" form of narcissism. It speaks of the lonely self seeking spiritual fulfillment by identifying the self with God. There is no Father out there to whom I can return or who will come and find me. I am lost in the cosmos, and my only hope is to declare my lonely self the only being that exists. And so I climb the staircase of mystical ascent in order to convince myself that I am the god I seek.

For Covey, God is not to be equated with the self but is rather the cosmic lawgiver who is known only to those who climb the staircase of moral achievement. My current position is one of exile. The god of Covey must be found by keeping his law. But it is the autonomous and exiled self who must keep that law, who, in fact, has all the power needed to keep that law apart from any help from God.

Our Own Stories of Exile

The African Woman is aware that stories control the lives of the people in that crowded room. As she admits in the story, "She doubted if those stories brought their owners any more inner liberation than her story of victimization had brought her." Instead, she was convinced that most of our stories hurt us. "We are all paralytics, she thought, withered by our private stories as truly as disease had withered the legs of the man on the mat." Her great longing was for a new story that would liberate each one from his or her dysfunctional story. "What would it be like, she wondered, if the hammer of a higher God broke through our stories?"

The African's statement that we are all "withered by our private stories" says something important about the master narratives of both the first century and the twenty-first century. The stories of the Theologian, the Philosopher, the Girl, although different in important respects, share a common denominator: They are all stories of exile. Living in exile means living in separation from God. It means conducting our lives with a profound sense of alienation—the experience of being a stranger or being alone. When it comes to the search for spirituality, stories of exile often motivate the search. But they also cripple the search before it begins.

One of the bitter fruits of our stories of exile is what they do to our concept of God. Such stories fill our minds with small thoughts of God and swollen thoughts about ourselves. We have become mentally imbalanced due to stories that distort the nature of God, the world, and human beings. G. K. Chesterton compared the intellectual impact of such stories to the mind of a madman. The great characteristic of the madman is not his loss of logic but his extreme use of it. He thinks he is Napoleon or the King of England or even Jesus Christ, and every objection one raises to his impossible view of the world is rigorously explained away. Raging narcissism not wayward reasoning is the real mark of the madman. His stories make sense to himself, so much so that he cannot see his insanity. He is convinced that he is the center of the universe and can explain away any objection to his master narrative.

How then does one break into the dark little dungeon of the narcissist? Chesterton's strategy was to appeal to their longings not their logic. To the man who pretends he is God one must politely comment:

> How sad it must be to be God; and an inadequate God! Is there really no life fuller and no love more marvelous than yours; and is it really in your small and painful pity that all flesh must put its faith? How much happier you would be, how much more of you there would be, if the hammer of a higher god could smash your small cosmos, scattering the stars like spangles, and leave you in the open, free like other men to look up as well as down.[9]

Our stories can prevent us from finding our true humanity and our proper place in God's world. To break through the twisted stories that distort reality and the true meaning of things one must find another master narrative, "the hammer of a higher god," to challenge and ultimately replace the stories that are killing us.

This is where Jesus comes in. As the African Woman wonders, "What would it be like if the hammer of a higher God broke through our stories?" She wonders if there is a controlling story that would enable us to "rise and walk." Most of all she wonders "whether the young preacher, leaning over the broken man, had just such a new story." Does Jesus have another story, one that could break through these stories of exile?

Why We Need the Jesus Story: The Story of Homecoming

In contrast to the exile stories of the Theologian, the Philosopher, the Girl, and the African Woman, Jesus tells a story about homecoming. When he mentions the forgiveness of sins before he heals the paralytic, he is not talking about just a theological concept but rather a whole new narrative of human life.

One way to summarize the difference between the popular models of spirituality referred to above and the model I see in Jesus is to look at Luke 15 and the parable of the two sons. Here Jesus retells the story of Israel's history in a surprising and subversive way in which even sinners, by the mercy and compassion of God, can find their way from the distant exile of the far country and enjoy the bounty of the Father's house. Nearby Jews, slaving in the fields of service, remain in exile despite their religious devotion, for they are in inner exile—living near home but still estranged from the Father and doubtful of his goodness and fairness. For Jesus, spirituality is not first and foremost about religious devotion or zeal. Rather, it is about a gracious gift of righteousness—right relation with God—to undeserving sinners who repent and humble themselves beneath the two hands of the Father—the hands of mercy and grace. For Jesus there are two different kinds of spirituality: the spirituality of homecoming versus the spiritualities of exile.

The great theme of Jesus' spirituality is not discovering I am the infinite God but that God is my infinite Father. This quest for spirituality must sail from the places of exile (including selfism and traditionalism) to the shores of home, where we will find the Father's house with its bounty and beauty. This is a daily journey.

Even more significant to Jesus' approach to spirituality is the importance of history for true spirituality. Both the mystic model and the moral model of spirituality call the individual to climb up the staircase of moral or mystical achievement in order to find either secret truths or effective habits. These models take us "up and away," that is, up the ladder of self effort to grab what one needs from the heavens. But for Jesus' model we must go "back to the future." In his model, only as we live in his story, as recorded by the apostles in the Gospels, can we find God and experience the bounty and beauty of his love in all of life. For both Chopra and Covey and other expressions of mysticism and moralism, history, the domain of time and space, is of only marginal interest in the pursuit of spirituality. In one sense much popular spirituality seeks to escape from history into the realm of infinite and super-historical reality.

Jesus makes the startling claim that spiritual reality is found not by going "up" but by going "back." He commands the seeker to move back into his story in all its historical detail. Only as we understand and internalize the personal biography of Jesus Christ can we experience spiritual transformation in the present. Jesus insists that we return to his story in order to remove the gap that exists between exiled humanity and our Creator God (see fig. 5).

How would going back into the Jesus story and experiencing the events of the life of Christ help me answer the nine life issues raised in the previous chapter? I believe that the homecoming spirituality of Jesus gives us the most satisfying answers to the great questions:

1. How do I restore color to my life when everything has gone gray? Only by going back to the Jesus story do I experience the love that turns water into wine.
2. How do I find love in a world that has forgotten how to love? Human sin has driven so much real love from our midst that the loss may seem irreparable. Most of our attempts to find love are made impotent by the exile stories that limit growth and real intimacy with God. Only by going back to the homecoming story of Jesus can I go forward with the power to love God and others. Faith in him, fueled by his story, opens up my future because it teaches me that love's power is unleashed by a story that leads us home.
3. How do I find community and peace in a world of diversity and differences? Because of the Jesus story, I know that love comes to me as a stranger from a strange land. By going back to experience the birth of Jesus, I can go forward with a God who breaks into our world to build unity amid diversity.

FIGURE 5

Jesus' Model of Spirituality: Back to the Future

Experiencing his:
1. promise
2. power
3. birth
4. baptism and temptation
5. kingdom vision
6. death
7. resurrection
8. return
9. demands

In this model, we do not go up to reach God, spiritual reality. Rather, we go back in time. We return to the story of Jesus, seeing in the same light what the apostles saw. As we experience the Jesus story (in at least nine ways),

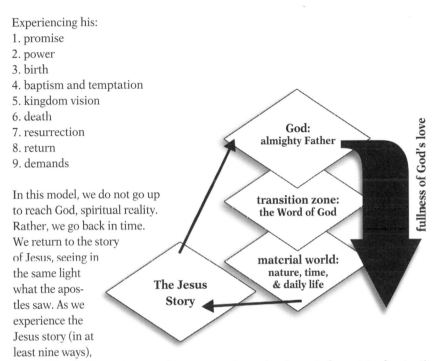

we are liberated from the up and away type of story (as shown in figure 1 in chapter 1) that dominated (and complicated) our lives. God as Father now sends all manner of beauty and bounty down into our daily lives, not because of our ascent but because of the connection we have with Jesus. When we enter the Jesus story anew, we experience God as Jesus did—full of grace, mercy, bounty, and beauty. This is the homecoming experience as opposed to the various spiritualities of exile in which God is seen as being far away and known only by our efforts to reach him.

4. How do I find a place to belong in a world of mobility, enmity, and alienation? The Jesus story teaches me that love brings in the new world order by first becoming the new world order. By going back to experience the baptism and temptation of Jesus, I can go forward with God as my Father and this world as my Father's house.

5. How do I find truth and wisdom in a world of confusing ideologies and competing theories? In this world without fathers,
without sources of wisdom and guidance, Jesus comes. The
Jesus story overcomes confusion and competing claims on truth
by teaching me the heart of wisdom: Love is found only by those
who lose it. By going back to the kingdom vision of Jesus, I can
go forward with a new master narrative that lights the path
ahead.

6. How do I find comfort and justice in a world of evil and suffering? The Jesus story teaches me that love conquers evil by
becoming its victim. By going back to the death of Jesus, I can
go forward into a future confident that evil and suffering are
not the last word but have been dealt with decisively by Jesus.

7. How do I find power to love and live in a world that drains my
strength and energy? The Jesus story teaches me that love is
stronger than death. By going back to the resurrection of Jesus,
I can go forward with the same power that raised him from the
dead.

8. How do I find hope and vision in a world that is uncertain about
the future? The Jesus story teaches me that love will never end
and will one day fill the world. By going back to the future of
Jesus, I can go forward into a future with Jesus.

9. How do I find direction and purpose in a world that has no
direction? The Jesus story teaches me that love demands all and
gives what it demands. By going back to the demands of Jesus,
I can go forward in union with him.

What is the relevance of Jesus and his story for the modern search
for spirituality? The power of Jesus is found only in the history of
Jesus, in the story told by the apostles. In other words, the only way
forward in the new quest for spiritual reality is to go back, back to
the story of the one who opens the way to God, the way back home.

In the chapters that follow, I want to take the homecoming journey of knowing God as our Father, not just as a force. This happens
only by going back in time and experiencing the nine realities of the
Jesus story. It does not happen by ascending to seven stages of consciousness or developing seven effective habits. We want more than
enlightenment or effectiveness. We want intimacy with God. We want
to know in greater depth of soul the fullness of the homecoming experience. We have begun our quest by asserting that the Jesus of the
biblical story is still alive and well in our world today and is the love

that turns water into wine. In this chapter, we have seen that the biblical story of Jesus is the true zone of personal transformation. That is homecoming truth 2: *Love's power is unleashed through a story that leads us home.* But what about the issue of religious diversity and spiritual pluralism? Can the story of Jesus help us find a spirituality that navigates the waters of pluralism and provides a path open to the world's diverse cultures? This is life issue 3 and beckons us to take a closer look.

OF ELEPHANTS AND ANGELS

EXPERIENCING THE BIRTH OF JESUS

If you saw yourself truly, you would no longer identify with this haphazard, ramshackle thing, your self. In truth you are the Self, created from the same spirit that in infinite form is called God.

Deepak Chopra, *The Path to Love*

God was reconciling the world to himself in Christ.

2 Corinthians 5:19

The Story: Of Elephants and Angels

I was in the kitchen singing away, chopping the onions," Mary explained to her four guests. The African Woman, the Girl, the Theologian, and the Philosopher were all sitting in her kitchen listening to her answer their joint question about the true identity of her son. "All of a sudden there was a strange man in the room. I almost cut my finger in surprise." She recalled the event like it was yesterday.

"'Greetings, you who are highly favored! The Lord is with you,' the stranger said. What kind of greeting is that? I thought. No 'How do you do?' No 'My name is Mr. So-and-So.' He was very strange. He spoke like I had won the lottery. While I was brooding on his manner, he dropped the bombshell: 'You will be with child and give birth to a son. You are to give him the name Jesus. He will be great and will be called the Son of the Most High. The Lord God will give him the throne of his father David, and he will reign over the house of Jacob forever; his kingdom will never end.'

"I hardly heard the part about David and the never-ending kingdom. I had trouble listening after the 'you will be with child' part.

"'How can this be since I am a virgin?' I blurted out and then wished I hadn't. The stranger said something even more terrifying.

"'The Holy Spirit will come upon you and the power of the Most High will overshadow you. So the holy one to be born will be called the Son of God.'

"I dropped the knife. His name would be 'Son of God'? I could hear the neighbors already.

"'What's the little one called, Mary?'

"'Oh, Joseph and I call him the Son of God.'

"And how would the local rabbi react? 'Everybody loves their kid, Mary, but we don't call our children "Jehovah," or "God," or "Son of God." And there's a simple reason we don't do that Mary. It's called blasphemy.' Explaining a miraculous pregnancy was one thing. Explaining blasphemy was another.

"This is all impossible, I thought. The stranger moved toward the doorway, and as if reading my thoughts he said, 'Nothing is impossible with God.' I agreed and mumbled something about being the Lord's servant and being willing to do anything. Then he was gone as suddenly as he had come."

Mary looked up at the four guests seated before her to gauge their reaction to this strange tale. They had come to Nazareth from Capernaum looking for answers about Jesus. They had little in common except intense curiosity about Mary's son.

"That's quite a story, Mary," said the African. "Back in my village the old women would sometimes predict the birth of a special boy child, someone who would become a hero to the tribe. But I never heard anyone called the Son of God."

"What do you think it means?" Mary asked the Theologian, afraid that she knew the answer.

"I think it means that your son is supposed to be God in human form. Your rabbi is not going to like that," answered the Theologian as gently as he could.

"Is it heresy to say that God could become human?" Mary asked the Philosopher.

"My problem is not so much with heresy. I have more problems with what that idea says about other religions," the Philosopher replied.

"What do you mean?" Mary asked.

The Philosopher took a deep breath. "If this son of yours is a unique expression of God, then other religions are left out in the cold. You would be saying that the mysterious God has revealed himself and his plan of salvation only through your son. That's a very offensive way to think nowadays. Wouldn't a universal God reveal himself in a universal way? Why would he speak through one person in a remote corner of the world when he could speak through nature? I think God has many faces and can be reached through many paths. I find it impossible to believe that he would limit himself to one tribe. Everyone needs to believe they are loved by God no matter what their religion is. This is what it means to be spiritual: To believe that God, whatever you conceive him to be, loves you totally."

At this point the Girl, who had been sitting quietly in her chair by the window, spoke.

"I remember a story a teacher once told me about why there must be many paths to God."

Mary was disturbed by these words but settled into her chair to listen.

"The story goes something like this," the Girl began. "Four blind men wandered out of their village one day and bumped into an elephant. They had never encountered such a beast before, and since the animal didn't seem hostile, they decided to find out what they could about the elephant in order to tell the other members of the village about him. One grabbed the elephant's tail and told the others that the beast was like a long stick. Another felt the elephant's foot and declared that the animal was like a tree. The third blind man touched the floppy ear of the elephant and concluded that the beast was like a large leaf. The fourth blind man grabbed the moist trunk of the elephant and announced to the others that the beast was like a huge snake. Anyway, you get the point. God is too big for any of us to know him fully, and so we all have our half-truths about him that we can mistakenly think are the whole truth. Every religion has truth about God, but no one faith has the whole truth. We are all blind men touching different parts of the elephant. Do you see what I mean?"

Mary did see what she meant. As a devout Jew she realized how heretical such a story was. She had been brought up to believe that only the God of Israel, not the gods of the nations, was the true and living God. Now she was challenged to consider that her thinking about God, and consequently, about the Son of God, born from her own womb, was narrow-minded and provincial.

It was late in the day now. The Theologian was the first to excuse himself. The others soon followed, thanking Mary for her time but feeling they had not found what they were looking for. Jesus remained a puzzle to them. Their search for clues would have to continue elsewhere.

Mary spent the rest of the evening alone, reading and sewing. The evenings were long now that Joseph was gone and her son was on the road. As she was sewing she grew drowsy and dozed off.

She began to dream. In the dream the angel of the Lord appeared to her again.

"You're doubting that your son is 'God with us,' 'the Savior of the world,'" said the angel.

"I don't mean to doubt," Mary replied. "The Girl told me a story about an elephant that has disturbed me."

"Yes, I know the story about the elephant and the blind men. But may I finish the story?"

"What do you mean? The Girl already finished the story. Nothing more happens. The blind men go back to their village and each holds on to his own partial picture of the elephant," Mary replied.

"Let me add another chapter," said the angel. "After they returned to their village, the blind men taught these four different perspectives to the people of the village, who were also all blind. Four groups of elephant worshipers were started based on the four views. The villagers were equally divided into tail worshipers, ear worshipers, leg worshipers, and trunk worshipers. These differences split the village into rival groups who sometimes became violent with each other. It was quite a sad state of affairs. Things got so bad between the four groups that the four blind men, who were now the supreme leaders of the village, got together to discuss a possible solution to bring the village together again. As they were discussing the issue, a breakthrough occurred. They came to realize that each of their views of the elephant was incomplete, so they pooled their information and came up with a fuller picture of an animal with a stringy tail, a leafy ear, treelike legs, and a long, snaky trunk. They felt that they had discovered the ultimate truth about the elephant and announced their latest discovery to the villagers. Many felt that the new composite picture of the elephant was far superior to the previous views. The four blind men had learned their lesson, however, and declared that no one in the village, on pain of banishment, had the right to proclaim that they had the final truth about the elephant. Everyone was required to admit that their view was limited and partial."

"Is that the conclusion?" Mary asked. "No one should be allowed to claim that they have the full and final truth about God?"

"Not quite. There's more. One day a strange man came to the village. He became the friend of the children of the village and claimed that he had been sent to deliver a wonderful message from the elephant. He claimed, in fact, that he was the Elephant Man—the original elephant that had now taken the form of a man in order to bring a message of hope to the village. He told whoever would listen that the elephant the blind men had discovered was not just a brute beast but was in fact the King of the Elephants who could do all kinds of wonders including restoring sight. The Elephant Man, to prove his point, gave sight to some of the children, who were overjoyed to see the real world for the first time. The Elephant Man went on to say that the curse of blindness had been given to the village because in the past they had killed elephants for sport. The Elephant King was willing to lift the curse of blindness if the people of the village would admit that they were wrong and would accept this good news from the Elephant Man. Many people in the village rejoiced to hear this message and began following the Elephant Man. More people claimed that they could now see."

"I think I'm getting your point. What happened to the Elephant Man?" Mary asked the angel in her dream.

"The four blind men met and discussed what they should do about the Elephant Man. None of the four leaders believed the stranger's story. After all, they were the ones who had discovered the elephant in the first place. What right did this latecomer have to tell them who the elephant really was and what he wanted to do? They denied that their ancestors had ever killed elephants, and they further denied that their blindness was a curse brought on by the King of the Elephants as a punishment for their evil. They concluded that the stranger was a liar who had broken the new religious law: No one had the right to claim that they had the full and final truth about the elephant. They called the Elephant Man to stand trial for making such claims. He was found guilty and was banished forever from the village. Before he left he organized his followers and told them that he would return one day to lift the blindness from all eyes. He then disappeared into the jungle."

The angel said much more in the dream about elephants and blind eyes, but it would be several years before Mary would fully understand the dream and unravel the mystery of the Elephant Man. When that day came, the angel would once again be present.

"Men of Galilee," the stranger would say, "why do you stand here looking up into the sky? This same Jesus, who has been taken from you into heaven, will come back in the same way you have seen him go into heaven."

These words would not trouble Mary this time because she would know they were absolutely true. She would know without a doubt that Jesus would come again. She would know he was the son of David and the King who would reign forever. She would know all this because she would finally figure out what the angel had meant when he said that Jesus was the Son of God, the son of the Elephant King.

She would know why water turned to wine when it touched his lips; why paralytics turned to pole-vaulters at the touch of his words; why roaring seas became purring pussycats when he rose from his slumber; and why gray stones, like soldiers under orders, rolled away from his tomb. The coming of the Son of God was the coming of God the Son. The stranger's words would come back to her. "Nothing," she would remember, "is impossible with God." (Based on Luke 1:26–38; Acts 1:9–14.)

Muslims in Memphis

Our story describes one of the New Testament's happiest events—
Christmas. For many North Americans, Christmas is little more than
a holiday break from the routines of school or work, filled with the
scent of evergreens and eggnog and little white lies about the fat man
from the far north. For millions of Christians around the world, however, Christmas is the celebration of the miracle of God becoming a
human in the person of Jesus Christ.

Christians further believe that the Christmas event is central to
spirituality. The quest for spirituality is the quest for the experiential
knowledge of God. When I pray or meditate as a Christian, I am not
just gathering information about God; I am attempting to deepen a
relationship with God. This relational knowledge of God so central
to Christian spirituality is tied up with the birth of Jesus Christ. Most
Christians would agree with Alister McGrath that "Christians believe
that Jesus Christ is the closest encounter with God to be had in this
life. God makes himself available for our acceptance or rejection in
the figure of Jesus Christ."[1]

Christmas and its message, however, have become increasingly
controversial. Public schools in North America and around the world
have to make sure that other traditions receive equal time. Many
Americans have left the churches of their youth and are searching for
spirituality in other world religions. Christmas has a different meaning for those who have embraced a rival faith.

I remember sitting next to a young woman on a plane. She looked
like an American college student. I couldn't help noticing, however,
that she was reading the Koran. Thinking that she was studying religion at school, I struck up a conversation.

"Are you studying Islam at university?" I asked.

"No, I'm a recent convert," was her reply. I probably looked startled but managed to recover enough to ask her about the details of
her conversion. She went on to tell me about the new mosque that
had been built in her hometown of Memphis, Tennessee, a place most
Americans would not associate with Islam. She had been attracted
by the zeal of some of her Muslim friends and the strong and simple
monotheism of the Muslim creed. I was struck by her sincerity and
commitment. When Muslims start coming from Memphis, I thought,
then religious pluralism is an undeniable fact of the modern world.

The four visitors in the story expressed the pluralist position well.
They were happy to see Jesus as someone of great religious impor-

tance. What they could not do was accept that Mary's child was the one and only God in human form. As the Girl said to Mary, "God is too big for any of us to know him fully, and so we all have our half-truths about him that we can mistakenly think are the whole truth. Every religion has truth about God, but no one faith has the whole truth. We are all blind men touching different parts of the elephant." In these few words, the Girl summarized the pluralistic belief that God can be reached through many paths and that no one religion is the only way.

Pluralism has many implications for spirituality. Spirituality must not be exclusive to any one tradition. It must be eclectic and syncretistic since all traditions contain truth about the realm of the Spirit and the divine. It also means that the practice of exclusivist Christian spirituality (that only believers in Jesus can have intimacy with God) cannot help but offend those convinced of the truths of pluralist spirituality. The Philosopher summarized a common opinion of pluralist spirituality in his conversation with Mary: "I think God has many faces and can be reached through many paths. I find it impossible to believe that he would limit himself to one tribe. Everyone needs to believe they are loved by God no matter what their religion is. This is what it means to be spiritual: To believe that God, whatever you conceive him to be, loves you totally."

Deepak Chopra has been one of the champions of this pluralist spirituality. In his book *The Path to Love: Spiritual Lessons for Creating the Love That You Need*, he describes his view of truly spiritual love. Love is the realization not only that you are loved by the universe but also that *you are that love* that fills the universe. "You know that you have fully experienced love when you turn into love—that is the spiritual goal of life."[2] He does not mean that we simply become loving people but rather that we realize we are God himself—expressions of infinite Spirit.

> If you saw yourself truly, you would no longer identify with this haphazard, ramshackle thing, your self. In truth you are the Self, created from the same spirit that in infinite form is called God. You are one grain of gold, compared to which God is all the gold that exists, and yet you can rightly say, "I am gold."[3]

This pantheistic vision of love and the self rejects the Christian and Jewish view. The Bible teaches we are creatures made by God but are not to be confused with God. Pluralism further rejects the Christian and Jewish identification of God with the God of Abraham, Isaac, and Jacob, the God who Christians believe became incarnate in Jesus. Chopra feels the biblical view of creation undermines true spirituality because it introduces the great roadblock to love: duality. Duality is the belief that there are separate selves. It is also the belief that God is distinct from us. If we are different from God, then we will begin to see ourselves as inferior and perhaps even sinful. Such duality in our thinking, Chopra explains, makes us feel unlovable, and therefore, produces unloving actions in our life:

> Duality is and always has been an illusion. There is no one out there waiting for you. There is only you and the love you bring to yourself. In spirit you are united with all other souls, and the only purpose of separation is for you to rejoin that unity.[4]

Chopra reveals the narcissistic master narrative underlying not only his view of spirituality but much of modern pluralism: God is the sum of all our thoughts about God and therefore is a projection of the self. Self-love is the only real love in a pluralistic world.

How then would Chopra address the second and third life issues? To the question, How do I find love and the ability to love in a world that has forgotten how to love? Chopra would tell me to look within and realize that I am the God of love who can therefore choose to love myself and others. I am the being who has ultimate meaning in the universe, and therefore, my pronouncements are final. To the question regarding how I find community and peace in a world of diversity and differences, Chopra would say that I must learn to see all concepts of God and all concepts of diversity within humanity as illusions. I must see that all reality is but the diverse expression of a single infinite self.

The birth of Jesus Christ presents a radical alternative to this pluralistic spirituality of pantheism and infinite self-love. In contrast to the idea that love is simply the self uniting with its cosmic protection, the story of Jesus presents love as coming from a source different from the self. From the story of the birth of Jesus, we identify a third homecoming truth regarding true spirituality: *Love comes to us as a stranger from a strange land.* To the question of how love can break through the divisions of our world and bring peace, the story of Jesus gives a simple answer: It is the birth of Jesus, as the angels said to the shepherds on that first Christmas, that is humanity's best hope for "peace on earth and good will toward men."

Before we can enter into the birth of Jesus, we must first answer some central questions: (1) Why do modern pluralists reject the uniqueness of Christ? (2) How should Christians respond to this pluralist challenge? (3) What are the implications of the birth of Jesus for the spiritual journey?

The Challenge of Pluralism

In the opening story, the angel builds on the Girl's parable of pluralism by describing how the village elders passed a law: "The four blind men had learned their lesson, however, and declared that no one in the village, on pain of banishment, had the right to proclaim that they had the final truth about the elephant. Everyone was required to admit that their view was limited and partial."

Today, in the global village, pluralism has become, if not a new law, at least a new religious orthodoxy. Those who insist that their view of God is the true one are viewed as breaking the rules of the religious marketplace. The old game of "my religion is better than your religion" is in very bad taste. In such an atmosphere, many Christians find it increasingly difficult to say with Peter in Acts 4:12, "Salvation is found in no one else, for there is no other name under heaven given to men by which we must be saved." For the modern pluralist, the only god that we should seek in prayer or worship is a familiar god from the familiar place of our world culture. The idea that the love we need to answer the great life issues could be given by a unique stranger different from the rest of us and our other religious leaders and who comes from a strange place beyond our time and space is not acceptable.

One of the shapers of this new pluralist orthodoxy is John Hick. In a series of important books and articles, he has called for a broadening of the concept of religion in general and salvation in particular. His call has been well received both in academic circles as well as among the wider public. His challenge to Christ's uniqueness can be summarized under five points.

First, since over 75 percent of the world is non-Christian and since most of the time a person's place of birth determines that person's religion, how can we claim that Christianity is the true revelation of God?

Second, serious study of other religions has made it impossible to be provincial about the superiority of Christianity. In addition, the migration to the West of millions of Muslims, Hindu, and Sikhs has exposed us to the quality of their worship and lives. We are therefore forced by the facts to reject the "older theology which held that God's saving activity is confined within a single narrow thread of human life, namely that recorded in our own Scriptures."[5]

Third, Hick rejects the idea that Christ saves all people, even those who do not believe in him. This position, known as inclusivism, is the attempt of certain Christian theologians to avoid a full-blown pluralism (all religions lead to God) by advocating instead that all humankind is saved by Christ working through the sacraments of the world's religions. Conscious faith in Christ is not needed to be saved by Christ. Why does Hick reject this Christian universalism? He sees in this inclusivism the old religious imperialism of traditional Christianity. It still clings to the old dogma that "only Christians can be saved: so we have to say that devout and godly non-christians are really, in some metaphysical sense, Christians or Christians-to-be without knowing it."[6] This is ptolemaic (human-centered) theology that falls into the trap of religious arrogance by making "our particular religion" the center of the spiritual universe.

What does Hick offer as an alternative? He calls for a Copernican revolution in our religious thinking that would put the "real" ineffable God in the center of the religious universe and would relegate all human religions to a fairly equidistant orbit around him. "He is the sun," writes Hick, "the originative source of light and life, whom all the religions reflect in their own different ways."[7]

Fourth, Hick denies that Jesus ever claimed to be unique. He believes that the science of biblical criticism has shown that Christ never made such statements. Hick agrees with those scholars who suspect that the early church fabricated much of the Gospel accounts in order to justify their faith in Christ. Given the fact that the evidence for the deity of Jesus has been tampered with, it is inadmissible, says Hick, in support of the supremacy of Christ. At the same time, a Christian is still free to regard Jesus as personally meaningful for him or her without regarding him as the only way.

Fifth, Hick sees his views as part of a story—the unfolding story of worldwide religious harmony. The future that Hick looks toward is not one in which a single world religion emerges supreme but one in which the various religions regard each other as of equal validity and quality and freely exchange elements of faith and worship. Pluralism is thus the path to a desirable future for the world community.

A more recent apologist of pluralism is Paul Knitter. Knitter takes a slightly different approach to pluralism than does Hick. While admitting that the Gospels and the Epistles all claim that Jesus is Lord and God, Knitter feels they do so with a limited intent. The claims of the New Testament, says Knitter, are intended to be true only for the Christian community and not for the world. Jesus was Lord for Christians. Jesus was God in the flesh for Christians. What is incorrect in the modern world, according to Knitter, is to assume that these ancient statements by a parochial religious community were ever intended for the vast majority of the world's people about whom Christians were not even aware. These claims for Christ's supremacy can still be maintained by the church as long as we realize we are using family language and not universal, metaphysical language. Adding Knitter's argument to Hick's, we have the broad outline of the contemporary case for pluralism.[8]

Identifying the Stranger from the Strange Land

What should we think about the challenge of pluralism? Our opening story suggests an answer. In her dream, Mary is given another parable to counteract the pluralist parable of the Girl. The new parable is a story about the Elephant Man, who breaks the pluralistic religious law of the village with truths that transcend the blindness of the village. Just as the Elephant Man challenged the neat religious arrangements of the four blind men, so too the Christ of the Christian story challenges the assumptions of modern pluralism and presents a different model of true spirituality. Seven witnesses identify the Elephant Man as none other than the one and only Savior of all humankind, the true Lord of the spiritual quest.

Witness #1: The Story of Jesus' Birth

First, the birth of Jesus points to his identity as the unique and only Lord and Savior. In the story, Mary describes the birth of her son and the remarkable words of the angel. While her four visitors are unimpressed with the story, much about the birth of Jesus should have attracted their attention.

The two Gospels that carry the birth narrative tell a simple but beautiful story, full of the drama of homelessness, the suspense of an evil, scheming monarch, and the pageantry of angels and wise men worshiping in a barn. But beneath the drama and pageantry are two very critical clues to the identity of Jesus. The first clue relates to the position of Jesus in Old Testament history. The second clue involves the role of the Spirit of God in the birth of Jesus.

Matthew gives us clue number one in his opening genealogy. He begins his Jesus story with "a record of the genealogy [literally, *genesis*] of Jesus Christ the son of David, the son of Abraham" (1:1). For Matthew, the Old Testament story falls into three periods of time marked by key events, events of which Jesus is the fulfillment. The first is the period from Abraham and his foundational covenant with Israel to the establishment of the Davidic line. Period two is the downward descent of Israel from the Davidic monarchy to the Babylonian "holocaust," which destroyed Israel as a nation. Period three covers the slow return of the people to the land, culminating in the return of the last and greatest of the Davidic kings, the Messiah himself. During each of these three stages in the story, something important is revealed about Jesus and his identity.[9]

Let's begin at the beginning. The first eleven chapters of Genesis not only reveal the identity of Israel's God (Creator of heaven and earth and thus a universal God sovereign over Israel and all other nations) but also the great problem Israel's God must solve. "Having created the earth and human beings to dwell with him upon it, God witnessed the rebellion of the human race against his love and authority." By Genesis 11 and the story of Babel, "we find the effects of sin have reached a 'global' scale, with humanity scattered in division and confusion across the face of the earth, an earth still under the curse of God." Genesis 12 provides God's answer to the problem of global sin. God refuses to save humankind through a Promethean hero like Hercules. Instead, he chooses a seventy-five-year-old man and his barren wife. They are to be the gracious recipients, says the Lord, of a son through whom all the nations of the earth will be blessed. When we begin to see the Old Testament story narrow its focus to Israel, we cannot forget that God's intentions are always global and that Israel's true role is not just to be blessed by God but to be a blessing to the nations.[10]

David's kingship is important for many reasons, but perhaps the principal reason Matthew mentions him is that it is during his reign that the Abrahamic covenant receives both an initial fulfillment and a revised future. Israel has truly become a great nation. But during David's reign God makes clear that he has a future and more extensive fulfillment in mind. In 2 Samuel 7:14, God promises David a son who will reign forever. Thus, period one in Matthew's genealogy comes to an end with the predication of a king unlike any other.

During the second period of Israel's history, mentioned by Matthew in the first chapter of his Gospel (from David to exile), that promise of the Davidic covenant is never fulfilled. The royal descendants of David, even Solomon in all his wisdom, are unfaithful to the covenant. They do not worship Yahweh first, nor do they provide a light to the nations. Prophets such as Jeremiah emerge in the sixth century B.C. who predict the destruction of the temple and the departure of Yahweh from Zion due to the sins of the nation. National unfaithfulness leads to exile in Babylon and the dismantling of the civic and religious institutions of the Jewish nation in 587–586 B.C. "The unthinkable had happened," writes Chris Wright. "God's people were evicted from God's land. The exile had begun and engulfed a whole generation. The monarchy had ended."[11] The great question in the face of this catastrophe was whether God's promises had failed (compare Isa. 40:27). The prophet Isaiah foresaw, however, that Israel's God would renew the covenant and restore the nation. In Isaiah 40–55, Israel is given the assurance "that Yahweh is not only still the sovereign Lord of all creation and all history . . . , but that he is about to act again on behalf of his oppressed people with a deliverance which will recall the original exodus, but dwarf it in significance."[12]

Within fifty years of Isaiah's prophecy, it looked as though the fulfillment of the Davidic covenant was just around the corner with the dawn of period three (from the exile to Jesus). In 539 B.C., Cyrus of Persia defeated Babylon and gave the Israelites their freedom to return home. Over the years that followed, the nation was rebuilt, but the Davidic line of kings was never restored. In 164 B.C., the priestly Maccabees family led a successful revolt against the Syrian colonial oppressors and established a royal dynasty that lasted roughly until the conquest of Palestine by Rome in 63 B.C. Though the non-Jew Herod the Great had been given the title King of the Jews, there was widespread opposition to his rule. The Davidic throne still had not been restored. Religious groups such as the reclusive Essenes, the puritanical Pharisees, the politically compromised Sadducees, and the militant Zealots jockeyed for position during the reign of Herod, as each group awaited, either with hope, fear, or skepticism, the fulfillment of the ancient promise of a Davidic king. It is no wonder that when Jesus arrived on the scene, he generated such interest among Israel's "royal watchers." Matthew implies in his genealogy that Jesus is the one who fulfilled not only recent messianic expectations but the older promises made to David and ultimately to Abraham. There seems to be little doubt that "one like the ancient of days" had come.[13]

Luke supports Matthew's view of history and his view of Jesus. In Luke 1:32–33, he records the prophecy of the angel that the coming of Jesus will open a new and never-ending chapter to the story of Israel and the world. Jesus will be called "son of the Most High." He will be given David's throne. Most significantly, "he will reign over the house of Jacob forever; his kingdom will never end." What kind of person can fulfill such statements? The modern reductionist Jesus, shorn of this framework of promise and deliverance, will not do. The only Jesus who fits the Old Testament story of Israel is one who came from God and possessed the power and authority of God.

The second clue about the identity of Jesus in the birth narratives of both Matthew and Luke is the emphasis on Jesus' birth through the Spirit. Luke 1:35 contains the words of the angel announcing the unique birth of the Messiah. The angel explains to Mary that "the Holy Spirit will come upon you, and the power of the Most High will overshadow you. So the holy one to be born will be called the Son of God." The identity of Christ as Son of God is directly linked to the nature of his birth. We have tended down through the history of the church to summarize this unique event as "the virgin birth." What does this event tell us about the identity of Jesus? Raymond Brown helps to answer that question. His *Birth of the Messiah* is the most extensive scholarly study of the subject in English. In this book, Brown studies the birth narratives in Matthew and Luke to learn as much as possible about the role they play in the Jesus story. The message of these narratives, Brown says in summary, is that "God has made Himself present to us in the life of His Messiah who walked on this earth, so truly present that the birth of the Messiah was the birth of God's Son."[14]

Thus, the first witness to the true identity of Jesus is the birth of Jesus itself. From its opening chapter, the story of Jesus militates against the concept that he was just an ordinary human person. His birth points to his extraordinary identity. This was no ordinary birth. This was no ordinary child. Though truly human, this Son of God was God the Son. For that reason, the Gospel writers present Jesus as the unique Son of God both by referring to the story of the Old Testament, which he fulfills, and the special activity of the Holy Spirit, which he receives.

Witness #2: The Claims of Jesus

Second, the words of Jesus himself require that he be seen as the only Lord and Savior. In the opening story, the Elephant Man reveals himself to the villagers as the Son of the Elephant King and the only one who can cure their blindness. These claims divide the village just as they divide the religious world today. Historically, Christianity has declared to the global village that Jesus was the "Elephant Man," the unique incarnation of the "Elephant King," the God of Abraham, Isaac, and Jacob.

What do we as Christians do then about the assertion by pluralists such as John Hick that Jesus never made claims of uniqueness? Modern biblical scholarship, pluralists argue, has shown that the statements in the Gospels, such as John 14:6 ("I am the way and the truth and the life"), were simply inventions of the early church and not original statements of Jesus.

While this is not the place for a full-blown discussion of modern biblical criticism, a little background on the stages of Jesus scholarship may help to put the skepticism of people like John Hick in perspective. Jesus scholarship in the last 150 years can be divided into three stages. The first stage is the *old quest* for the historic Jesus. Scholars in this phase tended to reject all claims of Christ's divinity and sought to recast Jesus in more human terms. Albert Schweitzer in the early years of the twentieth century exposed the main flaw in the old quest portrait of Jesus. Each scholar tended to view Christ in the image of a modern scholar. Reading one's own ideals into Jesus not only obscured the historical Christ more than orthodoxy had allegedly done, it also alienated modern scholars from the early church, which wrote the Gospels with a completely different vision about who Christ was.

After the old quest came to an end, it was eventually followed (after a rather lengthy period of anti-historical New Testament scholarship led by Rudolf Bultmann) by a second stage of scholarship called the *new quest* for the historical Jesus. Beginning in the 1950s, this movement was also extremely critical of the text of the Gospels. Culminating in the highly controversial Jesus Seminar, the new quest produced some useful scholarship but ended up with the same subjective and reductionistic view of Christ that hampered the old quest. When John Hick and other pluralists make the statement that Jesus never claimed to be unique or divine, they are basing their statements on the writings of new quest scholarship.

Since the 1970s a third stream in Jesus scholarship has appeared. Known as the *third quest*, this stage, characterized by studies such as Ben Witherington's *The Jesus Quest* and N. T. Wright's *Jesus and the Victory of God*, is less biased toward the early church and their view of Jesus.[15] Critical of the limits of the modern skeptical mind-set, yet committed to using the best tools of historical research, the third quest now takes the Gospels seriously as historical sources. Furthermore, these scholars are willing to take the portrait of Jesus that arises from these Gospels as the historical Jesus. Within this new stream of scholarship, the claims that Christ made about himself and his work are not dismissed out of hand as they were by new quest scholars. Christians who believe that Jesus understood himself to be unique can gain at least some encouragement from this new movement within Jesus scholarship.[16] Hick's statement that modern biblical scholarship disproves the deity and uniqueness of Jesus is thus inaccurate in light of third quest contributions.

But let's give Hick the benefit of the doubt. Let's agree not to use Christ's boldest claims to divine identity and authority. What evidence are we left with? Ironically, even the milder statements of Christ provide overwhelming indirect evidence that he understood himself to be the unique Son of God and Savior of the world. What kind of indirect evidence do I have in mind?

Consider first the parables that Jesus told. These pithy and picturesque mini-stories are regarded by even the most severe critics of the Gospels as authentic statements of Christ. We all remember favorites such as the lost sheep or the prodigal son. But there is more than wit and local color in these stories. They each assume that Jesus has the authority to change the Old Testament way of salvation. Christ's parables are unique. We find nothing like them in rabbinic literature. The rabbis used parables to illustrate Old Testament truths, not to challenge them. Christ, however, used parables to communicate new truths, thus implying that his authority to teach was divine. Christ's most famous parable, the prodigal son in Luke 15, is not only a story of sinners (Gentiles) coming back to a loving father. It is also about the father rebuking the elder son (Israel) when the latter rejects the welcome given to the prodigal (the widening of salvation to the Gentiles). Upon whose authority did Jesus base his retelling of Israel's story of salvation? His own authority. Jesus' words "but I tell you" reveal not only that he had the right to change the rules Israel's God had laid down in the Old Testament but also that Israel's God was in complete agreement with these changes. The powerful subtext of the stories Jesus told have led some scholars to conclude that "the parables' main aim is to let the recipients recognize Jesus' authority as the sole source of a salvific relationship with God."[17]

We could also point, secondly, to Christ's use of "Abba" for God. This familiar and affectionate Aramaic reference to God as a beloved and intimate father is rare in rabbinic literature. This use of Abba tells us that Jesus believed he had a special relationship with God. He claimed to enjoy a unique relationship with God as his Father. In the parable of the wicked tenants (Mark 12:1–12), Jesus describes himself as the uniquely loved son of the vineyard owner. In Matthew 11:27 and Luke 10:22, he claims that "no one knows the Father except the Son."

Consider, third, some of the other statements that Christ made about himself. In Mark 1:15 ("The time has come," [Jesus] said. "The kingdom of God is near. Repent and believe the good news."), the coming of the kingdom is equated with the presence of Jesus. This points to his superhuman status. In Luke 10:23, Jesus said, "Blessed are the eyes that see what you see." In Luke 11:31, he referred to himself as "greater than Solomon." He saw himself as the object of all prophecy in Luke 24:25–27. Jesus claimed to be in a category different from others. He was the "ransom for many" (Mark 10:45). His blood inaugurated a new covenant (Matt. 26:27–28). He told a crippled man in Mark 2 that his sins were forgiven, and when people in the crowd objected that only God could forgive sins, he healed the man to prove "that the Son of Man has authority on earth to forgive sins" (v. 10). Even one of his followers, Peter, after seeing him in action and listening to his teaching, was forced to conclude, "You are the Christ, the Son of the living God" (Matt. 16:16).

Christ's contemporaries heard these statements and responded accordingly. Socrates was killed by his enemies in Athens for "corrupting the youth," but he never claimed to be anything more than a mere mortal. Christ was killed by his enemies on a more serious charge. "'We are not stoning you for any of these,' replied the Jews, 'but for blasphemy, because you, a mere man, claim to be God'" (John 10:33). The statements of Jesus that drove his enemies to anger would drive his followers toward an understanding of his divine identity, which only the doctrine of the Trinity could properly capture.

We are forced by any reading of the evidence to conclude that Jesus saw himself as the unique Lord and Savior of humanity. There can be no reduction of Jesus to the level of teacher or rabbi. As C. S. Lewis states, "The discrepancy between the depth . . . of His moral teaching and the rampant megalomania which must lie behind His theological teaching unless He is indeed God has never been satisfactorily got over."[18] In short, even the most ardent deconstruction of the Gospels still gives us a portrait of the Jesus who was superhuman, spoke with divine authority, had a special Father-Son relationship with God, whose kingdom was equated with himself, and who loved sinners and believed he could save them.[19] Such statements leave no doubt that Jesus regarded himself as the divine Lord and Savior of the world.

Witness #3: The Actions of Christ

Third, the actions of Jesus can be explained only as the actions of one who was the unique Lord and Savior of humankind. In the story told earlier, the actions of the Elephant Man speak louder than his words. His power to cure blind eyes convinces many within the village to trust him as the Elephant King incarnate. In a similar way, the actions of Jesus help us to put his words in context. Alongside his lofty claims stand his self-giving acts of deliverance. Consider the fact that Jesus related to the socially marginalized of his day—lepers, tax collectors, prostitutes. Critics generally agree that the Gospel stories of Jesus and his association with the downtrodden are probably authentic because they would have little value in enhancing his reputation to later generations. Yet these stories of Jesus showing compassion to prostitutes, tax collectors, and lepers portray him as someone who loved sinners enough to die for them. They show him to be one of the most compassionate, moral, self-giving leaders in history.

Christ's compassion expressed itself in miracles that cured those afflicted by disease and deformity. When Christ fed the five thousand, gave sight to blind Bartimaeus, expelled the demons from the wild man of Gadarenes, and raised Jairus's daughter from the dead, he was doing more than merely displaying raw power. Jesus was doing things that only God himself could do. The miracles were signs that God in Christ was destroying Satan's kingdom and establishing his rule among humankind.

Mary, at the end of our story, understood this powerful connection between Jesus' actions and his true identity: "She would know why water turned to wine when it touched his lips; why paralytics turned to pole-vaulters at the touch of his words; why roaring seas became purring pussycats when he rose from his slumber; and why gray stones, like soldiers under orders, rolled away from his tomb. The Son of God was God the Son."

If Jesus cannot be accepted as merely a good teacher due to some of his amazing claims, then he might be dismissed as a liar or a lunatic. But is that really the impression he makes on the reader of the Gospels? Those who knew him best never charged him with being self-deluded or insane. He was a rational, composed, compassionate individual. There remains, however, another explanation for the enigma of Jesus and his identity: megalomania. But even though Jesus made the most outrageous claims about himself, his lifestyle of humble, other-oriented service and sacrifice refutes this charge. The best explanation for this combination of high claims and humble service is that he was in fact Israel's God in human form.[20]

Witness #4: The Testimony of the Early Church

Fourth, those who knew Christ best regarded him as the only Lord and Savior of all humanity. Acts 4 records the arrest of Peter and John and their trial in the Jewish religious courts for preaching about Christ. Peter's eloquent defense is recorded by Luke. As his critics listen, Peter reaches the climax of this courtroom drama in verse 12: "Salvation is found in no one else, for there is no other name under heaven given to men by which we must be saved." Such claims, augmented by the bold statements of John 1:1 ("The word was God") and Hebrews 1:3 ("The Son is the radiance of God's glory and the exact representation of his being"), are not ideas solely for first-century Jewish Christians living in the Mideast. They were intended to be universal truth about salvation, a universal truth that comes through a very special history, that of Israel's Messiah who is also the Savior of the entire world. The clear thrust of Peter's statement is that he is under moral obligation to proclaim Christ to all people, because without faith in Christ there is no salvation.

One of the strangest assumptions of modern Gospel criticism is that those who knew Christ best distorted the truth about him the most. Though some scholars cling to the older view that the Gospels were written over a hundred years after the death of Christ, more recent estimates tell us that they were all written within a generation of the events they record. Despite the firsthand knowledge that the New Testament writers had of Jesus, they are nonetheless treated by modern scholars as participants in a conspiracy of lies.

What makes this prejudice against the early church stranger still is the startling fact that within twenty years of his death, Jesus was regarded as God incarnate, the one and only Lord of creation and salvation. What was it about Jesus that inspired such claims? The words and deeds of Christ culminating in his redemptive death and miraculous resurrection are a better explanation for the early church witness to Christ than the conspiracy theory of new quest scholars. Once the resurrection is admitted as fact, then the claims of the early church accurately reflect the true glory of his person. Such claims in so short a time would be unimaginable without some basis in fact. Imagine a biography of the British leader Winston Churchill, written within the lifetime of people who actually knew him, that claimed he forgave sins, performed miracles, healed the sick, claimed he was God, and rose from the dead. There would be a huge outcry against such a portrait because of the large number of people who could refute such statements. But we have no such refutation of the claims of the Gospel writers by their generational peers.[21] Even the enemies of Christianity admitted that the tomb was empty. The portrait of Jesus drawn by the early church seems to have rung true to those who lived in Jesus' time, even if they refused to put personal faith in him.

I agree, therefore, with Jürgen Moltmann that the early church's witness to Christ should be taken seriously:

> Historically speaking, it is inadmissible to assume that on the basis of its experience with the risen and present Christ the Christian community projected anything into the history of Jesus which was inconsistent with the remembrance of him as he was during his lifetime. Historically it is more plausible to assume that the experience of the present Christ and the remembrance of the Christ of the past corresponded, and complemented one another.[22]

What of Paul Knitter's claim that the early church never intended to suggest that the titles of Jesus implied his lordship or saving relevance outside the Christian community? He attempts to distinguish between core beliefs ("Jesus is a savior"), which are of universal significance, and cultic expressions ("Jesus is the only Savior"), which are true only within the church. When the New Testament declares that "Jesus is Lord," it is speaking of the culturally conditioned faith of the church and its relationship with Jesus, not a metaphysical declaration of his universal supremacy. Alister McGrath's critique of Knitter's argument is on the mark: "This seems to represent a strategy designed with the sole objective of neutralizing the clear thrust of the New Testament proclamation."[23]

By way of analogy, imagine a medical researcher using such double-talk when she publishes a paper on the cure for cancer in a medical journal. Her discoveries, she writes, are absolutely true and have been proven by repeated experiments, but the cure for cancer is true only for other researchers. She never intended to imply that her science was true for all human beings. Such an approach is not only unacceptable in scientific literature, but it is an offense to common sense. If something is really true in the thought world of the biblical writers, then they believed it was true for everyone, not just for the smaller circle of believers. We have no right to read back into biblical times or into the minds of biblical writers the relativism of our own confused age.

In light of the evidence, I can only affirm that the portrait of Jesus painted by the early church is the best likeness available. And that portrait is of a Jesus who is both true man and true God.

Witness #5: The Worldwide Expansion of the Gospel

Fifth, the worldwide expansion of the gospel refutes the charge that the gospel of Jesus Christ is not universally available and therefore not universally valid. Pluralists such as John Hick argue that a universal truth (such as God and his way of salvation, for example) must be universally available. It is not fair, he argues, for God to communicate saving truths about himself to only a particular people at a particular time. How could a universal God withhold such crucial information from most of the world by revealing himself to only a small group tucked away in a corner?

Is it so strange, however, for God to reveal universally valid truths through the narrow channel of a particular individual in a particular time and place? Isn't the entire history of science a history of particular discoveries at particular times by particular people that only slowly spread around the world, where they were recognized as universally valid? Take the case of antibiotics. Penicillin was discovered in 1928 by British bacteriologist Alexander Fleming. Since its discovery in England, the use of penicillin and its family of antibiotics has spread around the world. Wherever it has gone it has healed diseases and alleviated suffering, yet no one complains that this universally valid medical breakthrough should be discounted because it came to light through a particular person at a particular time.

The same God who reveals medical truths to his world through special individuals in a given time and place acted similarly by revealing spiritual truths to his world through the person of Jesus Christ.

Furthermore, the worldwide mission of the Christian church has brought this universal message around the globe. There are now more Christians in non-Western cultures than there are in the West. In 1998, there were 238 countries in the world. In 150 of these countries, Christianity was the religion of more than 50 percent of the population. In another 58 countries of the world, Christianity was the professed faith of a significant minority of the population. Only in 29 countries out of 238 was Christianity held by less than 1 percent of the population.[24] Along with this testimony of the growth of non-Western Christianity is the growth of non-Western missions. It is estimated that there are nearly ten times as many non-Western Christian missionaries as there are Western ones. The claim that religion is merely an accident of culture and geography is no longer true. Christianity is the most global of all the world's religions, and the ongoing work of missions means that those who have never heard of God's cure for sin and death will one day learn of this unique and miraculous gift. The claim of the pluralist that Jesus' message of salvation is too geographically and culturally limited to be true for all humanity is thus a distortion of the facts.

Witness #6: The Experience of Faith

Sixth, the experience of Christian faith leads to the affirmation that Jesus is the only Lord and Savior of humanity. In the elephant story, the village was divided between those who accepted that the Elephant Man had ultimate truth and could take away blindness and those who did not. Those who believed trusted in him, while those who were skeptical rejected him. What this part of the story teaches is that a commitment to faith is necessary to know the truth about Jesus. This is the special work of the Holy Spirit, who can open minds and convince hearts.

The experience of a Spirit-engendered faith enables one to see that the Jesus of the Gospels was the God of Abraham, Isaac, and Jacob come to earth as a real human being. That's the message of Christmas. He turned water into wine. He healed the sick and raised the dead. He calmed the storms and commanded demons to depart. He gave sight to the blind and made paralyzed bodies new again. He then rose from the dead, validating his claims to be the Creator God of the universe. The Spirit of God, speaking through the written Word of God, produces this understanding of Christ in ways that are deeper than reason or evidence.

It is wonderful that there is so much historical, textual, and archaeological evidence for the reliability of the Gospels. It is a great support for faith in the Christian story. We must remember, however, why we believe the Bible and its Gospels are reliable. Faith in the Christian story is a result of encountering Christ and accepting him as Lord. This means that I accept his judgments on truth and morality as the final word. I am no longer an autonomous thinker or ethicist. I accept his views on all things. John Frame states the difference that the experience of faith makes in affirming the reliability of the Bible:

> And if one is a Christian—if his or her ultimate loyalty is to Jesus—cannot one muster from that loyalty the courage to stand against even the frail reed of modern biblical scholarship? Many ancient Christians (and some modern ones) have had to do much more—to be burned alive, crucified, or thrown to lions—rather than renounce Christ. If Christ calls us to love God with all our heart, soul, mind, and strength, and to follow Jesus in all of our activities, how can we deny to him the small favor of adopting unpopular, but Christian positions on biblical scholarship.[25]

Frame's words apply just as aptly to the question of pluralism. To be a follower of Jesus means adopting Christ's view of himself. He claimed to be the Son of God. He claimed to be the only way, truth, and life. He claimed to be the Savior of the world. Does not our experience of faith in him require that we submit to his claims?

Christ taught that the Holy Spirit would lead his followers into all truth (John 16:13). This promise has led to the production of a reliable written canon of Scripture that teaches all we need to know about Jesus in order to love, enjoy, and serve him. When this Spirit-inspired faith fills the heart, the unique claims of Christ cut through the static of modern pluralism and convince the mind that humanity's one and only Savior has appeared.

Witness #7: The Arrogance of Pluralism

Seventh, only by affirming Jesus as the only Lord and Savior can we avoid the arrogance of pluralism and cultivate the humility of the cross. In the story, the claims of the Elephant Man are rejected by the village pluralists. But the reaction of the Elephant Man is fascinating. He does not act arrogantly. He is banished by people who (if his claims are true) are powerless over him. Yet he meekly accepts his banishment. What is the story trying to say?

Christians are often accused of religious arrogance and spiritual imperialism for affirming the supremacy of Christ. It is certainly true that Christians, as sinners, have been and will at times continue to be arrogant in their claims and behavior. Christians are not always consistent with their Christ. But the claim that Christian exclusivism is arrogant distorts the true Christian position. The true Christian position is that we approach other faiths from a position of weakness, not of superiority. The nobility of thought, the sensitivity to the spiritual dimension, the lofty ethics, and the intensity of zeal and devotion found in other religions often surpass that of the Christian. The Christian looks up at other religions around him and rejects them not out of arrogance but out of humility.

What do I mean? Christ reveals to the Christian that religious achievement, however noble, however lofty, is not the place where God has chosen to meet humankind. Lesslie Newbigin pictures the world's religions as a staircase reaching toward God and adorned with spiritual achievements of all kinds. But "the central paradox of the human situation is that God comes to meet us at the bottom of our staircase, not at the top, that our ascent towards God . . . takes us further away from the place where he actually meets us."[26]

Martin Luther declared that only a theology of the cross (one that rejects any human contribution to salvation) and not a theology of glory (one that emphasizes human morality or devotion) can lead us to the place of cleansing and mercy. Justification by faith is therefore the great scandal of religion. Man's work will not be accepted. God will not be pleased except by his own work in and through his Son. The Christian thus feels that it is the other religions of the world that in the last analysis project the very arrogance that they impute to Christianity. Though God has spoken to the world through Christ, the world continues to climb its staircases, pile up its achievements, and create its own religious solutions. With Paul the ex-Pharisee, members of other religions must come to the point at which they leave their achievements behind and even "consider them rubbish, that I may gain Christ and be found in him" (Phil. 3:8–9).

We can only conclude that the blind men of our day who claim that they have a God-centered view of religion cannot be believed. The god of John Hick is a god who agrees with his ideas and instincts about what God should be. The real center of Hick's religious universe is Hick's theory of religion. Pluralism is yet another human-centered perspective on truth that robs God of his glory. A truly God-centered view of religion depends on a reliable word from God—not a theory developed by our village blind men. That reliable word has come to us in the person of Jesus Christ and in the canonical writings that witness to him.

As the story makes clear, the discussion about Christianity and world religions should not be about "whose religion is better." It should not be an exercise in human pride. The discussion should be about who can make the blind villagers see. If the Elephant King alone can lift the curse of blindness and the Elephant Man is his chosen means of self-disclosure, then the village must seek him. If the blind men are right, then the villagers should follow them.

In the face of the arrogance of pluralism, the Elephant Man surprises us with his compassion. But he did not come to earth to complain about human pride. He didn't rise from the dead simply to show up other religions. He came as a "ransom for many." This means that God came down in the person of Jesus Christ not to condemn us for our rebellion and treason against him but to take our capital punishment upon himself. The Jesus of John 14:6 humbles himself before a world that snubs his true identity and washes the feet of his critics with his mercy and grace.

Experiencing the Birth of Jesus: Implications for Spirituality

The Philosopher in our opening story summarized pluralist spirituality in words that reflect popular thinking today: "I think God has many faces and can be reached through many paths. I find it impossible to believe that he would limit himself to one tribe. Everyone needs to believe they are loved by God no matter what their religion is. This is what it means to be spiritual: To believe that God, whatever you conceive him to be, loves you totally."

How should we respond to this pluralist spirituality and the challenge it brings to the quest for an authentic Christian spirituality? We must retell the story of the elephant and the blind men. We must declare that the Elephant King has come to us in human form to restore our sight. To confront the story of the Elephant Man is to confront the necessity of a decision. Not to decide is to decide. The voice of the King has spoken. Any response but glad submission leads to enmity with the

King and ultimate misery. The church of Christ is therefore under obligation to proclaim Christ as the only hope for those searching for union with God. The birth of Jesus as the return of the God of Israel to his creation is thus foundational to Christian spirituality. It is the key truth we tried to capture in homecoming truth 3: *Love comes to us as a stranger from a strange land.* In light of this truth, let me mention a few implications of this homecoming rule for spirituality.

First, spirituality must now be redefined in terms of what it does with Jesus. We cannot simply measure spirituality by ethics or passion. Gandhi would certainly outstrip most Christians in those categories. The great test of any spirituality must be what it has done with the Jesus story. How does it answer the question, Whose son is he? Many forms of spirituality today, captured by the therapeutic movement or New Age approaches, do not pass this test. Jesus' stature as the God of Abraham, Isaac, and Jacob come in human form puts him at the very center of the spiritual universe. Not to recognize that is to begin the search for spiritual reality in the wrong place and with little chance of success.

But can't one love God without believing that Jesus is God? The Christian response to this is that whatever god a person might claim to love is simply an invention of the mind. It is easy to love a god that we create. Designer gods match perfectly what we want them to be. One figure in the history of spirituality who captured the significance of this critical point was the eighteenth-century American pastor and theologian Jonathan Edwards. In his classic on true spirituality, *The Religious Affections*, Edwards refutes the idea that any image of God can produce authentic spirituality.

> Self love may be the foundation of an affection in men towards God, through a great insensibility of their state with regard to God, and for want of conviction of conscience to make them sensible how dreadfully they have provoked God to anger. They have no sense of the heinousness of sin as against God, and of the infinite and terrible opposition of the holy nature of God against it. *And so having formed in their minds such a God as suits them* [my emphasis] and thinking God to be such an one as themselves, who favors and agrees with them, they may like Him very well and feel a sort of love to Him, when they are far from loving the true God.[27]

In contrast, says Edwards, true spirituality and the love that is truly spiritual are marked by an appreciation for the inherent beauty of the person of Jesus prior to any thought of his benefit to us.

The first foundation of the delight a true saint has in Christ is His own perfection; and the first foundation of the delight he has in Christ, is His own beauty; He appears Himself the chief among ten thousand and altogether lovely. . . . They first have their hearts filled with sweetness from the view of Christ's excellency, and the excellency of His grace and the beauty of the way of salvation by Him, and then they have a secondary joy in that so excellent a Savior and such excellent grace are theirs.[28]

There is a place for sanctified self-love, but that place comes later. A God-centered appreciative love that focuses on Jesus must come first and is the mark of a love that is truly spiritual. It is a love for a stranger from a strange land whose inherent beauty as the infinite personal God become flesh fills the soul. I recall my own spiritual pilgrimage as a child seeking for something to fill the emptiness I felt. I had an idyllic childhood in many ways. I grew up surrounded by the wonders of nature and spent long hours fishing and walking in the beautiful forest behind my house. Yet for all the experience of God as Creator, it was only when I heard the message that the Creator had come into history to find me that my heart responded in true appreciative love for him. Though there was no doubt a measure of self-interest in my turning to God, what I remember about my decision to follow Christ was the sense of ecstasy my soul experienced in simply thinking about the beauty of Christ's person and work. He was the incarnation of the love that my soul desperately needed. But more than simply being the answer to my need, he appeared to me in my mind as full of beauty and glory in and of himself. This appreciative love for God in Christ preceded my "need love" for him. True spirituality, then, must be redefined in terms of what it does with Jesus.

Second, spirituality must be open to all. Someone might wrongly conclude that if we accept the uniqueness of Jesus as the gateway to the love of God, we are thereby closing the door to the rest of the world. The third life issue we stated earlier concerns this very thing: How do I find community and peace in a world of diversity and differences? The answer is in loving the world with the love that we have been given by the stranger from a strange land. The one who has come is for the whole world not just for a single tribe or culture. He seeks to tell the story of his coming and our homecoming through him to all the world. Into this world of diversity and difference comes a story of one who loves his exiled enemies. He seeks to pour out his transforming love on all those estranged exiles living in every culture, in every part of the earth, and in every age of history.

If Jesus is the one true God and Savior of humanity, being spiritual means being active in sharing him with the world. There can be no Christian spirituality without Christian missions. For all of our spiritual disciplines and practice of prayer, any spirituality based on the truth about Jesus as the God man must be activist and open to the world. We cannot be tribal or parochial. We cannot be selfish or privatistic. That is the sign that we are still living under an exile story.

Does this mean we should be arrogant crusaders imposing the Jesus story on innocent cultures? The very nature of the Jesus story is about rejecting the way of power and force and submitting humbly to the way of weakness and servanthood. No mission worthy of Christ's name would try to duplicate the misguided methods of the medieval Crusades. No spirituality worthy of the name would betray the example of Jesus by boasting of its superiority and imposing itself on others. The only authorized mission-oriented spirituality is one carried on in the spirit of John 20:21: "As the Father has sent me, I am sending you."

Third, spirituality involves worship of the historical Jesus. Jesus is more than an example to follow or a miracle worker to admire. He is the true and living God worthy of our worship. This Christ worship was not borrowed from first-century hellenism but was a necessary conclusion drawn from the understanding of the historical Jesus as the fulfillment of Jewish eschatology. But it is possible to turn from the historical Jesus as the object of our love and spiritual vision to an idealized image of him in his ascended glory. We no longer have to see Jesus in the story told by the apostles, one might wrongly conclude, because we can approach the cosmic Christ directly.

One of the problems of Corinthian spirituality addressed in Paul's first epistle to them is the denigration of the historical Jesus. The Corinthian "super saints" despised the material world of time and space. They wanted an "ahistorical" Christ as opposed to the Jesus of history. Paul warns against speculating about a heavenly Christ when he writes in 1 Corinthians 4:6, "Do not go beyond what is written," which is to say, the Jesus of the Gospels. When he defines the essence of the Spirit's work in the life of the believer in 1 Corinthians 12, it is to produce the conviction that "Jesus is Lord" (v. 3) and not just the confession that "Christ is Lord." The opposite of true spirituality according to that same verse is to despise the historical Jesus. True spirituality, even when one believes that Jesus is God, cannot bypass the Jesus of the Gospels. True spirituality is still living in and living out the Jesus story. This means that the Jesus who is risen and ruling our world today insists on being known in and through the Gospels. We cannot simply meditate on an idealized Jesus and bypass the incarnate Jesus. The birth of Jesus tells us not only that Jesus has taken on flesh but that he will always bear that incarnate form and wants us to know him and relate to him in his historical self-disclosure. Visions of the cosmic Christ that people have today and have had down through history should not confuse us. Such visions are at best secondary spiritual experiences. Seeing, loving, embracing, and serving the historical Jesus presented to us in the written Word is the heart of authentic Christian spirituality. The transformation zone of true spirituality is the past. We must go back to the historical Jesus in order to unleash the powers of heaven.

Fourth, spirituality is not about our quest for God but rather about God's quest for us. In the previous chapters, we talked about the mystic model of Deepak Chopra and its way of ascent. We also talked about Stephen Covey's moral model and its way of achievement. Both of these models begin with humanity as the new Ulysses sailing off to find God. The Jesus story, in its very opening chapter, ushers us into a new reality: Love comes to us. God is seeking us. He is the new divine Ulysses traveling the path of danger to find his wounded and defeated family. He is the father in the story of the lost son. He runs out to meet us as we stagger up the road. He is the shepherd who leaves his larger flock to find the single lost sheep. This is the God we need to know. The personal knowledge that we can have of him is that he is a God whose love moves him to know us, even in our exile. No Promethean model of spirituality fits into this fact about God. Any model that sees humanity as the lonely hero seeking an indifferent or distant God begins with such a deep exile mentality that it cannot know the God who has returned to Zion to make his dwelling place with human beings like you and me. To find God in the spiritual quest means being found by God. This is the meaning of the birth of Jesus, a birth that we must internalize by declaring that what Jesus did in Bethlehem he did *for us*. History crashes into the present and leads us back to the stranger from a strange place who gives us a greater gift than the wise men gave to him—the gift of a divine lover who seeks us out in order to bring us home.

Back to the Muslim from Memphis. At one point in the conversation I asked this young American convert to Islam a question that I'm sure many others had asked her.

"Would you mind my asking what attracted you to Islam? After all, it isn't widely regarded as being very friendly to women." I was not ready for the answer she gave.

"For me it wasn't an issue of convenience or comfort. For me it has always been a question of truth. I follow Islam because I believe it's true."

A question of truth. This is an answer that rebukes those of us who have become pragmatic about questions of religion and spirituality. Christian spirituality has much to commend it. But ultimately the most important reason for embracing the Jesus model is not just its benefits or its ability to fulfill our longings. It must be the question of truth. Pluralism may be more convenient in the modern world or more in line with the spirit of the age. But the truth about Jesus testified to by his birth must be the deciding factor. If he is just one of the world's many religious gurus, then take your pick. But if he is the true and living God come to earth to seek an exiled humanity, then "there is no other name by which we must be saved." He, the historical Jesus, is where God chose to reveal himself and to meet with humanity. He, the historical Jesus, is the source of salvation. He, the historical Jesus, is the Christ of the creeds, the maker of heaven and earth, and the last word about true spirituality. The Jesus of history is definitive in our search for God because the Jesus of history is both the God we seek and the God who seeks us.

4

PETER'S DREAM

EXPERIENCING THE BAPTISM AND TEMPTATION OF JESUS

In a century or two, or in a millennium, people will live in a new way, in a happier way. We won't be there to see it but it's why we live, why we work. It's why we suffer. We're creating it. That's the purpose of our existence. The only happiness we can know is to work toward that goal.

Anton Chekhov, *Three Sisters*

As soon as Jesus was baptized, he went up out of the water. At that moment heaven was opened, and he saw the Spirit of God descending like a dove and lighting on him. And a voice from heaven said, "This is my Son, whom I love; with him I am well pleased."

Matthew 3:16–17

The Story: Peter's Dream

After visiting Mary in Nazareth, the Theologian, the Philosopher, the Girl, and the African found themselves seated on the same bus heading back to Capernaum. They were going to continue their investigation of Jesus the wonderworker. They agreed that the key person to talk with this time was Peter, who was emerging as Jesus' right-hand man. When they arrived in Capernaum a few hours later, they intercepted Jesus and his disciples just as they were about to sail to the opposite shore for more preaching and wonder-working. The group of investigators pulled Peter aside and requested an interview. With his characteristic mixture of gruffness and good humor, Peter granted their request.

"Jump in the boat. We'll talk as we ride the waves."

The four looked at each other, glanced at the blue and cloudless sky above them, and followed Peter into the boat. The Girl saw Jesus at the back of the craft settling down for a nap. Peter hoisted the sail. Once they were underway, he told them the story of how he met his Master:

"I was having bad dreams. I'd wake up in the middle of the night, breathing heavy, eyes bulging out of my head. But once I was awake, I couldn't remember the dream. All I could remember was the feeling of terror. What kind of horror can you see in your dreams that would frighten your conscious mind so badly that it simply refuses to replay it? It was a question I couldn't answer.

"The nightmares had started soon after my brother Andrew and I had come to the Jordan to hear the message of John and prepare ourselves for the coming of the Messiah. I would spend entire days watching the crowds that had fought their way through the rush hour traffic in Jerusalem and made the twenty-mile journey to the Jordan to hear John the Baptist.

"I never failed to be amused by the typical reaction of the religious tourists. They would start by complaining about the prices at the kiosks by the Jordan, and then they would wonder what the big deal was anyway about a guy running around in animal skins. Then they would see him, John the Baptist, and would hear his message about the coming of the Messiah. Before you could say Shadrach, Meshach, and Abednego, they would take off their cameras and hats and dive right into the brown waters of the Jordan begging to be baptized. It happened so routinely that Andrew and I stopped keeping count. Messiah mania was growing.

"I soon realized that the big attraction was not the immersions of John but rather the message about the Messiah whom John was announcing. People were convinced that the Messiah was about to land and turn the world upside down. Every time the subject of the return of Israel's King came up, I would go over the grocery list of messianic facts I'd been taught since Sunday school. He would be the anointed one—that is, ordained by some sign for his kingly work. He wouldn't just be a king because he also had a role as a prophet and a priest. He would be a prophet, telling the people the liberating truths of God and restoring the Torah. He would be the last priest, restoring the temple and covering sins and bringing in the new covenant.

"But most of all he would be the great King, heir of the Davidic throne, who would conquer Rome and all the enemies of Israel and establish the kingdom of God on earth forever. When John told people that the Messiah was coming, visions of heavenly sugarplums started dancing in a thousand heads, and in no time sensible people were stripping down to their skivvies and diving into the Jordan. A chicken in every pot, two cars in every garage, no more death and taxes—all these things would be true when the Messiah came. Angels would descend on Jacob's ladder, and the glories of heaven would come spilling out like fish from a full net.

"And then just a couple of months ago the great day came. I was watching John baptize an attractive redhead, when all of a sudden he stopped and the poor girl almost drowned. John was looking at the top of the hill at a small figure walking all alone—looking a little lost. John pointed and at the top of his lungs yelled out, 'Behold, the Lamb of God, who takes away the sins of the world!' I looked at Andrew and told him, 'This is it.' I hadn't been this excited since my wedding day. Then I and the hundreds who lined the banks of the Jordan listened for the drumroll and waited for the lower end of Jacob's ladder to pop through a cloud.

"But nothing happened. A little man, maybe thirty, who was dressed as badly as I was, walked through the crowd and down to the water's edge. He took off his sandals and stripped down to his underwear. He walked into the Jordan, stood in front of John, and said in a whisper, "I want to be baptized." They exchanged some words, which few could hear. The little man was dwarfed by John. It was all so ridiculous, I thought. This small, quiet man in his underwear was the Messiah? What kind of Messiah gets baptized for the remission of sins? If this was the Great Physician, shouldn't he heal himself?

"Just when the scene looked like it couldn't get any more ridiculous, a bird landed on the Lamb of God. I couldn't believe my eyes at the absurdity of the scene. The man was standing in the muddy water, making John look like a giant. There were no chickens in the pot, no cars in the garage, no angels, no Jacob's ladder, and on top of this, a bird lands on the Messiah's head. The bird man was supposed to be the 'one to come.' I almost laughed out loud. And I would have if it were not for what happened next.

"There was a light from the sky. The clouds parted. I heard a voice from heaven that made the waves of the Jordan stand at attention. Everyone heard it. It was impossible not to hear it. 'This is my beloved Son, in whom I am well pleased,' the voice said, plain as day. Eleven simple words that shook the Jordan. I had heard the words before. They were words from the Hebrew Scriptures that spoke about the heir of David, perhaps referring to the Messiah, although I'd never heard them applied directly to the coming one. I couldn't help wondering if this was the sign from heaven showing that the bird man was in fact the one who would turn the world upside down.

"While I was puzzling over the words from heaven, the bird man disappeared. I asked around to find out where he had gone, but no one seemed to know. Weeks went by while I tried to figure out his next move. Then some hunters came in from the wilderness saying they'd seen a mysterious figure out there in the wilds that fit his description. They gave me a rough idea of where they had spotted him. I determined to find him and confront him. I needed to know for myself if this Jesus was truly the one who would turn the world upside down or whether I should wait for another.

"For seven days I searched the wilderness for the bird man, following the crude map given to me by the hunters. On the seventh day just as the sun was setting, I came over the top of a hill and saw him standing on a cliff with another figure. I got as close as I dared and hid behind a rock. Even in the soft and forgiving reds and golds of the dying sun, Jesus looked terrible. He looked like he hadn't eaten or slept in weeks. The person standing next to Jesus looked like an angel. He was the most beautiful creature I'd ever seen. Jesus once again looked small and weak next to the dazzling figure from another world. If I'd been asked to pick the King of the Jews at that moment, I'd have voted for the angel of light.

"I could hear the two talking together but could barely make out what they were saying.

"'If you are the Son of God,' said the beautiful creature, 'tell these stones to become bread.'

"Jesus answered 'It is written: Man does not live on bread alone, but on every word that comes from the mouth of God.'

"The angelic figure scowled at this answer and gave a second challenge to the bird man. 'If you are the Son of God, throw yourself down. Isn't it written somewhere that God will protect you?'

"'Isn't it also written: Do not put the Lord your God to the test?' was the quick reply.

"The angel grew furious at his words, and with a mad motion of his hands pointed to the great valley below them. At this point I was shaking like a leaf and my eyes were bulging out because as the angel spoke, all the kingdoms of the world were on display. I don't know how he did it, but it was all there. Jerusalem lay just below them, and the city-states of Greece and even the imperial capital of Rome were visible on the horizon. The lights of the cities stretched out before us like fallen stars.

"'All this I will give you,' spoke the angel in a voice as regal as Caesar's, 'if you will bow down and worship me.'

"I couldn't believe my ears. This was blasphemy. The beautiful creature was no angel. The moon was out now, and I could see the face of Jesus clearly in the cold light. There was no doubt about it—Jesus had smiled.

"'So you would give me my kingdom all at once, would you? Wipe out all my enemies in an instant? I'd get to have my visible rule before the whole watching world in the twinkling of an eye? I must admit it's faster than building it in two stages: First loving my enemies and then ending all enmity. My way is longer and more painful.'

"I could see Jesus look toward the kingdoms of the world with their twinkling lights, and then I saw him turn back to the fallen angel.

"'Away from me, Satan. For it is written: Worship the Lord your God and serve him only.'

"Suddenly the devil was gone, and I saw more shining angels fall at the feet of Jesus than I could shake a stick at. They offered him food and drink and water to wash. 'Angels,' I recalled, 'would descend on Jacob's ladder, and the glories of heaven would come spilling out like fish from a full net.' I realized suddenly why I had not seen the new world order appear at the Jordan when Jesus arrived. I realized that the new world order was Jesus himself.

"And just at that moment when the true identity of Jesus was beginning to dawn on me, I remembered my nightmare. I remembered a face from the nightmare and five words that I had spoken in the dream. The face was that of the bird man, the Messiah, the true prophet, priest, and king who resisted Satan and passed the test of obedience. There was no horror in that face. And the words were innocent enough. In my dream I said them to a young girl who asked me a question I can't remember. 'I don't know the man,' was my reply. Simple words. Yet every time I think of these words the sweat forms on my forehead and my hands began to itch. What do you make of that?"

Peter's question hung in the air as his four listeners reviewed their own private utopias and the relevance of Jesus. The Philosopher envisioned an age of spiritual enlightenment and universal mysticism. The Jesus Peter described didn't seem to fit in that dream. The Theologian, like Peter, longed for the restoration of Israel's glory through a kingly Messiah who would conquer Rome. Jesus didn't fit the bill. The Girl daydreamed about a society of unrestricted personal freedom. The African Woman imagined a world free of racism. Jesus didn't really seem to fit either of their stories of the future. They were each about to tell Peter their private doubts about Jesus when suddenly a fierce storm exploded on the lake. Castles of dark clouds formed over the boat. Torrents of rain pelted down. Waves began to curl over the sides of the boat, and the sail ripped. The African looked back at Jesus. He seemed to be sleeping peacefully right through all the chaos. Peter yelled commands to the others and then went to the back of the boat and shook Jesus awake.

"Master, Master, we're going to drown," he yelled above the gale.

Jesus got up. He moved past his cowering disciples and the four interrogators and walked to the bow. Grabbing on to a rope, he held out his hand and commanded the storm to stop. In seconds the wind died down and the waves returned to their normal pitch and roll. He turned back to his frightened friends in the boat. With his eyes on Peter and his guests, he asked, "Where is your faith?"

Peter turned to the Theologian, the Philosopher, the Girl, and the African, who were looking puzzled and terrified.

"Who is this?" Peter asked them. "He commands even the winds and the water, and they obey him." (Based on Matthew 3:13–4:11; Luke 3:21–4:13.)

From Dream House to Haunted House

The Smiths recently had a lifetime wish come true. They were able to build their dream house. They had planned and saved for years. Finally, everything had come together, and their little utopia in the suburbs had been built. They had their pond out back. They had their barn for the horses. They had their quiet street for the children. Everything was ideal. Then the Joneses, a retired couple, moved in next door. The Joneses complained about the pond. They complained about the Smiths' children. They managed to prevent the Smiths from legally keeping horses. The Joneses criticized everything the Smiths did. They complained about the Smiths repeatedly to the local neighborhood association and turned the whole neighborhood against them. They threatened to sue the Smiths over minor things real and imagined. In short, the Joneses made the life of the Smiths miserable. The Smiths thought they were building their dream house. They ended up with something closer to a house of horrors.

The case of the Smiths and the Joneses reminds me of the double edge of utopian dreams. Like Peter and his friends in our opening story, when it comes to dreams, we can't live with them and we can't live without them.

Let me start with the positive side. One of the most characteristic features of being human is the dream for a better world. We are not just *Homo sapiens*. We are also *Homo utopians*, restless for a better place, a better world, a better home. Lest you think I'm exaggerating, just examine the evidence. Plato's *Republic*, the future visions of Isaiah and Ezekiel, Thomas More's *Utopia*, and Edward Bellamy's *Looking Backward* are the tip of the iceberg when it comes to utopian literature. From *Star Wars* to Bill Gates's *Road Ahead*, humanity longs for utopias fueled by such things as technology or "the force." In Anton Chekhov's *Three Sisters*, one of the characters, Colonel Vershinin, describes the power of utopian dreams: "In a century or two, or in a millennium, people will live in a new way, in a happier way. We won't be there to see it but it's why we live, why we work. It's why we suffer. We're creating it. That's the purpose of our existence. The only happiness we can know is to work toward that goal."[1]

Chekhov was convinced that we needed our utopian dreams in order to be happy. Steven Weinberg agrees. In an article in *Atlantic Monthly*, Weinberg describes some of the current utopian visions of twenty-first-century daydreamers. Even though most of the twentieth-century fantasies about the future (like communism's classless society and a world of universal peace and prosperity) have run out of steam, there are still plenty of smaller utopias to go around. He mentions "five and a half" in particular that "seem to be emerging in the public debate." Consider these slightly updated castles in the clouds:

- *The Free-Market Utopia.* Weinberg describes this as a world in which "government barriers to free enterprise disappear. Governments lose most of their functions, serving only to punish crimes, enforce contracts, and provide national defense." In the world of free trade and open markets, "the world becomes industrialized and prosperous."[2]

- *The Best-and-Brightest Utopia.* This is the dream that "public affairs are put in the hands of an intelligent and well-educated class of leaders." This is the blueprint drawn up by Plato in his *Republic,* and it lives on in pockets of corporate America and in Asian communities such as Singapore, where Lee Kuan Yew, senior minister of Singapore, has said "that only an elite, consisting of the top three to five percent of a society, can deal effectively with public issues."[3]

- *The Religious Utopia.* This is a dream of many conservative Christians and the nightmare of secularists. "A religious revival sweeps the earth reversing the secularization of society that began with the Enlightenment. Many countries follow the example of Iran, and accept religious leaders as their rulers. America returns to its historical roots as a Christian country. Scientific research and teaching are permitted only where they do not corrode religious belief."[4]

- *The Green Utopia.* The Green movement wins. "The world turns away from industrialism and returns to a simpler style of life. Small communities grow their own food, build houses and furniture with their own hands, and use electricity only to the extent that they can generate it from sun, wind, or water."[5]

- *The Technological Utopia.* Bill Gates wins. "The development of information processing, robotics, synthetic materials, and biotechnology increases productive capacity so much that questions about the distribution of wealth become irrelevant.

National borders also become irrelevant, as the whole world is connected by fiber optic cables."[6]

- *The Civilized Egalitarian Capitalist Utopia.* Weinberg's own modest utopia takes small pieces from the above and envisions a world he believes is just within reach (hence, he calls it only a half utopia). He describes it as a world flowing with art and opera: "Production remains mostly in the hands of competing private corporations, overseen by a democratic government that is itself overseen by independent courts; these corporations continue to use high salaries along with status authority to attract workers and managers with special talents, and dividends to attract capital. Those who receive a high income are able to keep only part of it; to prevent the rest of their income from being simply taken by taxes they give much of it to museums, universities and other institutions of their choice, reaping benefits that range from moral satisfaction, to better seats at the opera."[7]

So utopianism is alive and well and makes our pulses beat a little faster. But let me point out the dark side of future dreams. Weinberg's proposed utopias seem mild by past standards, but the story of the Smiths and the Joneses is a cautionary tale that applies to even moderate proposals for paradise. Let me state the problem bluntly: *We cannot seem to solve the problem of people.* As has been pointed out by many of our most insightful prophets and thinkers, such as Aldous Huxley and George Orwell in the twentieth century and John Calvin and Martin Luther in the sixteenth, human nature is the problem. We are the rain that spoils the parade. We are the ants at the picnic. We are the snake in the Garden. In Chekhov's play a character responds to the utopian visions of his friend:

> Well, maybe we'll fly in balloons, the cut of jackets will be different, we'll have discovered a sixth sense, maybe even developed it—I don't know. But life will be the same—difficult, full of unknowns, and unhappy. In a thousand years, just like today, people will sigh and say, oh, how hard it is to be alive. They'll still be scared of death, and won't want to die.[8]

Yet for all the sensible skepticism about utopianism by a Chekhov, a Huxley, or an Orwell, it simply will not go away. In fact, the current global quest for spirituality may well include a healthy dose of this utopian obsession—at least a desire for a highly private utopia in which the self can find its own personal island of happiness amid the wider dysutopia of a violent and decaying planet.

Why is utopianism so appealing? What need does it fulfill in the human heart? There are a number of answers to these questions. One of the reasons for the persistence of utopian dreams is our sense of homelessness. For all of our technology, progress, and industry, many of us still feel like aliens on this planet and long for a day when this world is turned into a place where we can feel at home. Hungry people dream of food. Homeless people dream of homes.

Why this sense of homelessness? To put it bluntly, most of us believe that the world as it is, is not the world as it should be. Suffering and hatred make living miserable. What does it matter that I can create a wireless network in my home if my kids hate me and my wife files for divorce? What good is a dream home in a neighborhood of malice? One test of the effectiveness of any spirituality is this utopian test. It is one of the great life issues mentioned in chapter 1: the issue of homelessness. How do I find a place to belong in a world of enmity and alienation?

The spirituality that we long for must give us hope about a future home on this planet, hope about a changed world and an end to enmity and alienation. In a world of racism, materialism, hatred, and war, we must insist that any spirituality contending for our allegiance must address the issues of changing society and transforming the world order. One of the reasons why Promethean and narcissistic stories control our lives is because we use them as bulwarks against the despair of daily living in a world that we feel is increasingly hostile. Unless Christian spirituality can show that the Jesus story answers this longing for a place to belong, a place to feel at home, rival master narratives will continue to produce an exile mentality in our search for God.

And here's the rub. One of the great objections to Christian spirituality is that it appears to fail the utopian test. Like the characters in our opening story, we see Jesus as irrelevant to our dreams about a golden age on earth. The inescapable fact is that though Christians claim that Jesus came in the first century as the Jewish Messiah to fulfill the Old Testament's prophecies about a new world order, after he left, there was no new world order anywhere to be seen.

This is the charge of at least one spokesperson of modern Judaism, philosopher Martin Buber. Modern Jewish rejection of Christ is based primarily on one fact. Jews were expecting the Messiah to bring in a new world order. When Jesus came, nothing changed. A purely spiritual change wrought within the soul is not true to the Old Testament Scriptures. This was Buber's main complaint as he wrote in 1933. "The church rests on its faith that the Christ has come, and that this is the redemption which God has bestowed on mankind. We, Israel, *are not able to believe this.*"[9]

Note that Buber does not say that Israel does not want to believe. Israel is unable to believe. Why? Buber continues:

> We know more deeply, more truly, that world history has not been turned upside down to its very foundations—that the world is not yet redeemed. We *sense* its unredeemedness. . . . The redemption of the world is for us indivisibly one with the perfecting of creation. . . . An anticipation of any single part of the *completed* redemption of the world—for example the redemption beforehand of the soul—is something we cannot grasp.[10]

Like most of us, Peter knew what alienation felt like. He also had firm ideas about what utopia would look like. Political freedom, personal prosperity, spiritual renewal through the dawning of the messianic age—that was his dream. The trouble was that Jesus didn't fit Peter's utopian stories. Jesus' actions both at his baptism and during his temptation contradicted most of the pleasing dreams that Peter desired and expected the Messiah to fulfill. Jesus not only contradicted Peter's expectations about the messianic age, but did so intentionally. Why? Jesus reveals that the utopian future humanity longs for has already come, not in the world around us but in the personal experience of Jesus himself. Just as the Theologian, Philosopher, Girl, and African were about to write off Jesus as irrelevant to their dreams, he arose in the midst of a storm and brought peace. One with such powers has entered into a new order of reality that each of us only dreams about. To get at that new order of reality, I want to take you on a tour of two key events in the life of Christ: his baptism in the Jordan and his temptation in the wilderness. As we tour this familiar ground, I believe we will discover a truth about true spirituality that will help liberate us from the rival utopias that have stolen our hearts.

I want to answer the utopian objections to Jesus by developing homecoming truth 4: *Love brings in the new world order by first becoming the new world order.* To persuade you of this truth, let's join Peter and the others by the waters of the Jordan and in the wild mountains of the wilderness.

The Jesus Dream Defined: Four Signs of the New World Order

In the opening story, Jesus' appearance at the Jordan is underwhelming for many, including Peter. As he tells the story, Jesus just arrived and waded into the Jordan, asking to be baptized by John. Peter felt the scene was ridiculous. After all, people were getting baptized in order to get ready for the King's appearance. It made no sense, if Christ was the long-awaited King, for him to get baptized. Plus, the messianic King was expected to come in a show of force and power. Jesus came in meekness and without an army. Adding to the oddness of the scene was the descent of the dove and the booming voice from heaven. Yet the New Testament writers saw the baptism of Christ as anything but ridiculous. "This event, the baptism of Jesus, was so important," writes Christopher Wright, "that it is included in all four Gospels and is frequently also the starting point of the apostles' preaching in Acts."[11]

What Peter and other Jewish observers found disorienting about the appearance of Jesus as the long-awaited messianic King was that he did not look the part. What did the part call for? The Old Testament is full of messianic expectations. Let me mention four of the most common items on the Jewish wish list.

First, the Messiah would take away the sins of Israel. Zechariah 9 is a famous messianic passage. There the prophet predicts the coming of Israel's God as a great king, regaining dominion and conquering enemies. But at the heart of this political renewal and military victory is the promise of cleansing. "Because of the blood of my covenant with you, I will free your prisoners" (Zech. 9:11). In Zechariah 13:1, we are told that in the age of the Messiah "a fountain will be opened to the house of David and the inhabitants of Jerusalem, to cleanse them from sin and impurity." This theme of the Messiah acting as a priest cleansing Israel is developed in Isaiah 52:13–53:12. This is the fourth and longest of the so-called "servant songs" in Isaiah and is the climax of the messianic visions found in chapters 40–66. The servant of the Lord, though an exalted being (52:13), will also be disfigured (52:14). This disfigurement seems to be the symbol of sacrifice, for once the servant is disfigured, he will "sprinkle many nations" (52:15), that is, he will perform the priestly function mentioned in Leviticus of sprinkling the blood of the sacrifice on sinners so that they will be morally clean in God's eyes. This theme of the suffering servant who may also be the kingly Messiah is developed in Isaiah 53, where the servant of God becomes the sin bearer of many (v. 5: "He was crushed for our iniquities; the punishment that brought us peace was upon him").

Second, the Messiah would bring the rule of God back to earth. The most frequent theme in Jewish messianic prophecy is the theme of royal rule over Israel and the world. This is the great homecoming of God after centuries of holy exile from his sinful people. In Zechariah 9:9, the messianic King enters Jerusalem in humility and peace ("riding on a donkey") and establishes control over the world such that "his rule [extends] from sea to sea" (Zech. 9:10). In 2 Samuel 7:13, God promises to "establish the throne of his kingdom forever." One way to recognize the messianic King is the intimacy that he has with Israel's God. God will "be his father, and he will be my son" (2 Sam. 7:14). Mysteriously, God will punish this son king ("I will punish him with the rod of men, with floggings inflicted by men," v. 14) but "my love will never be taken away from him" (v. 15), and despite his suffering he will rule forever as the eternal Davidic King (v. 16). Similar prophecies of the kingly rule of the Messiah can be found in Daniel 7:13–14 in which a son of man from heaven, that is, a human being unlike the beasts who rule the other kingdoms of the world in Daniel's vision, "was given authority, glory and sovereign power; all peoples, nations and men of every language worshiped him." Because the messianic King would be a descendant of David, there were specific messianic prophecies linking him to the city of David (Bethlehem) and to Davidic styles of leadership (worship, wars against the enemies of Israel, and the special place of Jerusalem as his capital city). More important than these details, however, was the scope of the messianic King's rule. Political rule over the entire earth was a necessary function of any true Messiah (Dan. 7:14). Failure to establish this universal political rule would invalidate a candidate's claim to be the Messiah.

Third, the messianic King would change the world. Not only would he cleanse and rule the world, but the world would be transformed under his sovereign administration. Some of the most famous messianic passages describe this new world order. Isaiah 61:1–4 envisions the visible transformation of the world under the rule of the Spirit-empowered messianic King:

> The Spirit of the Sovereign Lord is on me,
> because the Lord has anointed me
> to preach good news to the poor.

He has sent me to bind up the brokenhearted,
   to proclaim freedom for the captives
   and release from darkness for the prisoners,
to proclaim the year of the LORD's favor
   and the day of vengeance of our God,
to comfort all who mourn,
   and provide for those who grieve in Zion—
to bestow on them a crown of beauty
   instead of ashes,
the oil of gladness
   instead of mourning,
and a garment of praise
   instead of a spirit of despair.
They will be called oaks of righteousness,
   a planting of the LORD
   for the display of his splendor.
They will rebuild the ancient ruins
   and restore the places long devastated;
they will renew the ruined cities
   that have been devastated for generations.

The King will not simply announce the new world order but will in fact usher it in through the power of the Spirit of Yahweh that rests upon him. The true King would be known by this fundamental test: Did he change the world?

Fourth, the messianic King would lead Israel in a great holy war through which she would conquer her enemies. The only Messiah that Israel expected was one who would lead them in a great holy war against the Gentiles. This holy war is predicted in Zechariah 14:3. The Lord will allow the nations to surround Israel, but at the eleventh hour "the LORD will go out and fight against those nations, as he fights in the day of battle." Daniel 2:44 predicted that the messianic kingdom would "crush all those [Gentile] kingdoms and bring them to an end, but it will itself endure forever." This was the great holy war that would usher in the kingdom or rule of God. The sons of Maccabee had begun such a holy war in the second century B.C., but their movement fizzled. The first-century world of Jesus was rife with would-be leaders of the great holy war, which would expel the foreigners and open the way for the return of God to Zion. As N. T. Wright affirms: "The praxis that would demonstrate Messiahship thus included leading the victorious battle against Israel's enemies. . . . A Messiah who was executed by the occupying forces was not, after all, the true Messiah."[12]

I can begin to appreciate the confusion of Peter and others over the claims that Jesus was the long-expected King. We might see his death as the promised cleansing from sin, but what of the establishment of his rule, the change of the world, and the conquest of Israel's enemies? How can we face this apparent failure on Jesus' part to fulfill these aspects of Jewish expectation? Some Christians have divided the work of Jesus into two phases: the spiritual and the political. They argue that Jesus came to accomplish only a spiritual victory in the first century. His political victories lie in the future when he returns a second time to earth. Jewish thinkers such as Buber and Jacob Nuesner reject out of hand this spiritualizing of the work of the Messiah as being unbiblical and dualistic. I agree. The proper Christian response to an overspiritualized spirituality can be found in the Gospel writers' sketch of the baptism and temptation of Jesus.

The Old Testament, as we have seen, demanded at least four signs of the Messiah and his rule. The Gospel writers as they record the baptism and temptation of Jesus show that he delivered on all four signs. They do not divide the work of Christ into a spiritual phase and a future political phase. Rather, they see that Jesus fulfilled all four expectations in an unexpected way. *Jesus begins the new world order by becoming the new world order.* He becomes on our behalf the new world we seek in four ways: (1) He begins the new world order of cleansing from sin by taking on himself the role of sin bearer; (2) he begins the new world order of the rule of God by accepting the rule of God from his Father; (3) he begins the transformation of the world by receiving the Spirit's empowerment; and (4) he begins the conquest of Israel's enemies by defeating the ends and the means of the kingdom of Satan.

Sign #1: Becoming the Sin Bearer

When Matthew records the baptism of Jesus, he relates the conversation that passed between John the Baptist and Jesus in the brown currents of the Jordan. It went like this:

John: "Why are you doing this? I'm the one who needs to be baptized by you. I'm the sinner here. Why on earth are you, as the Messiah, getting baptized at all?" (paraphrase of Matt. 3:14).

Jesus: "You've got to baptize me, John, and you need to do it right now. This is the only way to begin the new world order, when everything is made right again after being crooked and broken for so long" (paraphrase of Matt. 3:15).

Jesus' actual phrase explaining why he wanted to be baptized was "to fulfill all righteousness." What does this mean? For Jesus and his world it meant "making everything right again." When we use expressions such as "everything is going to be all right" with a troubled friend or "everything's just right" with a waiter who asks us how we are enjoying our meal, we are closer to the meaning of the term *righteousness* than if we confine it to a narrow religious meaning. Jesus believed that his baptism was the trigger event to "making everything right again." Jesus saw the Jordan event as the first step toward the inauguration of the new world order.

How does Jesus' baptism trigger this new world order? By allowing Jesus to take on a new role that would change the world. The muddy water is an anointing of a new Adam. Most importantly, however, Jesus becomes the new Adam, beginning a new humanity by bearing the sins of the old humanity. At the same time, he becomes the second Adam—reconstituting a new humanity. The head of the old order, Adam the first, brought sin into the world. That's what messed up the world. That's how things went wrong. The second Adam, the new representative head of the human race, was now taking on his new role as the one who would make everything right again. His baptism in the wilderness of the Jordan valley and in the waters of the Jordan River connects back to Genesis 2 and the creation of the first Adam from the dust of the ground. From the waters of the ancient river, a new Adam would emerge who would remove the curse from all of life just as the first Adam had imposed it. He himself becomes the first member of that new order of life.

Sign #2: Becoming the King through Whom God Will Rule

Not only does Jesus take on the role of the new Adam who will make the world right again, but at his baptism he takes on a second role. Jesus becomes a new David at his baptism. The baptism of Christ was an announcement of the kind of Davidic King that he would be. David was known as a great king not only for his wars but also his worship. He was not allowed to build the temple of God because of his wars, but he gathered all the material for it and commissioned his son to complete it. He danced before the ark as he brought it into Jerusalem and penned song after song of timeless praise. The great trademark of his reign was his war against idolatry and his passion for Yahweh's supremacy. He was willing to suffer and die in order to restore the worship of Yahweh, putting his life on the line time and again against Goliath, Saul, and even Absalom his son to advance the glory of God. In a moment when we see Jesus fighting for the supremacy of God in all of life in the face of the wilderness temptations of Satan, we will see him in his role as this new Davidic King.

Israel had lost David's passion for God and his willingness to suffer for God's cause. Israel, unfortunately, was willing to suffer for the cause of Jewish nationalism but not for the cause of global blessing. Genesis 12:3 still controlled Yahweh's agenda with its promise of a great homecoming to himself of all the earth's peoples. Israel was willing to die for Israel but not for the nations. Jesus at his baptism becomes the new Israel, the new Davidic King of wayward Israel who will restore the rule of God among his people.

With Jesus as the new Adam and the new David, God is ready to return to earth in a dramatic homecoming. In fact, the words from heaven reveal the meaning of the baptism as the homecoming of God. Matthew 3:16–17 describes the momentous event with great economy: "As soon as Jesus was baptized, he went up out of the water. At that moment heaven was opened, and he saw the Spirit of God descending like a dove and lighting on him. And a voice from heaven said, 'This is my Son, whom I love; with him I am well pleased.'" This first phrase, "this is my son," is a reference to Psalm 2:7, a royal psalm referring to King David originally and then to all the kings who came after him. In the opinion of Christopher Wright, this psalm

> was probably said at the coronation or enthronement of Davidic kings as God's way of endorsing their legitimacy and authority. However, the fall of Jerusalem and the exile in 587 B.C. was the end of the line for the Davidic kings. So this Psalm was given a future look and applied to the expected, messianic, son of David who would reign when God would restore Israel. The heavenly voice at his baptism identified Jesus as that very one.[13]

No Jew with any scruples would have sung that psalm about the Jewish Hasmonean kings or Herod the Great. None of these were from the house of David. Now suddenly the true Davidic King has arrived. Like his father David, who was anointed while still a humble shepherd boy, this young Messiah, though humble in appearance, receives the sacred words and the oil of the Spirit's anointing to at last destroy that long-vacant throne.

This experience of enjoying the Father's full favor and love is what we referred to in an earlier chapter as the homecoming experience.

This experience of being filled by the Father's love is produced by the action of the Holy Spirit, who came to do in the life of Christ what the words of the Father declared. The Spirit of God would communicate to Jesus the favor of the Father, the love and delight of the Father, and the sublime good pleasure of the Father. What did this homecoming experience mean for Jesus? Wright explains:

> The awareness of God being his Father and himself being God's Son is probably the deepest foundation of Jesus's selfhood. This is something on which most New Testament scholars would agree. Even those who sift the texts of the Gospels with rigorous suspicion as to what may be regarded as authentically from Jesus himself, agree that the Father-son language regarding Jesus himself survives the most acid skepticism. And they would also point out that for Jesus, God's Fatherhood and his own sonship were not merely concepts or titles. Nor were they merely part of his teaching curriculum. They were living realities in his own life. Jesus experienced a relationship with God, of such personal intimacy and dependence, that only the language of Father and Son could describe it. It was deepest in his prayer life, and that was also where his closest friends observed it, as they heard him habitually use "Abba," the intimate Jewish family word for father, in personal address to God. This was something new and unprecedented that Jesus brought to the meaning of being children of God.[14]

Sign #3: Receiving the World-Changing Power of the Spirit

The descent of the Holy Spirit means that Jesus is now endowed with the powers of the new world order. The Spirit that descends on Jesus is the Spirit that participated in the original creation. In Genesis 1, the Spirit of God moves over the waters as he forms and shapes the old creation. He has now returned to move over new waters and to empower a new Adam to restore the creation that has been lost to sin.

We are now in a position to answer Martin Buber's challenge. For Buber, Jesus came but nothing changed. A whole new world order was expected, but no new world order was visible. Rome was in charge both before Jesus came and after he left.

Yet the picture of the baptism tells a very different story. The old world order was characterized by the experience of exile. Yahweh had departed due to human sin, leaving Israel defenseless against her enemies. The Spirit had departed, leaving the forms of worship empty. The kingship had departed, leaving the throne of David vacant.

With the coming of Christ, anointed by the Spirit and approved by the Father, all that changed. A new world order came in, which the Father returned to rule through his Son, the Spirit returned to renew and empower the new creation, and the throne of David was filled by one who would defeat Israel's true enemies. How, you may ask, did all these things happen? Where do we see the return of the Father, the coming of the Spirit, and the renewal of the Davidic line? The answer is unmistakable. We see this new world order of the return of Yahweh and his Spirit to remove the curse of sin and unleash the age of blessing and joy *in the person of Jesus*. The Father's favor returns to earth by resting not in the temple but in the person of Jesus. The Spirit renews creation by coming not to Israel at large but to the new Adam only. The rule of God is restored not in the palace of Herod but in the person of the Son of God. God's plan of renewal of the world begins not in the creation at large but at only one point in the creation—that point represented by Jesus, the embodiment of the new creation. Beginning with his baptism, then, Jesus carries around within him the powers of the new age, the forces of the new creation and the new world order—the power to cleanse from sin, the return of the Father's royal favor and presence, the Spirit's power, and the ability to defeat Israel's enemies. The kingdom has landed on earth. The exact touchdown point has been identified. The touchdown point is in the waters of the Jordan and in the person of the man from Nazareth.

What does the baptism of Christ mean? Jesus was taking on himself the role of the prodigal as he enters the water to be baptized by John. At the Jordan, the Father leaves his self-imposed exile from Israel and runs out to meet this new King, who has returned home on behalf of Israel. His words are the fatted calf of favor, the bright robe of delight, and the golden ring of love. The Spirit of God takes these relational realities deep into the mind and soul of the new Davidic King and feeds him with a power and joy that sustains him throughout his ministry. This is the homecoming experience: the full assurance of the Father's full favor. It is the key ministry of the Holy Spirit in the life of Christ. It is the secret of Jesus' power. It is the basis of his boldness, confidence, and personal identity. It is the greatest experience in life, one that his ministry would make possible for all others who would return to the Father and come home to his rich house in the name of Jesus. It means that the new world order has come in the person of Jesus.

This homecoming experience is the heart of the new world order that the utopian impulse seeks. The original creation was ruined by the estrangement of the first Adam from God through sin. The restoration of the great commandment takes place through the new Adam. Christ will now live a life of love—loving God totally and loving others unselfishly. There will be no Jewish tribalism, no Promethean arrogance and bitterness, no narcissistic self-absorption. He has entered paradise, the paradise of Yahweh's return and homecoming. Fullness of joy will be his daily meat and drink despite the anger of his critics and the rage of his enemies.

Sign #4: The Defeat of Evil—Rejection of the Way of Seizure

Peter tracks Jesus into the wilderness to learn more about this puzzling figure. He stumbles on the scene of the temptation in which Satan, as an angel of light, puts the second Adam through the paces of temptation in an attempted replay of Genesis 3. There in the wilderness Peter becomes convinced—in our opening story anyway—that this man from Nazareth truly is the Messiah. What did Peter see in the temptation of Christ that confirmed what should have been seen in his baptism?

We find the account of the temptation in Matthew, Mark, and Luke but not in John. Only Matthew and Luke provide an extended look at this crucial event. In each account the three temptations involve (1) turning stones to bread, (2) tempting God by falling from the temple, and (3) becoming king of the world by worshiping Satan. The order is slightly different in Matthew and Luke. Luke's account in his fourth chapter is distinctive in being preceded by a genealogy at the end of chapter 3. His purpose is to show the reader the connection between the second Adam, the new Son of God, and the first Adam, the earlier son of God (Luke 3:37). Note four points about the temptation of Jesus and the defeat of evil.

First, Jesus redefines the enemy that he must fight as messianic nationalism. When Jesus goes into the wilderness, driven by the Spirit of God, he does so in the role of a new Israel, a new Adam, and a new King who will also be a priest. But fresh from his creation as the new man and the new head of a redeemed humanity, he is compelled to undergo the ordeal that the original human head of humanity had to undergo in the opening chapters of the Bible. Once again the enemy comes with a particularly juicy temptation.

This time Satan does not use a fruit to entice the new Adam. This time he uses the greatest temptation of them all—the utopian temptation—to lure Jesus into his trap. Jesus needed to experience this ordeal, for as the King of his people he needed to fight and defeat their enemies. What was the great enemy? The enemy was Satan and his false utopia of militant messianic nationalism. As Jesus faces this great temptation, he confronts what we all must confront: the temptation to give our hearts to a utopian dream, however great or modest, and then to enter the story that the dream creates and become its slave. The great temptation is always to finish one's story—to act it out. This is the inescapable lure of a compelling utopian vision. It takes control of our hearts and insists that we be consistent with the character required by our master story of tomorrow. Getting into the wrong story is disastrous.

But why fight Satan? Why didn't Jesus turn his attention to the more visible of Israel's enemies—Rome itself? N. T. Wright answers this question convincingly.

> Jesus' analysis of the plight of Israel went beyond the specifics of behavior and belief to what he saw as the root of the problem: the Israel of his day had been duped by the accuser, the "Satan." That which was wrong with the rest of the world was wrong with Israel, too. "Evil" could not be located conveniently beyond Israel's borders, in the pagan hordes. It had taken up residence within the chosen people.[15]

Jesus, says Wright,

> aimed precisely at telling Israel to repent of her militaristic and messianic nationalism. Her aspirations for national liberation from Rome, to be won through a great actual battle, were themselves the telltale symptom of her basic disease, and had to be rooted out. Jesus was offering a different way of liberation, a way which affirmed the humanness of the national enemy as well as the destiny of Israel, and hence also affirmed the destiny of Israel as the bringer of light to the world, not as the one who would crush the world with military zeal.[16]

The real enemy that Jesus would attack and defeat was Satan. His clearest manifestation was not in pagan Rome but in the paganized people of God.

Jesus was thus redefining the real battle and the real enemy. What was keeping Israel in exile? Not insufficient zeal for their religion and culture. Not the presence of the colonial power of Rome. Rather, it was satanic bondage to idolatrous tribalism and nationalism that was the root and branch, the real enemy that must be fought.

Second, to fight this enemy Jesus rejects not only the enemy's ends but also the enemy's means. Jesus identified the real enemy as the satanic politics of militant and messianic nationalism. But one can fight such an ideology by using the very methods of violence and idolatry that characterize the enemy. Jesus would have none of that. To reject the ideology he would have to reject the methodology of this ideology. Violence and power were the compromised means to the idolatrous ends. Jesus would fight for Israel and defeat not only satanic ends but the misdirected means to those ends. Promethean means lead us into exile as much as Promethean ends. Satan had destroyed the worship of Yahweh around the world by imposing hostile stories of exile. His greatest coup was changing the story of Israel, a story of salvation for the nations and the return of Yahweh to all the people, into the militant tribalistic mockery—of Jewish nationalism. In both the temptation and the baptism, Christ announces that the new Davidic monarchy would reject *both satanic ends and satanic means.*

Third, the three temptations are all temptations for Jesus to live a life of seizure and self-reliance rather than sonship and surrender. What was the exact nature of these temptations? Why did Satan dangle before the Son of God the possibilities of turning stones to bread, recklessly falling into miraculous deliverance, and turning a minute's worth of false worship into an eternity's worth of global kingship? These famous temptations have inspired much profound analysis over the centuries. Some see them as a rejection of materialism, fame, and power. They see in these particular temptations universal truths about sin, righteousness, and true spirituality that are relevant to everyone today.

I agree that the temptation of Christ contains universal truth about sin and its conquest, but we must be careful not to tell this story in a way that bypasses the story Jesus was living out and trying to retell and transform. What happens if we look at the temptations in light of the story of Jewish nationalism?

I agree with Sinclair Ferguson when he writes that

> the significance of the event does not lie in ways in which our temptations are like his, but in the particularity and uniqueness of his experiences. . . . His testing is set in the context of a holy war in which he entered the enemy's domain, absorbed his attacks and sent him into retreat.[17]

Specifically, Satan was asking Jesus to enter the same idolatrous utopian story of violent Jewish nationalism that Israel herself had fallen into. He called for this new King to give in to the compelling visions of economic security (symbolized by the bread), religious fanaticism (the leap from the temple), and political domination (the kingdoms of this world) that were the main features of the Jewish militants. Satan also tempted Jesus to seize these idols in a Promethean way through his own independent will and apart from submission to his Father and the prompting of the Spirit.

The words of Jürgen Moltmann underscore the drama of this decision by Jesus:

> We have to see this potential messianic "seizure of power," which Jesus and the early Christians rejected, against the background of Jesus' helplessness in the story of the passion and his death on the cross. Filled with the Spirit, Jesus becomes the messianic Son of God; but through the temptations into which this same Spirit leads him, he is denied the economic, political and religious means for a "seizure of power." Here . . . his passion in helplessness is prefigured: his victory comes through suffering and death. At his triumphal entry into Jerusalem he offers the people no bread, at his entry into the temple he does not perform the messianic sign, and before the Roman Pilate he does not call on the heavenly legions in order to win a military victory. From the story of the temptations the way to the cross follows.[18]

This battle against Satan and his methodology of the idolatrous use of creation (bread), religion (cast yourself down), and the kingdom (autonomous earthly rule) begun in the wilderness will continue throughout the story of Jesus. At every point Jesus will reject the way of "seizing power" and instead give himself over to the way of the Spirit, gladly depending on the favor of his Father and the renewing power of the Holy Spirit to unleash the forces of the new world order that were now present in his person.

Like the first Adam, Christ is tempted by the devil. He is tempted to bow before the idols of fallen humanity and a compromised Israel: a misdirected sensuality (stones to bread), a misdirected spirituality (tempting God), and a misdirected sovereignty over creation (power and status through idolatry). Christ's response to these temptations is a resounding no. "Away from me, Satan," we read in the story, "for it is written: Worship the Lord your God and serve him only." Christ passed the test and retained his sinless perfection. Hebrews 4:15 is correct when it declares that "we do not have a high priest who is unable to sympathize with our weaknesses, but we have one who has been tempted in every way, just as we are—yet was without sin."

Fourth, the temptation indicates that Jesus will establish his kingdom in two stages, first in himself and then in his world. The story of Jesus will be radically different from the story of Israel and the story of the nations. He will live a life of love even for his enemies. He will die to cover the sins even of those who killed him. Christ will create a new world order by loving enemies. This is the beginning of the new world order, and it is found in Jesus himself. Loving enemies, therefore, is stage one. Stage two will mean that Jesus will end all enmity. Moltmann speaks of the stage to come:

> Jesus of Nazareth, the messiah who has come, is the suffering Servant of God, who heals through his wounds and is victorious through his sufferings. He is not yet the Christ of the parousia, who comes in the glory of God and redeems the world, so that it becomes the kingdom. He is the Lamb of God, not yet the Lion of Judah. What has already come into the world through the Christ who has come and is present, is the justification of the godless and the reconciliation of enemies. What has not yet come is the redemption of the world, the overcoming of all enmity, the resurrection of the dead, and the new creation. The love of God has become manifest through Christ. But the glory of God has not yet broken forth out of its hiddenness.[19]

I would add one additional item to Moltmann's list of what has "already come." Not only do we already have the justification of the godless and the reconciliation of enemies, we also have the redeemed world, the end of enmity, the resurrection, and the new creation—in Christ himself. He has these powers already within him. He walked around on this earth, endowed as the second Adam with the new world order—life in the power of the Spirit. This is stage one: Christ embodying and enjoying the true utopian vision of God himself and enabling sinners and prodigals to enter that reopened paradise through a relationship of faith with him. Stage two will be when Jesus reappears to transform all things into the new world order he has inaugurated. Stage one is initiation in himself. Stage two is consummation in the cosmos.

Jesus rejects the way of seizing what one wants. That is the way of the old order that is passing away. At his baptism he is filled with the joy of the homecoming of God and of the joys of living as the Son of such a God. He has no worry about his future. His good Father will give him every good thing. He can gladly surrender to the Father's will and way, even though the path will lead through the cross, because he trusts the Father's heart. This is the one who even as he sleeps in the back of a boat in a storm has the power to rise and command the winds and seas to obey him. This is the one, the only one, who though hidden from our eyes by the veil of history, stands behind that veil amid the raging storms of our world with the power to command them to cease.

Experiencing the Baptism and Temptation of Jesus: Implications for Spirituality

At the end of the opening story, the four spiritual seekers struggle with the relevance of Jesus for their dreams. "The Philosopher envisioned an age of spiritual enlightenment and universal mysticism. The Jesus Peter described didn't seem to fit in that dream. The Theologian, like Peter, longed for the restoration of Israel's glory through a kingly Messiah who would conquer Rome. Jesus didn't fit the bill. The Girl daydreamed about a society of unrestricted personal freedom. The African imagined a world free of racism. Jesus didn't really seem to fit either of their stories of the future."

Yet the Theologian, the Philosopher, the Girl, and the African are as astonished as Peter when the sleeping Jesus rises from his slumber to still the storm. He has powers within him that can make seas grow calm and make dreams come true. In our own journey, the hidden Jesus of the Gospels, the Jesus who doesn't appear on CNN or in the pages of the *New York Times,* is the one who controls the powers of the new world order we need. This chapter has followed Christ to the side of John the Baptist and the tempter in the wilderness in order to discover homecoming truth 4: Love brings in the new world order by first becoming the new world order.

As I reflect on the story of Jesus' baptism and temptation, let me suggest two implications for Christian spirituality.

1. *Giving up our private utopias.* Whether the sugarplums dancing in our heads are plucked from the tree of philosophers or harvested from more modest sources such as the pragmatic dreams of Steven Weinberg, modern utopian schemes collide head-on with the story of Jesus. There can be no union with Jesus unless we turn from our own utopian visions and enter his. Whether our utopian dreams are mystical or moral, whether they are political or patriotic, true spirituality must dream of the kingdom of God and its inauguration in Jesus. Jesus did not come to support the deadly dream of militant

and ethnocentric Jewish nationalism. He does not come into our lives to support the five and a half utopias outlined by Weinberg. Christ rejects something at the heart of most of our dreams—the underlying Promethean plot that trusts in the skill and daring of humanity to establish our private worlds. Jesus challenges our utopian stories not only by rejecting their Promethean spirit but also by affirming that the true utopia is not something out there in the future but rather is something here and now present in the person of Jesus. Union and communion with Jesus daily permit me to taste the powers of the new age and enjoy its firstfruits.

What we must not do is simply spiritualize what Jesus intended to do. Jesus is intent on complete transformation of the world in every way. No stone will be left unturned. He who turned water into wine is committed to transforming all of life by his power. Moral models and mystic models emphasize changing oneself and minimize changing the world. Jesus' story is about someone who is committed to bringing in a new world order but does so by first becoming that new world order himself. But he does it for us, for our benefit. After he first becomes what the whole world should be, he then unleashes that new world for others. This new world order is not spiritual in the sense that it is just inward. It is relational. The key to the new world order is not just introducing more external beauty or bounty. There was nothing wrong with the beauty and bounty of Eden in Genesis 3. What was wrong with that first utopia was Adam and Eve and their ruined relationship with God and one another. Paradise became a place of exile because of the damaged relationships that Adam and Eve experienced as a consequence of their sin and rebellion against God. There was nothing wrong with the dream house of the Smiths. What turned the dream sour was the negative relationship with the Joneses.

The key to the world we want, then, is not just a new environment, such as Martin Buber insists on. It must begin with a new quality of relationship with God and others. Jesus' entrance into this new world order of transformed relationships with God and others marks the beginning of the new world order in human history. Jesus inaugurates, as our representative and leader, those new relationships that will characterize the world to come. At the waters of the Jordan he becomes the new Adam, ready to remove sin and its curse. He becomes the new David, ruling the world out of the power and joy of the homecoming of his Father. He becomes the new man in the Spirit, empowered to transform the world. He becomes the man of glad surrender, rejecting the way of seizure because of his complete confidence in the riches of his sonship. Jesus did this in himself and for us. He enters this new world of Spirit empowerment, intimacy with the Father, and renewed rulership of all things not only for himself but also for his people—those who will follow him in faith. In order to follow him into the new world that opens up in him and through him, we must renounce our old utopias and hang our hopes on his star alone.

2. *Seeking the homecoming experience.* The experience of Jesus at the Jordan, when the voice from heaven declares God's love for his beloved Son, is the heart of true spirituality. For the spiritual seeker today, just as for Jesus then, the path to paradise is the experience of the return of the Father to us in love, acceptance, and approval. It marks a new way of life for those of us who have been living in the internal exile of Promethean or narcissistic master narratives. This is the homecoming experience that Paul describes in Romans 8:15–17 and 8:28–39. In those passages, Paul shows that we can have the same experience today that Jesus had at the Jordan. We can hear the Father speak words of love and acceptance to us in the midst of our muddy waters or stormy seas. We can have the assurance of sonship so that we can cry out "Abba." We can experience the descent of the dove each day, calling us home and filling us with the power and riches of our Father's house because through Jesus we have become heirs of all good things. When we enter into this part of the Jesus story, we become gradually liberated from a mind and heart full of exile stories. We awake each day confident that nothing can separate us from the love of God.

This is the secret of happiness. This is the utopia we must seek. This is the power of the Jesus story—to lead us into this homecoming in which dreams come true and our humanity is restored.

If Jesus is the Messiah, why hasn't anything changed, the world continues to ask. Where's the new world order? Our story gives an answer to these questions. Peter made the breakthrough discovery that we must make if we are to understand Jesus as the Messiah, and find an authentic Christian spirituality. We will not see the new world order that Jesus brought unless we see Jesus himself as the new world order.

How is he the new world order in and of himself? The new world order cannot be only a change in the environment and institutions of civilization. It must also be a transformation of individuals and their human relationships. Human beings must be changed from being hateful, selfish narcissists to being men and women who love God with all their heart and soul and mind and strength and who love others as much as they love themselves. Christ was this kind of person—

full of love for God and others without blemish. He showed the perfection of his love by loving his enemies—sinners like you and me. He came first to love his enemies and then to end all enmity. He came to change me into someone like himself.

At the end of Arthur Miller's *Death of a Salesman*, Willy Loman lies in his grave. His wife and son stand at the graveside wondering what made his life so tragic and so empty. "I can't understand it," the mother says, wondering whether this tragedy could have been averted.

"Nothing could be done," the son explains, "because he had the wrong dreams."

The quest for spirituality is doomed to fail unless we get the right dreams. In Jesus at the Jordan, dripping with the waters that anointed him as the new Adam and highly favored royal Son, we see the dawn of a new world that can be ours as well. How to enter that world in which dreams come true is the subject of the next chapter, as we look at Jesus and his teaching about the kingdom of God.

5

The Homecoming

Experiencing the Teaching of Jesus

Here I am, a fool with a heart and no mind, and you are a fool with a mind and no heart, both of us are unhappy, both of us suffer.

Fyodor Dostoyevsky, *The Idiot*

> Blessed are the poor in spirit,
>   for theirs is the kingdom of heaven.
> Blessed are those who mourn,
>   for they will be comforted.

Matthew 5:3–4

The Story: The Homecoming

I n your kingdom, Lord, how do people find happiness?" the Girl asked, dragging on a cigarette. Her eyes were hard, but her question seemed sincere. The disciples were irritated that she had interrupted the Master, but Jesus didn't seem to mind.

A great throng had gathered on the mountainside to hear Jesus teach them about the kingdom of God. Scattered throughout the crowd were familiar faces. Peter recognized some businessmen there on the mountainside still wondering, he imagined, whether there was any profit to be made on the miracle worker. Next to the Girl he saw the Theologian. The Philosopher was also there. Back in the shadows near a tree was the African. The Girl's question had hushed the crowd. All eyes were now directed at Jesus.

Before he could answer, a man in a suit and tie rushed through the crowd and fell before Jesus.

"Master, I plead with you to come to my house immediately," the man said, out of breath. "My daughter is sick and dying." Peter recognized him as Jairus, a ruler in the synagogue. Tears were flowing down the troubled father's face. His suit was soiled, and there was a rip in the shoulder seam. He looked terrible.

Jesus said nothing. He helped the man to his feet and motioned for him to lead the way to his daughter. The crowd moved with him as he walked. The Girl, the Philosopher, the Theologian, and the African pressed close to Jesus, waiting to see if he would answer the Girl's question.

"In my kingdom," Jesus said, "the way to be happy is to learn how to weep, the way to be satisfied is to learn how to be hungry, and the way to getting everything you want is to give up everything you have." Jesus smiled at the Girl.

The Girl looked puzzled but said nothing. The Theologian, struggling to keep up, spoke.

"Teacher, we certainly appreciate your sense of humor, but don't you think the Girl deserves a more direct answer? The law of Moses is clear. The way to happiness is by serving and obeying God and his law. There are no shortcuts. Whatever you sow you reap." A hum of approval swept through the crowd. The Girl scowled and blew her smoke in the Theologian's face. She spoke again.

"You certainly seem to love your paradoxes, Rabbi. And you theologians certainly love your Moses. But I find both of you a bit tedious for my taste. Happiness can be found by a quicker path than either of you admit. Here's my theory. Point one: Happiness is getting what you want. Point two: When you want something bad enough, go after it until you get it. Point three: Once you grab what you want, you have grabbed happiness. What are my wants? Simple. I want good wine, fast horses, romance, total freedom, great music, and money in the bank. I go after the things I want. When I get them, I get happiness. You have heard it said, 'All things come to him who waits,' but I say, 'All things come to him who grabs.'" Several of the young people laughed.

Jesus stopped and looked at the Girl. He smiled. Jairus's face dropped when Jesus stopped.

"Master, please. My daughter," he said. Jesus ignored his words. He began to tell a story.

"Once there was a man who had two sons. They each had very different ideas about how to find happiness. One day the younger son said to his father, 'Father, give me my share of the estate. I'm bored with you and with this place and know that my happiness lies out in the world.' The father was rich and had put aside a vast inheritance for his boys. Though he pleaded with his son not to take this path, the son would not listen. The father gave the son his portion of the inheritance and watched as he went off down the road to the far country. Once the son arrived he devoted himself to the pursuit of pleasure. 'Happiness is getting what you want,' said the son, walking into a bar. 'And I intend to get what I want.' He got his wine. He got his women. He got his happiness. Until the money ran out. Once that happened, the wine dried up and the women disappeared. Jobs were hard to come by, but the young man went out and using his drive and initiative grabbed one of the few openings left in the far country. He became a pig feeder.

"One day while he was feeding the pigs he asked himself, 'Don't the hired hands in my father's house have plenty to eat?' He made up his mind. 'I know I have lost my father's love and respect forever. After all, I've squandered the wealth he worked hard for. I've brought shame on his name and spurned his love. Since he is a just man, he will have disowned me as his son. And this is as it should be. But I will come crawling to him and ask him to hire me as a farmhand. There may be just an ounce of mercy left in his heart.'

"And so he got up, brushed himself off, and started for home.

"Meanwhile, back at the ranch, the elder son was working in the fields, deep in thought. He knew his younger brother had been a fool. He knew that happiness was not found in the far country of self-indulgence. As he leaned on the plow and scanned the long straight furrows he had cut, he reminded himself where happiness was found. Service and sacrifice—those were the twin truths that led to happiness. He had left nothing to chance. Happiness was getting what was coming to him. Happiness was the day when his father, whether he liked it or not, would have to give him the farm because he had earned it through his service and his sacrifice. There was nothing his father could do about it. He was a just man, his father was. When he saw the logbook of all the hours he as the elder son had spent working the fields and slaving away on the farm, his father would realize that the only proper payment would be to give him everything.

"On the day when his father would be forced to pay up, the elder son would demand a party. There was one very fat calf that he would slaughter for that feast with his friends. He thought of his father's beautiful robe. He would ask him to give it to him because, after all, hadn't he earned it? He would wear it in front of his friends as a badge of honor and glory. The elder son had it all figured out. There was no way the old man could weasel out of it.

"Leaning on the plow, he looked down at the main road that ran by the farm. He saw a lonely figure walking along the road, head bowed. He knew immediately who it was. 'So, he's dragging his hungry carcass back to the farm after all the pain and shame he has brought upon his father. He'll get exactly what's coming to him,' the elder son thought.

"As he watched the lonely figure move along the road, a strange thing happened. The door of the farmhouse flew open, and out the door came his father, running like a man half his age. He had shaving cream on his face. His shirt was unbuttoned and flapping in the breeze. The old man had his arms stretched out and was calling out the name of the younger son, a name that had not been spoken for many months. The younger brother had dropped to his knees on the road. The father was still running full force when he reached his son. They both tumbled over, rolling on the road, locked in one another's arms.

"By the time the elder son had unhitched the plow and headed back toward the house, it was too late. His father had killed the fatted calf that he had wanted and had given the young failure the gold ring and the beautiful robe that he himself had desired. The elder son stood in the front yard, while the party was cranking up in the house. Finally his father came out to him to tell him the good news about his younger brother. It didn't take long for the elder son's anger to boil over.

"'All these years I've worked like a slave on this farm and what did I get? I never got the fatted calf. I never got the gold ring. I never got your beautiful robe. But this good-for-nothing drags himself home as a miserable failure, smelling of prostitutes and cheap wine, and what does he get? Everything that should be mine!'

"The old man looked at his son and spoke to him in a soft voice. 'You are always with me, my son, and everything I have is yours. You did not have to work for happiness like a slave. I am your father not your pharaoh. I *had* to slaughter the fatted calf and give away my beautiful robe and my gold ring because this is one of the happiest days of my life. This is a day when forgiveness, acceptance, love, and hope have filled our lives to overflowing. Don't you see? We had to be glad and celebrate because those four things are the secrets of happiness, and they have come to our house today. But you will not be able to enjoy this happiness until you weep over your bitter spirit, hunger for love more than legalism, and empty your hands of all that you have earned so that they may be filled with all that can be given. Your brother has discovered these things and now his joy is full.'"

Before anyone could react to Jesus' story there was a shout.

"Your daughter is dead," a servant said, rushing out from a nearby house and falling before Jairus. Jairus crumpled into a heap on the cobblestones. Mourners poured from the house, wailing and weeping. The servant looked up bitterly at Jesus while he spoke to his devastated master.

"Mr. Jairus, you don't need to bother the teacher anymore. It's too late for him to do anything now," the servant said. Jairus sobbed as he rocked back and forth on the ground.

"Don't be afraid," Jesus said to Jarius. "Just believe and she will be healed." He then helped the weeping Jairus to his feet and went into the house.

The smell of death was everywhere. Various relatives and friends turned away from the swollen face of the father as he accompanied Jesus toward his daughter's bedroom. Jesus entered the room taking only a few disciples with him. Candles had been lit. Incense was burning. The dead girl lay on her bed, pale and still. Loud wailing came from the living room. The Girl, the Philosopher, the Theologian, and the African peered through the bedroom doorway. They watched as Jesus moved next to the body.

"Stop wailing," Jesus said with authority. "She is not dead but asleep."

The crying stopped as his words trickled through the house. Bitter laughter replaced the wailing. Jairus could not believe the insensitivity of Jesus' words. He was about to ask Jesus to leave when Jesus took the dead girl's cold hand.

"My child, get up," he whispered.

As everyone looked on in anger and disbelief, the young girl's eyelids fluttered and then opened. She sat up. Several people screamed. She stood up and embraced her father. Tears returned to his face. He looked at Jesus but could not speak.

Jesus returned the man's gaze and then turned to the Girl in the doorway.

"In my kingdom the way to be happy is to learn how to weep, the way to be satisfied is to learn how to be hungry, and the way to get everything you want is to give up everything you have." The crowd was amazed at his teaching because he taught as one who had real power over life, death, and happiness and not just words and opinions like the philosophers and theologians. (Based on Matthew 5:3–6; Luke 15:11–32; 8:40–56.)

The Challenge of Secularism: A World without Fathers

I can think of no other parable of Jesus that has made more of an impact on my life, or on the lives of millions, than the simple tale about fathers and sons. The true theme of the parable is the kingdom of God. Most scholars agree that Jesus' teaching can be summed up in the great theme of the kingdom. In parables and in displays of power, Jesus inaugurated the new story of the kingdom not only in Jewish life but in all of human history. The episode of the raising of Jairus's daughter reminds us of what the crowd discovered after hearing his story and seeing his power: "He taught as one who had real power over life, death, and happiness and not just words and opinions like the philosophers and theologians." This chapter reveals what kind of kingdom story Jesus was telling and what spiritual power that story can unleash in our lives.

Let me first, however, review where we have come thus far. In chapter 1, we looked at the issue of modern boredom as a central reason behind the new quest for spirituality. We interacted with Deepak Chopra and Stephen Covey, suggesting that they are representatives of two types of spirituality. Chopra represents the mystic model, which seeks union with God through meditation and higher states of consciousness. Covey represents the moral model, "which seeks effective living through following the character ethic" of the past. Jesus presented a third alternative. For him a life regains meaning not just by thinking differently. Rather, a living relationship with him by faith transforms the water of daily existence into the wine of gladness.

In chapter 2, we looked at the importance of master narratives. There is no spirituality outside our master narratives. Every model of spirituality assumes a certain controlling story often of the Judaistic, Promethean, or narcissistic kind. I said that most of our master narratives hurt us in the spiritual quest but that the story of Jesus liberates us from our dysfunctional stories. I also made the point that the way forward in the spiritual quest is not simply to go "up" (through mysticism or moralism) but to go "back." The transformation zone is not in our minds but in the past. As we rediscover the story of the historical Jesus and experience its truth, we are changed.

In chapter 3, we looked at pluralism and its conviction that Jesus is only one (and not necessarily the best) guide to spirituality in our global community today. By examining a number of witnesses to the birth of Christ and the facts that flow from that event, we established the supremacy and uniqueness of Jesus in the quest for true spirituality.

Finally, in the previous chapter, we dealt with the power of the future on our present lives. We examined the role that utopianism plays in shaping us and our values. Standing against humanistic utopianism is the messianic order of Jesus Christ. We saw that the temptation and baptism of Christ reveal Jesus not only as the Son of God but also as the King of a new world order. That new world order is full of powerful forces that we need in order to turn from our dangerous dreams and enjoy the new reality of Jesus himself. We thus established the human identity of Jesus as the new Adam who is also the Lord of life. Only he can restore creation and regain paradise. He is not only the dream breaker as he rejects our humanistic utopias, but he is also the dream maker who in himself shows us the homecoming experience in which sins are removed, God returns as a compassionate and generous Father, and the Spirit fills us with all the powers and riches of the new age.

Having dealt with some of the main challenges to authentic Christian spirituality (the issues of boredom, relevance, pluralism, and utopianism), I need now to deal with another contemporary challenge to spirituality: *secularism.* All of us have felt the cold hand of this modern specter and experienced its reductionism, which drains life of meaning, beauty, and happiness. Among the jewels it steals from our lives is the diamond of hope. Secularism and despair go together. As I said earlier, the modern resurgence of interest in spirituality is partly a reaction to secularism and its reductionism.

One modern parable of this secular despair is the Clint Eastwood movie *Dirty Harry*. In a series of commercially successful films (*Dirty Harry*, 1971; *Magnum Force*, 1973; *The Enforcer*, 1976; *Sudden Impact*, 1983; and *The Dead Pool*, 1988), Eastwood plays Inspector Harry Callahan, a tough cop alienated from the system. In Harry's world, it is not just the killers who are evil. The entire system is evil. Harry's world is "urban, ominous, dangerous and violent without warning. . . . No god looks on from the horizon. . . . Callahan is defined by silence and isolation."[1] He forms his own brand of spirituality without a god by becoming an "urban ascetic," alone and disconnected from family, friends, and society.

If life seems at heart to be evil or empty, then many of us turn inward to find a refuge from the harsh outer world. Such a spirituality can be called a spirituality of despair. Such a spirituality is caught up in a story of exile. It attempts, without success, to escape the story through inwardness or a gritty existentialism. We become like Eastwood's Dirty Harry, a lonely crusader in an urban wasteland. In our opening story, Jesus shows another way. The kingdom of God is the response to the world of Dirty Harry, a world in exile and despair. But we would be wrong to think of the kingdom of God as an idea or complex of ideas. The kingdom is actually a story—a story that gives meaning to life and direction to our search for true spirituality. What I hope to show in this chapter is that Jesus' story of the kingdom is about sharing with us the happiness he experienced as Yahweh's Son. The kingdom of God is therefore at heart the experience of the return of the God of the Bible to us as a Father through Jesus and our return to him as forgiven and beloved sons and daughters.

Our opening story focused on fathers and the challenges they face. In the parable Jesus told, two sons struggle with their attitudes toward their father. One, whom no one ever expected to darken his father's door again, returns home to a loving relationship with his father, while the other, who actually lives at home, is left burning with anger, envy, and hostility. At the end of the opening story, a father in despair comes to Jesus to ask for help with his daughter, who lies at death's door. Finally, our opening story is full of the presence of a third father, the one Jesus called Abba. This is the Father in heaven, the Father to whom Jesus prayed. He too is an object of controversy in the story, for not all of Jesus' hearers trust him as the source of life nor believe that his kingdom rule is the secret of life and happiness.

This struggle in the story over the relationship that various characters have with fathers raises an issue that is relevant to our times—the issue of fatherlessness. As autonomous individuals, we have parents but no fathers—no one on whom we depend for life and direction. For those of us inflicted with the secular fever of fatherlessness, stories of exile make more sense of our grim reality, hopeless though they may be.

But the Jesus story calls for a different response to our loneliness. Jesus in word and deed teaches homecoming truth 5: *We overcome the tragedy of fatherlessness through a love that is found only by those who lose it.* I'd like to unpack this truth by focusing on Jesus' most famous sermon—the Sermon on the Mount. What it teaches about the spirituality of the kingdom of God is just the antibiotic we need to tame the fever of secularism in our souls.

Understanding the Teaching of Jesus: The Story of Homecoming

A great deal of academic ink has been spilled trying to define what Jesus taught about the kingdom of God. The intentions of this book do not allow me to enter into the major theories. Instead, let me cut to the task at hand and offer my own conclusions on the matter.

For Jesus, the kingdom of God is a story of coming home, that is, of Yahweh returning to earth in the first century of our era in the person of Jesus Christ. As the prophets foretold, the return of the God of Israel to rule and reign on earth would be a time of judgment on his enemies but of the restoration of paradise for his people. Jesus himself is the beginning of that world transformation. But what happens in him is also for us and will be done in us. So the kingdom of God is not only the personal rule of Jesus but also the experience of the homecoming of God by his repentant people. For us the kingdom experience involves living at home on earth with God as our all-sufficient Father. It is a story of what it is like to be liberated from an exile mentality and to enjoy the fullness of the Father's house.

In the Sermon on the Mount in Matthew 5–7, Jesus declares that the happiness of living at home in the Father's house is greater than the dubious pleasures of living in exile either in the far country of indulgence or the near fields of Pharisaic arrogance and anger. The sermon is a detailed look at life lived from within the homecoming experience.

It would be fair to ask why I am so certain that the homecoming experience is the great theme of the Sermon on the Mount. Let me offer three reasons in support of this view. First, consider the strong testimony of the context. The previous two chapters in Matthew's Gospel dealt with the baptism and temptation of Jesus. I demonstrated in the previous chapter how these events were dominated by the homecoming experience. The baptism of Jesus climaxes with the words "this is my beloved son." The temptation is dominated by the testing of this homecoming experience. The tempter constantly prefaces his words with "if you are the Son of God." We should not be surprised that Matthew wants to continue this important theme in chapter 5 and following.

Second, not only does the context support the theme of homecoming, but the content of the Sermon itself demands it. Within the sermon we have overwhelming evidence that Jesus is talking about the great themes so powerfully depicted in the Luke 15 parable of the lost sons. This evidence comes in the form of references in the sermon to knowing God as Father and living as sons of God. There are eighteen different references to the relationship with the Father (seventeen direct references to the Father and one reference to being a son of God).[2] *Pleasing, trusting, and enjoying the Father is the great concern of the entire sermon.* To see how important these eighteen references to the Father and the sonship experience are, consider the number of references within the sermon to the kingdom of heaven (Matthew's phrase for the kingdom of God). Though there are eighteen references to the Father in the sermon, there are only eight references to the kingdom. We can therefore say with confidence that for Jesus the restoration of the kingdom of God concerns the enjoyment of God as an all-sufficient Father in all of life. The commands of the sermon in each instance must be understood not as a new law but rather as the new behavior that flows from leaving an exile mentality and sharing in the new homecoming mentality. When the Father's love, favor, and wealth are enjoyed as the basic realities of life, we are living inside the Jesus story. The entire sermon, then, is a commentary both on the parable of the two sons as well as Jesus' own homecoming experience begun at the Jordan River.

Third, as additional proof that we are on the right track, we note how the clash between an exile story (that God is far away) and the homecoming story (that God has returned to earth forever in Jesus) makes sense of the two kinds of righteousness mentioned by Jesus in Matthew 5:20: "For I tell you that unless your righteousness surpasses that of the Pharisees and the teachers of the law, you will certainly not enter the kingdom of heaven."

While Jesus came not to end Mosaic spirituality (keeping the law) but to fulfill it, he nonetheless rejects the spirituality of the "Pharisees and teachers of the law." Why? Weren't they also committed to the same Mosaic spirituality that Jesus was? The answer is that though the Pharisees were committed to the same law, their spirituality was permeated by the exile mentality of first-century Judaism. Their spirituality was not yet liberated by the new story of Yahweh's return in grace and mercy that Jesus had come to tell and to inaugurate. Because they were blind to the return of the almighty Father to earth as King, their "righteousness" was prone to be the carefully orchestrated behavior of the insecure and the legalistically calculated love indicative of a "scarcity" mentality. By this I mean the perspective that God never provides enough, and therefore, I must be "tight" with whatever resources I have. Because the Pharisees were still in inner exile in their colonized country, they were far from God and not yet truly home. Jesus' perspective is sharply different. He displays an "abundance" mentality based on a generous Father who was near at hand and eager to show his love.

How then do we read the Sermon on the Mount in light of the homecoming story of the return of Yahweh to us and we to him? Just as the father in the story of Luke 15 gave four magnificent gifts (sandals, fatted calf, ring, and robe) to the returned prodigal, so too our heavenly Abba wants to give priceless gifts to those of us who make the journey home, back to the Father's house. Jesus teaches in the sermon that his Father and ours wants to give six gifts to those who come home to his rule.

Gift #1: The Gift of Happiness (Matt. 5:1–12)

In our opening story, Christ answers the Girl's question by saying, "In my kingdom the way to be happy is to learn how to weep, the way to be satisfied is to learn how to be hungry, and the way to get everything you want is to give up everything you have." This is a reference to the beatitudes, which provide the dramatic opening to the Sermon on the Mount. In Matthew's Gospel, the actual promise of Jesus is that a special kind of happiness associated with living in the kingdom of God (Matt. 5:3) will be granted to those who are poor, meek, hungry, merciful, pure, peacemakers, persecuted, and those who mourn (Matt. 5:3–11). This opposes common sense, which says that weeping leads to sadness not happiness, or that hunger leads to misery not satisfaction. What did Christ mean by these paradoxical statements?

Dallas Willard offers an explanation. The beatitudes

> serve to clarify Jesus' fundamental message: the availability of God's rule and righteousness to all of humanity through reliance upon Jesus himself, the person now loose in the world among us. They do this simply by taking those, who, from the human point of view, are regarded as most hopeless, most beyond all possibility of God's blessing or even interest, and exhibiting them as enjoying God's touch and abundant provisions from the heavens.[3]

In other words, Jesus is not teaching the moral condition that leads to happiness (poverty, meekness, purity, or mercy) but the gracious provision of happiness to anyone no matter what their inner state. Relationship with Jesus, not inward worthiness, is the key to experiencing the new world order and its joys.

What has sometimes been missed is that the Sermon on the Mount is at heart a comedy about kingdom happiness not an ethical treatise about impossible moral obligations. I am *not* saying that the Jesus story of the kingdom has nothing to do with ethics. It most certainly does.

Stories are not innocent entertainment. When millions of Americans read *Uncle Tom's Cabin* in the 1850s, they wanted to change the praxis of slavery. When millions of Westerners heard the story of the Holocaust after the dust of World War II settled, they created organizations that would forever attempt to change the praxis of racism and anti-Semitism. So it is with Jesus' story of the kingdom. When we get it straight, it produces a desire within us to live differently. Note that believing and entering the story produces the new behavior, not the other way around. No amount of outward action brings us into the story. It is the story that creates authentic action.

And what is that new behavior? It means no longer living with a poverty mentality but rather with an abundance mentality. To live in the kingdom means to "live like kings." To hear the Jesus story correctly is to hear that in our Father's house we have enough for every situation. Our calculated love and carefully measured acts of righteousness can now be abandoned in favor of a radical love and an exuberant otherness.

The key text that points to this new kingdom praxis is Matthew 6:8: "Do not be like them." This suggests that Christ is describing a way of life that stands in contrast to "business as usual." John Stott spells out the implications of this verse:

> There is no single paragraph of the Sermon on the Mount in which this contrast between Christian and non-Christian standards is not drawn.... The pagans love and salute each other, but Christians are to love their enemies (5:44–47); pagans pray after a fashion, "heaping up empty phrases," but Christians are to pray with the humble thoughtfulness of children to their father in heaven (6:7–13); pagans are preoccupied with their own material necessities, but Christians are to seek first God's rule and righteousness (6:32, 33).... And this Christian counterculture is the life of the kingdom of God, a fully human life indeed but lived out under the divine rule.[4]

What is being rejected by the follower of Christ? Behind the rejection of non-Christian behavior stands the rejection of non-Christian beliefs. To accept the story of the kingdom is to reject the rival stories of the Gentiles and the Jews. Rival stories shape life and lead to every kind of sin (Rom. 1:18ff.). The kingdom story of Jesus rejects the rival stories of the world and leads to life and salvation. It unleashes the power to live in a radically new way.

But how does it do that? How does believing the kingdom story empower us to be different in Dirty Harry's rotten world? How do we live in Christ's new world of joy and shalom when everywhere we are surrounded by the emblems of death and despair? We will miss the real difference between kingdom living and living in the world if we miss the fact that happiness is what the Sermon on the Mount is all about. This points to the fact that the kingdom is a comedy in the Shakespearean sense of a story that leads to a happy ending, that is, an ending in which the characters find true happiness.

The beatitudes show this. Happy are the poor in spirit, the meek, the persecuted, the merciful, the hungry, and the forlorn, Jesus proclaims. How does such weeping, such hunger, and such emptiness lead to a happy ending? The answer is that leaving the old stories of Israel, Greece, and Rome, and, in fact, living in conflict with those stories means that I have entered another story, the rival master narrative of the kingdom wherein true happiness is found.

This is the story of the parable of the prodigal son. God has now returned to his estranged sons. He opens his arms to the returning Gentiles. He entreats the stubborn sons of Israel to join the celebration of this great homecoming event. To those who like the prodigal were empty and in rags, the kingdom comes as a gift. Even to the pure it comes as a gift. Once we embrace this new story of the kingdom, a happiness like falling in love comes our way.

Gift #2: The Gift of Love (Matt. 5:13–48)

But how does living in the story of the kingdom produce true happiness when we are expected to turn the other cheek, give up our clothes, and pluck out our eyes? In Matthew 5:13–48, Jesus tackles these issues as he discusses thorny human conflicts such as anger (5:21–26), adultery (5:27–30), divorce (5:31–32), integrity in speech (5:33–37), justice (5:38–42), and loving enemies (5:43–48).

What ties these various topics together is that they all have to do with the difficult task of loving other people. We are full of such selfishness and contempt for others that it is difficult for us to hold our anger, control our lusts, keep our vows, be reliable in our words or merciful when wronged. The root problem is stated in verse 43: "Love your neighbor and hate your enemy." Jesus criticizes that teaching and replaces it with the new command to love even our enemies.

Anger is a pervasive problem in our culture. Statistics tell us that in America alone there are twenty-five thousand murders each year, including a thousand that take place in the workplace. Anger is a component of each of these crimes. The destructive effects of anger on marriage, family life, friendships, and personal health are probably incalculable.[5] So when Jesus offers both a critique of anger (5:22: "anyone who is angry will be subject to judgment") and hints that in his kingdom, in the new order of things, anger can be replaced by love, we all should sit up and take notice.

But how can we do this? How can we avoid the anger of the person who demands too much or slaps us on the face? How can we avoid even the suppressed anger of giving up our coat to the enemy or turning the other cheek to the unjust? The answer lies in finding out how Jesus was freed from such anger and lived with such generosity to the undeserving. To understand Matthew 5, we must go back to Matthew 3 and 4 and the dynamics of the new world order begun there by Jesus. The secret, therefore, of overcoming anger is to enter into the sonship experience with Jesus and to enjoy the riches of the Father's house, namely, life in the Spirit.

Don't miss how much this liberating gift of love rocks the old order. In Gerd Theissen's historical novel of Jesus, *The Shadow of the Galilean,* two of his characters debate the Sermon on the Mount and its commands to turn the other cheek and give away one's possessions to the needy. One character accuses Jesus of teaching a slave ethic, a "morality for little people." The other character, Joanna, sharply disagrees:

> What irritates you about this Jesus is precisely the opposite of the limited morality of little people. He gives little people attitudes which previously were your privilege. Isn't it the privilege of the upper class to be able to live without care? But Jesus says that the privilege is there for everyone, including those who have nothing. . . . And isn't it a privilege of the powerful not to have to fear their enemies? The powerful can be magnanimous, since they know that their enemies cannot harm them but must come to terms with them. But Jesus says to everyone, and not just to the powerful: "Love your enemies . . . that you may be children of our Father in heaven." All are to be sons of God. People used to call only the kings of Israel sons of God. But Jesus applies that term to anyone who is generous to his enemies. Everyone is then a king.[6]

When one enters the comedy of the kingdom, paupers become princes and children become kings. Life in the Spirit enables us to live with these hilarious attitudes of confidence in the Father's splendid control of all of life down to the little details. I don't need to try to seize power or pleasure in order to gain control or put up defenses. The Spirit fills me with the attitudes that enable me to live like a rich man and sleep like a baby. I don't need to live in anger and contempt of others. My welfare will be looked after by the King of kings. I don't need to find happiness in illicit sex. My Father who is rich in love can give me all the love imaginable to renew my marriage and keep me full of desire for my wife. I don't need to lie and swear in order to get people to do things for me. My rich Father will take care of my needs. I don't need to worry about losing a coat or being taken advantage of. My Father's house is a place of abundance, so that while I should live wisely, I do not have to hate those who wrong me. My Father will right every wrong. When we come home to the Father's house, "everyone is then a king." The path to happiness is possessing this new mind-set, a mind-set that sees the new world order as already existing in Jesus. Such a kingdom mind-set frees me to love.

Gift #3: The Gift of Spirituality (Matt. 6:1–18)

Little is said in our opening story about spirituality. The Theologian, however, makes one important statement on the subject: "The law of Moses is clear. The way to happiness is by serving and obeying God and his law. There are no shortcuts. Whatever you sow you reap." We know this type of spirituality well. This is the piety of the fundamentalist, the spirituality of the performance mentality. Jesus warns against keeping God's law in a Promethean way, a way that focuses attention on one's autonomous efforts to give, to pray, to fast.

In dramatic contrast to the spirituality of the Pharisees, Jesus paints simple pictures of how children, living at home with their rich and powerful father, should talk to him and act before him. The key feature of the kingdom spirituality Jesus describes is the childlike dependence on the Father in all of life.

This simple childlike spirituality is seen in what Jesus teaches about the Lord's Prayer (Matt. 6:5–15). I like the way Dallas Willard paraphrases this most famous of all prayers:

> Dear Father always near us, may your name be treasured and loved, may your rule be completed in us—may your will be done on earth in just the way it is done in heaven. Give us today the things we need today, and forgive us our sins and impositions on you as we are forgiving all who in any way offend us. Please don't put us through trials, but deliver us from everything bad. Because you are the one in charge, and you have all the power, and the glory too is all yours—forever—which is just the way we want it.[7]

One of the most dramatic features of the prayer is the emphasis on asking for things. There seems to be an economy of adoration and an emphasis on the outreached hand. This model prayer is a "gimmie" prayer in which Jesus asks us to ask. He wants us to realize we are dependent children safe at home. He wants us to see God as the all-sufficient Father who gets glory and gives joy by meeting needs.

Willard reflects on this central lesson drawn from the Lord's Prayer, the way Jesus taught us to pray:

> The teaching about prayer that emerges from the life and teaching of Jesus in the gospels is quite clear. Basically it is one of asking, requesting things from God. . . . Prayer simply dies from efforts to pray about "good things" that honestly do not matter to us. . . . Prayer is a matter of explicitly sharing with God my concerns about what he too is concerned about in my life.[8]

For all of our good talk about contemplative prayer or adoration in prayer, Jesus wants us to talk about life, our lives as they are lived every day. He wants us to talk about our concerns, where our hearts are every day. By doing this we begin to see God as a friend, someone we can share real life with and someone whose listening ear and loving responses draw us to him in love and trust.

Praying this way in faith is not as easy at it may seem. The great problem of course is that we often come to prayer with such negative and suspicious thoughts of God that we have great difficulty in letting our lives tumble out happily into the Father's lap. Given the exile stories that have twisted our minds, we are more likely to address prayer to the "Marquis de God," described by Willard as the divine counterpart to the namesake of sadism:

> The Marquis de God. Ready to show how much he cares by punishing you. . . . In a moment of rage, continents convulse with seismic activity. In a fit of moral indignation, he demonstrates the latest craze in viral mutations. . . . The Marquis de God is simply a god who hates. This is a deity who despises sin and sinners with such passion that he'll murder in order to exterminate them.[9]

What gives us the power to overcome this false view of God? What enables us to barge spontaneously into our Father's presence at any time day or night, climb up on his lap, and pour our troubles and longings out to him? Because we are at home, and he is our loving Father, crazy about us because of Christ.

Gift #4: The Gift of Wealth (Matt. 6:19–34)

In the opening story, the Girl summarizes the secular approach to the pursuit of happiness: "Point one: Happiness is getting what you want. Point two: When you want something bad enough, go after it until you get it. Point three: Once you grab what you want, you have grabbed happiness. What are my wants? Simple. I want good wine, fast horses, romance, total freedom, great books, and money in the bank. I go after the things I want. When I get them, I get happiness. You have heard it said, 'All things come to him who waits,' but I say, 'All things come to him who grabs.'"

While this may sound bold and confident, it actually hides a life of constant worry and anxiety. Without money, a fatherless Promethean cannot hope to be happy. Jesus understands the exile mentality that controls so many people's lives. The kingdom story of homecoming offers liberation from the worry produced by our exile narratives. In

Matthew 6:19–34, Jesus addresses the twin issues of what we treasure and what we worry about. The two things tend to be related. What I treasure most, I worry about most. The major issue here is worrying about material things and consequently treasuring money as the way to get these material things such as food and clothing. In contrast to the grasping anxiety of the world, Jesus points to the trusting nature of birds and flowers. "They do not labor or spin," he tells his audience, and yet the Father provides all they need. If the Father so cares for birds that have not entered the sonship experience, how much more will he care for those who have? The experience of homecoming as the prodigal son in the parable discovered means not only that your relationship with the Father has improved but also that the riches of his house are now open to you.

The rule of God must be seen to be comprehensive, covering all of life. What must not be lost in our focus on the redemptive rule of Jesus is that the sovereign rule of God is over all of life. When Psalm 47:2 declares, "How awesome is the LORD Most High, the great King over all the earth," it is pointing to this comprehensive aspect of the kingdom. God as creator and sustainer is the universal King over all people at all times and in all places.

What is often lacking in the church's understanding of the kingdom is that this all-encompassing epic dimension of the kingdom must be kept together with the more familiar redemptive aspects of the kingdom story. God's rule involves law, redemption, and the transformation of all things. As we shall see below, it is only a proper focus on the historical Jesus that can enable us to integrate these dimensions of the kingdom and the sweeping changes they are effecting in all of life. The Jesus who turns water into wine, stills the storm on the lake, and conquers death itself is not only the Savior of our sins; he is also the comprehensive King of creation.

Thus, the kingdom story is an epic story that speaks of the comprehensive scope of God's rule and reign. The kingdom is a gift of wealth that frees us from worry about daily life.

Gift #5: The Gift of Influence (Matt. 7:1–12)

In the opening verses of Matthew 7, Jesus addresses the problem of changing people's minds. The subject seems to be judging others, but it is a manipulative judging. It is a judging meant to control and condemn. "Do it my way or else" is the attitude that stands in contradiction to the kingdom way of life. How do you persuade them to adopt your viewpoint or your values? In the old order of things, there's nothing like a little arm-twisting or a little name-calling. Put people on a guilt trip and watch them respond. But the way of Jesus in the new order of things is quite different. He commands that we give up the way of intimidation through judgment and condemnation (7:1–6). Instead, he calls us to ask, seek, and knock. For what are we to ask? Luke record's Jesus' answer to that important question: "How much more will your Father in heaven give the Holy Spirit to those who ask him!" (Luke 11:13).

The Spirit of God is the great persuader. Paul was convinced that the Spirit alone could convince people about the truths of homecoming. "My message and my preaching," declared the apostle in 1 Corinthians 2:4–5, "were not with wise and persuasive words, but with a demonstration of the Spirit's power, so that your faith might not rest on men's wisdom, but on God's power." This does not mean that I don't have to work hard to communicate well with others. It does mean that I can stop playing god in my attempts to manipulate others. I am now free to enjoy the Father's gift of influence.

Gift #6: The Gift of Salvation (Matt. 7:13–29)

Jesus closes the Sermon on the Mount with a series of metaphors that contrast the way of death with the way of salvation. Salvation is like a narrow gate that is hard to find. The way of death is easy to find and full of traffic. Salvation in the kingdom is like a good tree that bears good fruit. The lost are like a bad tree that bears terrible fruit. Trimming up the branches won't help. There is something terribly wrong at the root. False prophets are like bad fruit trees. They work hard, but their labors bear the bitter outcomes of unbelief and judgment from God. Finally, salvation is like living in a house built on a rock. The storms of life cannot destroy it. Death is like living in a house built on sand that gets swept away by the tides of life.

What are we to hear in these metaphors of life and death? The key phrase is found in verse 23: "I never knew you. Away from me, you evildoers!" We can avoid this fate and find the way of salvation by entering into the story of Jesus. This is the will of the Father: to live in and live out the new world order inaugurated by Jesus. Thus, the sermon ends as a love story about knowing the Father through his unique Son.

This love story is Bible wide and history long. By love story we mean that the story of the kingdom is at heart about the covenant between God and his people. Don't stumble over the unromantic sound of the word *covenant*. In the Bible, the covenant speaks not primarily of rules but of relationship. It speaks of God's love commitment to be the husband of his bride—the people of God. The key word in this kingdom love story is *covenant*. Adrio König defines covenant as "a gracious relationship of love between God and humanity, a relationship in which God takes the initiative."[10]

The kingdom of God throughout history is God's pursuit of fallen humanity in order to restore their covenant relationship with him. The covenants in the Bible, therefore, are more like marriage covenants than business contracts. König summarizes the Old Testament covenants in the new covenant phrases of Jeremiah 31:33: "I will be their God, and they will be my people." This new covenant promise reaches it climax in Christ as König explains:

> "I shall be your God" is the first part of the covenant—God's part, God's responsibility. What we hear and see throughout the Old Testament is confirmed in Jesus. In the covenant relationship, God is for us: he is neither antagonistic nor neutral toward his creation. In John 3:16 we read, "God loved the world so much . . . ," and in John the "world" is fallen humanity. God's love for the world is finally and fully revealed in Jesus. That is how God is, since Jesus is God's revelation, and that is how Jesus is. Jesus is for humanity. Even in the second part of the covenant "and you will be my people" he fulfills for us and then through the Holy Spirit, in us.[11]

The kingdom as love story explains why Jesus' first miracle took place at a wedding, where he turned water into wine. It also explains why the Book of Revelation calls the great celebration at the end of time the wedding feast of the Lamb. The kingdom is not just a Jewish story about political restoration. It is on a wider and more intimate level a love story that reaches its climax in Jesus.

Experiencing the Teaching of Jesus: Implications for Spirituality

The opening story portrays Jesus not only as a teacher but as Lord of life and death. He raises the daughter of Jairus to new life after all hope is gone. This aspect of the Jesus story, his authoritative and life-giving teaching, must be experienced today by modern Jairuses if we are to know true spirituality, one that can liberate us from the wrong stories and bring us into the happiness of coming home.

In the Sermon on the Mount, we heard Jesus describe the gifts that come to those who enter his new story about the return of God to us and our opportunity to leave our states of exile and return to him. In an age of exiled Dirty Harrys and chronic fatherlessness, a fifth homecoming truth must be heard: *We overcome the tragedy of fatherlessness through a love that is found only by those who lose it.* We saw in the parable of the prodigal son and the Sermon on the Mount that the gift of sonship and the inheritance of happiness, love, wealth, spirituality, influence, and salvation that come with this gift are offered to undeserving prodigals who are willing to leave their autonomy in the far country and find their way home. To those today who ask the question about finding happiness that the Girl asked Jesus, he offers the same answer: "In my kingdom, the way to be happy is to learn how to weep, the way to be satisfied is to learn how to be hungry, and the way to getting everything you want is to give up everything you have."

As the story unfolds, we realize the meaning of these strange words. The father in the parable of the two sons explains their hidden message: "I *had* to slaughter the fatted calf and give away my beautiful robe and my gold ring because this is one of the happiest days of my life. This is a day when forgiveness, acceptance, love, and hope have filled our lives to overflowing. Don't you see? We had to be glad and celebrate because those four things are the secrets of happiness, and they have come to our house today. But you will not be able to enjoy this happiness until you weep over your bitter spirit, hunger for love more than legalism, and empty your hands of all that you have earned so that they may be filled with all that can be given." When forgiveness, acceptance, love, and hope fill our lives, we experience a high level of joy. But how do we get that experience? The Sermon on the Mount gave us some hints. Let me mention a few more lessons about spirituality that we can learn from Jesus the teacher and storyteller.

First, Christian spirituality is caught in the tension between the "already" and "not yet" aspects of the kingdom of God. The homecoming experience has begun, but it has not yet been consummated. Raising this question brings up one of the most mysterious aspects of the kingdom teaching of Christ: His kingdom is both already here and not yet come. Note the two different tenses of the kingdom. Some passages speak of it as already here (Matt. 12:28; Luke 11:20). Other passages speak as though it is still to come (Matt. 26:29; Mark 14:25;

Luke 22:18). The last century saw scholars divide into two camps over this issue. One view has been called "consistent eschatology" (Albert Schweitzer) because it teaches that the kingdom lies wholly in the future. The kingdom is a radical break with the space-time world. Jesus expected it to arrive at the end of his earthly ministry but was sadly disappointed when it did not. At the other extreme was C. H. Dodd, whose "realized eschatology" argued that in Jesus all the expectations of the kingdom had been met, and therefore, no future apocalypse should be expected.[12]

The truth about this question of the now and the not yet of the kingdom seems to lie somewhere in the middle. The term *inaugurated eschatology* describes the view that sees the kingdom as already here and yet not yet consummated. A. M. Hunter and W. G. Kümmel developed this middle position in which, though a final consummation was yet to come, nonetheless "in Jesus' person and actions the future was already realized since he who was to usher in salvation at the end was already present." The kingdom was both to be fulfilled in him at the consummation of all things but also had been fulfilled in his person, teaching, and work.[13]

Thus, the story of the kingdom is the story of the return of God to earth in two stages. In the first stage, the kingdom comes fully in Jesus, who is filled with the powers of the new age not only for himself but also *for us*. After the coming of the Spirit (Acts 2), these same powers of homecoming are unleashed *in us*. We will later describe the final stage in the kingdom's progress in world history when Christ will consummate his lordship and kingship *with us* and *around us*.

We live in the tension between this already and not yet, between the love already experienced and the love that is yet to come. But tension is not always a bad thing. Like the strings of a guitar, just the right tension produces beautiful music. At the heart of this tension is the person of Jesus himself, who contains both the already and not yet aspects of the kingdom. He is the bridge between this contradiction and the resolution of this tension.

I like John Stott's insight into this tension:

> The essence of the interim period between the "now" and the "not yet,"
> between kingdom come and kingdom coming, is the presence of the
> Holy Spirit in the people of God. On the one hand, the gift of the Spirit
> is the distinctive blessing of the Kingdom of God, and so the principal
> sign that the new age has dawned. On the other, because his indwelling
> is only the beginning of our kingdom inheritance, it is also the guar-

antee that the rest will one day be ours. . . . He is the guarantee that the new world of God has already begun, as well as a sign that this new world is still to come.[14]

Second, faith in Christ is necessary for true spirituality. In the raising of Jairus's daughter, the faith that the father had in Jesus was critical to the miracle of her restoration to life. In the Sermon on the Mount, faith in God as a loving, caring Father is critical to happiness and blessing. We must believe that the hidden new world order in Jesus is more real, more valuable, and more lasting than the visible old world order around us. This kind of faith enables us to live in the Spirit and to believe the promises of the kingdom that guarantee all future grace to us in this life and the next. Worry, anger, bitterness, and anxiety are dispelled. Slowly the world of Dirty Harry fades away, and space is made for a world brimming with the fruits of the Spirit and the emblems of faith.

But faith is only as good as its object. A life-giving faith is one that focuses on the giver of life. As Jesus said, "Whoever believes in me, as the Scripture has said, streams of living water will flow from within him" (John 7:38). When we thus recognize that the baptized and tempted Jesus is now the King of all creation and history, we must make him the focus of our faith.

Because of the centrality of faith in Christian spirituality, we must watch out for the New Age trap of simply equating the lordship of Jesus with the forces of nature or evolution. Donald Bloesch warns us of this pitfall:

> Still more drastic is the reinterpretation of the lordship of Christ in New Age theology and philosophy. Christ is portrayed as the eros of the universe rather than the lord of the universe. Or he is the "reason" and "mind" of the cosmos rather than the ruler of the cosmos (Matthew Fox). He is the energy that rejuvenates the universe rather than the power that controls the universe. We may speak of him as lord but only in the sense of "one who makes the universe go around." Instead of the infinite-personal God of traditional Christian faith, New Agers uphold the evolutionary creative force that is realizing itself in conjunction with the strivings of a humanity seeking to be reborn. Jesus is the paradigm of heroic manhood who shows us how to draw upon the energy of the cosmic Christ within us.[15]

This is not the faith that leads to true spirituality. We must reject this New Age concept of the lordship of Christ and return to Jesus' statement in the Great Commission of Matthew 28:18 that "all authority in heaven and on earth has been given to me." Jesus is not just a symbol for the creative force. He is the personal, living Lord of creation, judgment, redemption, and final consummation. In him the kingdom story is a story that grants the gift of salvation. Faith in him opens up the fountain of true spirituality. Faith in anything else poisons that fountain.

Third, prayer is important. Prayer is central to those who want to move back home. Talking with one's father is a necessary part of every healthy father-child relationship. This is why Jesus taught about prayer in the Sermon on the Mount. And he practiced what he preached. He is seen praying regularly in the Gospels and teaching his disciples to pray. As Marcus Bockmuehl writes, "Perhaps the single most important practical expression of both participation in Christ and imitation of Christ was prayer." For Jesus, "prayer conveys most profoundly the openness, trust and dependence which characterizes a true relationship with God."[16] The conversation that Jesus taught us to have with our Father in heaven is to be filled with such openness, trust, and dependence, qualities appropriate to those who have truly come home.

But while prayer is an honest conversation with God as our Father, it is also a complicated conversation with him. Prayer is not a simple matter of dropping requests and waiting for answers. Our Father does not robotically answer each request in the affirmative. Often he does not. Prayer is a conversational relationship with God. Parents do not automatically respond to requests. They talk things over with their children, and good children do not just fill in request forms; they talk their needs over with their parents. Wise parents figure out the best way to respond that will do the maximum good for their children. So, too, our Father in heaven, though all things in the universe are subject to his will and word, responds to our conversational relationship with him not with mindless approval but with loving strategies that will maximize our joy and growth as mature children.

The Kingdom of God and the South Bronx

And so the kingdom of God has come. The King of a new world order has come and is still in our midst. Yet the secular dream resists him and his kingdom. At the height of secularism in the mid sixties, Harvard theologian Harvey Cox celebrated the city as the triumph of the secular dream—the true expression of the kingdom on earth. By the

1990s that vision had vanished, and the alienation and desolation that the story of secularism created was written large across our cityscapes. There were many who bore witness that the secular city was not the kingdom of God. Jonathan Kozol, in his sociological study of the children of the South Bronx in New York City, found one such witness.

Anthony is a remarkable boy who lives on St. Ann's Avenue in one of New York's bleaker neighborhoods. The South Bronx is home to some six hundred thousand people. St. Ann's Avenue is the center of the poorest area of the South Bronx, where the largely black and Hispanic population lives below the poverty line. It is considered the "deadliest block" in the "deadliest precinct" of the city. It is home to four thousand heroin injectors. Prostitution is a major line of work for the neighborhood's single women. It is a world without fathers. This is Anthony's home.

When asked, Anthony says that life on St. Ann's Avenue is like the plagues of Egypt.

"Sadness is one plague today. Desperation would be a plague. Drugs are a plague also."

"Anthony, what should we do to end this plague?" Kozol asks.

"Mr. Jonathan," Anthony replies, "only God can do that."

"But when will God bring an end to the plagues?" Kozol probes.

"Mr. Jonathan," Anthony says again, "I don't know when. I think it will only happen in the Kingdom of Heaven. . . . I only know that this is not his kingdom."[17]

Anthony, in the midst of the far country of the South Bronx, knows that his fallen world is not his true home, that the world plagued by the sins of modernity is not yet the kingdom of God. He looks for a story different from the broken narratives of capitalism and secularism and their failed promises. He needs a story that rejects all stories with proud human heroes and their failed attempts to bring in the kingdom. He looks for a transcendent story about one from heaven taking action to deliver this good but fallen world. Jesus told the kind of kingdom story that Anthony was looking for.

When it comes to understanding the story of the kingdom of God, Anthony's starting point may be the beginning of wisdom. That is the starting point for hope. The kingdom story is a story about a Father who cries out to the world, "I shall be your God," and about a Son on earth who cries back on behalf of a deaf and blind humanity, "And we shall be your people." The kingdom story is not just about the power of God coming to earth. It is about the compassion of God finding his children, forgiving his prodigals, and bringing them into the joys of the Father's house, where golden rings and fatted calves testify to his love and care.

I find in myself so much of the alienation that I see in the secular city. The nub of this alienation is a chronic doubting of the goodness of God. I am in constant battle with my own unbelief. The story of the kingdom, the story that Yahweh has returned to be a loving King to his people and to fulfill the promises of the new covenant, is the story I need to erase the droning tape recording of modern alienation that plays somewhere in my head. I need this new story to open my eyes to the reality that has broken into the South Bronx and into the secular self. This new reality is the inbreaking of the kingdom. The difference this inbreaking makes is forever captured in the words of the father in Luke 15:31: "You are always with me, and everything I have is yours." Because of Jesus these words are now true.

THE SCARECROW GOD

EXPERIENCING THE DEATH OF JESUS

How seriously would we take a person who said, "I have faith in Adolf Hitler, or in John Dillinger. I can't explain why they did the things they did, but I can't believe they would have done them without a good reason." Yet people try to justify the deaths and tragedies God inflicts on innocent victims with almost these same words.

Rabbi Harold Kushner, *When Bad Things Happen to Good People*

God presented him as a sacrifice of atonement, through faith in his blood. He did this to demonstrate his justice, because in his forbearance he had left the sins committed beforehand unpunished—he did it to demonstrate his justice at the present time, so as to be just and the one who justifies those who have faith in Jesus.

Romans 3:25–26

Story: The Scarecrow God

The African was in her rented room in Jerusalem. It was now midnight on the Friday night of Passover. Jesus was dead. The disciples had scattered. Her eyes were swollen and her hand was shaking as she wrote in her journal:

Dear Diary,

I have just been through a very emotional week, and I must write down all that has happened. This has been either the worst week of my life or the best. I cannot yet sort out which it was.

It all began this past Sunday. I had followed Jesus and the others to Jerusalem. Our hopes were high. I had actually begun to believe that he was the King foretold in prophecy. Apparently thousands of others had come to that same conclusion because when Jesus approached Jerusalem riding on a donkey, the people followed after him, spreading their cloaks on the road. The entire crowd of his followers began to praise God in loud voices because of the miracles that they had seen Jesus do.

"Blessed is the King who comes in the name of the Lord," they chanted. "Peace in heaven and glory in the highest." Peter and the other disciples walked behind the Master, eyes wide with surprise at this royal reception.

I was there with my companions of the last few years. The Girl was there watching Jesus ride through the gates of Jerusalem. I could tell she wanted to talk with him. From what she had told me, she was almost ready to become his disciple. What was holding her back, however, was her struggle with the whole issue of suffering and evil. A few days before, we had gone shopping together in Jerusalem. I had begun confiding in her about my growing faith in Jesus. She had been skeptical. On our way to the supermarket we had passed a row of begging mothers clutching their tiny, dirty babies. The Girl pointed at the babies and said, "If God is so good, why does he allow so much suffering? If he is the King of the world, how come the world is in such a mess? Multiply these dying babies by millions and you have some of the reasons that are holding me back from following Jesus." She then said something that startled me even more.

"I believe in God too, only I don't believe in an all-powerful God. I believe that God is good but that he is limited in his ability to overcome human sin and suffering. If he could he would, but he can't so he won't. That has helped me deal with the problem. This Jesus is a good man, but he is no more able to deal with the problem of evil than anyone else is. I'd like to be a 'spiritual' person, but I can't get past all the evil that surrounds me."

While I was trying to think of something to say, she changed her direction.

"It's not just the dying babies in Jerusalem that bother me. I also blame God for my screwed up family life." The Girl went on to describe growing up in a home dominated by an angry father and his verbal abuse. She described how his rage made it difficult for her to believe in a loving God. Consequently, she had eased the pain of her early years at home by her defiant lifestyle and her denial of God. She looked down at the box that contained her addictions.

"But recently, Jesus has made me wonder whether there was an answer to all the garbage in my life," the Girl said to me. "One reason I've followed him to Jerusalem is to find out once and for all if he really can make things new again. Don't you think I could use an overhaul?"

I laughed with her and said something about all of us needing some spring-cleaning. I then went back to my room and did some thinking. There was a personal dimension to this discussion of the goodness of God and the existence of evil. My mother died giving birth to me. My father had been beyond consolation and blamed me for her death. She had been beautiful, others told me, and he had loved her more than life itself. I carried around with me a treasured picture of her in a blue dress. It was my only memento. As soon as I was old enough to be useful, my father sold me into slavery. That was how I ended up in Israel. Always in the back of my mind was the nagging question about the goodness of a God who would allow such things as death and slavery. The Girl had touched an old wound, and it was throbbing again. Was the Girl correct that the best way to soften the blow of evil in the world was to reject God's omnipotence and revise my expectations about Jesus? If I couldn't accept the Girl's solution to the problem, what other solution was there?

I decided to talk with the Philosopher and the Theologian about the problem of evil. It wasn't until Sunday that I saw them again.

While we were waiting for Jesus to enter Jerusalem as the new King of the Jews, I asked the two of them for their thoughts about evil and suffering.

The Philosopher agreed with the Girl that there was no God such as the Old Testament described. The only God he believed in was an energy field that lay behind all of life. This God was the sum of all things, both good and evil. Evil was just a primitive way of thinking, he argued. He had developed a higher level of consciousness, he reported to me, that went beyond the infantile categories of good and evil. God just was, he told me. Whatever is, is right. True spirituality recognizes that evil is just an illusion.

What the Philosopher didn't tell me but what I had found out from other sources was that his philosophy of living beyond good and evil had destroyed his marriage. His wife, Miriam, just before she had left with the kids and the dog, had said that he cared only about himself. He was locked into the story of narcissism. She had been right too. The Philosopher carried with him an old notebook in which he recorded his reflections on the great questions of life and God. His notebook justified every selfish act he had ever committed, every gross infidelity that he had performed. Miriam had left before he had filled his notebook. She had known about his womanizing. She had watched him assemble his me-centered theories and realized that she could never mean much to a man so completely in love with himself. When she couldn't take it anymore, she had left. She got the kids and the dog. He got the notebook and his narcissism. That day of the triumphal entry I realized why the Philosopher kept following Jesus around. He wanted to get rid of his notebook. The trouble was that he couldn't bring himself to do it. Hundreds of attempts to part with his personal philosophy had failed. He had only one hope left. If he could give it to the man on the donkey, he might be freed. I felt sorry for him but at the same time was confident that Jesus had an answer to his problem.

The Theologian had a different explanation, as I suspected. Evil was a result of the curse upon sin. After Adam and Eve fell from innocence through their act of disobedience, God cursed them and every aspect of life. Misery, suffering, sin, and death were all a result of the just punishment of sin. Only after human sin was completely removed would there be any hope for alleviating suffering. He pointed to the golden dome of the temple, the most prominent structure in Jerusalem.

"My hope is in that building," he told me. "That is the place where sin is covered and where the wrath of God is appeased. If anything happens to that structure, or to the system of sacrifices that it sustains, then all hell will break loose. You think things are bad now. You can't imagine how much worse they would be without the temple. When the Messiah comes one day, perhaps things will change. Until then, the forgiveness of sins through the sacrifices of the temple keep the world afloat. Maybe this Jesus we have been following around has a better system to take away sin. But I doubt it."

So the four of us followed him, the King on a donkey, into Jerusalem. Each of us believed on the basis of what we had seen in the last couple of years that only Jesus could help us find what we were looking for. If there was a solution to the problem of evil and misery, he just might have it. But as the week unfolded, all our hopes were dashed.

On Friday morning I heard the news that Jesus had been arrested. He had been found guilty by both the Sanhedrin and Pilate. He was sentenced to die on Friday afternoon so that the dirty deed could be done before the beginning of Passover at sunset.

At the appointed time I made my way to Skull Hill, just outside the city, where Jesus was hung up with nails on a wooden cross placed between two thieves. The irony of it all was that for the first time since the triumphal entry I finally had access to Jesus. Most of his followers and well-wishers had disappeared, and only a handful of the faithful stood at a distance watching their dreams die with the young man on the cross. The Girl was there as well as the Philosopher and the Theologian. Some soldiers and a few hecklers amused themselves by yelling, "Aren't you the Messiah? The one who will save the world? Why don't you save yourself?" After a while the hecklers became bored with their own words and stopped.

I will never forget how he looked, this miracle worker from Nazareth. He looked to me like a limp scarecrow in a farmer's field. But scarecrows are supposed to scare evil away so that the crops can grow. This scarecrow seemed to gather evil around him. The crows of sin and death were pecking at him and eating his flesh. How could the God whom Jesus proclaimed, a God who had returned to be a loving Father to his people, allow this to happen? There was no solution to the problem of evil here, I thought, only another charge against the God who had taken my mother, had turned his back on the Girl, had given up the Philosopher to his narcissism, and had abandoned the Theologian to his dead orthodoxy. How could I have come to believe in a scarecrow God, powerless to save either himself or others?

As I was deep in thought, the crowd began to react to the man on the cross. I heard someone behind me yelling. "It's him," a man shouted, and the crowds pressed in around the dying healer. I looked around at the faces of the crowd. Every face was full of anger.

"You let my little sister die," said one attractive woman in a business suit. "You cannot be good."

"You let me lose my job," said another.

"You cannot be good," the crowd shouted.

"You robbed me of my sight," said a blind man in rags.

"You cannot be good," the crowd shouted.

"You took my husband from me and gave him to another," said an older woman.

"You cannot be good," the crowd shouted.

"You let my father rot in prison," yelled a young man.

"You cannot be good," the crowd shouted.

"You have permitted corruption to run riot in our land," said a young journalist.

"You cannot be good," the crowd shouted.

"You have sent plagues upon us that have killed the innocent," said a doctor.

"You cannot be good," the crowd shouted.

"You have watched while our race has been enslaved and humiliated by the world," said a student.

"You cannot be good," the crowd shouted.

"You watched while I sank into my addiction," said a teenager holding up a syringe.

"You cannot be good," the crowd shouted.

"You have allowed our sex to be exploited and oppressed," said a distinguished-looking woman in glasses.

"You cannot be good," the crowd shouted.

"You watched while I was sexually abused by my father," said a young girl with a face full of tears.

"You cannot be good," the crowd shouted.

"You have allowed your followers to be imprisoned and killed and you haven't even lifted a finger to help them," said a man with a clerical collar.

"You cannot be good," the crowd shouted.

"You destroyed my faith by putting me in a family full of rage and hypocrisy," said the Girl who had joined the crowd.

"You cannot be good," the rest shouted.

"You allowed me to sink into my narcissism and watched it destroy me and my marriage," said the Philosopher.

"You cannot be good," the crowd shouted.

"You have broken your promises to Israel and allowed us to be colonized and raped by heathens," said the Theologian.

"You cannot be good," the crowd shouted.

The accusations went on for hours until at last someone yelled, "He's dead!" It was true. Jesus hung from his nails as a lifeless and defeated scarecrow. And then the beating started.

One by one, the wretched of the city spat on him and beat him with their fists. The first one to spit on him was a woman with a shriveled arm. After she spit on him and moved away, her arm was straight and whole. The first one to hit the accused was blind. After pounding on Jesus, he moved away and discovered that he could see. The teenager whose arm was full of holes from his many drug injections took his syringe and stabbed Jesus in the leg. The teenager moved away and felt a strange sensation creep over his arm. He looked down and saw that all the holes were gone. He felt like his appetite for the drug had been taken away.

I watched the Girl take a stick and beat Jesus. As she was beating on the dead man, she dropped her box at the foot of the cross. Just then someone came up behind her and took the stick away. It was her father. I saw them speak together. Each was crying. Then they embraced. I saw them leave arm in arm. She left the box behind.

I watched the Philosopher take his pen, the one he used to write in his notebooks, and jab at Jesus with wild fury. The notebook fell at the foot of the cross and fresh blood from the dead man splattered upon it. After the Philosopher vented his rage, he stopped and turned around. He dropped his pen when he saw his wife, Miriam, the kids, and the family dog standing there.

"I'm not sure why we've come," Miriam said, "but we want to give you one more chance." Soon there was a heap of adults and children hugging and weeping and laughing. The Philosopher kissed Miriam with a passion I had not seen him express in the two years I had known him. He looked back at the dead man on the cross. He then walked off with his family, dazed by joy.

I watched the Theologian bang the cross with his fist.

"You ruined everything," he sobbed. "I was beginning to believe that you were the one. Now you are dead." He buried his face in his hands, then turned away.

Suddenly a young temple intern came running.

"The temple curtain has been ripped," the young man shouted, out of breath.

"Who did this outrage?" the Theologian demanded.

"No one. It just happened. I was standing in front of the Holy of Holies about fifteen minutes ago, and all of a sudden the curtain ripped in two and the sacred place was exposed."

The Theologian looked at Jesus. He had died fifteen minutes ago. "The dead have been seen rising from the graves, sir," the intern said. "God seems to have escaped from the temple and is now running around Jerusalem changing everything."

The intern's words triggered my imagination. I imagined standing before the curtain and hearing the rustling of God behind the veil. Suddenly I saw Yahweh, ripping the partition with his bare hands and smiling on a world that he had been separated from for centuries. He tossed the curtain aside. This was not about gaining access to Yahweh. This was about Yahweh running out of the temple and into the world, just as the intern said. I imagined him running through the streets of Jerusalem, shirt unbuttoned and flapping in the breeze, like a father going to meet his returning son.

The Theologian, however, didn't seem to be listening to the intern. He was looking at the scarecrow man on the cross.

"Somehow you did this," he said with wonder in his voice. He then turned back to the intern.

"Let's run. I want to see this sight."

I watched the two of them run off down Skull Hill like a pair of schoolboys. The Theologian was the faster of the two.

I myself was too caught up in the mob mentality to realize what was going on. I pushed my way to the front and stood before the dead man. I picked up a rock and threw it at his face. I was right on target. The lifeless head jerked from the force of the stone.

"That was for my mother," I said and felt no remorse. I moved out of the crowd. I left the hill and returned to the city. I was on my way back to my room when somebody called my name.

I turned around. Standing in front of me was an African woman in a beautiful blue dress. I recognized her immediately from the picture I carried with me. It was my mother. She looked radiant. I ran to her and clutched her like I had wanted to do all my life.

"I'm alive forever, now, my little one," my mother said to me.

"But how? You died when I was born."

"Him," said my mother, pointing across the street toward Skull Hill.

"You mean the dead man?"

"Yes," my mother said.

"But he cannot be good," I said, repeating the chant of the crowd.

"Don't you yet see?" my mother asked, talking to me like I was still a little girl. "He was innocent of all the evil that you accused him of today. He suffered with every victim of every crime and injustice that has ever been committed, so great was his hatred of evil."

"I don't understand."

"The evil he permitted," my mother explained, "was the evil he saw in your hearts. He knew that allowing the evil would lead you to accuse him and kill him. And he also knew that dying as an innocent man at the hand of those who accused him of being evil would be the way to cleanse each of you and all the world of evil. But that is not the best part. Once evil is washed away by his death, life in all its fullness returns."

"Are you saying, Mother, that he permitted evil so that he could become its victim in order to take it away? Couldn't he have done it another way?"

"Not really. He had two choices. He could take away evil by destroying the human race since the source of evil was the human heart, or he could take it away by letting himself be destroyed. He chose the latter way. I for one am glad he did."

"Doesn't this mean that he who is supposed to be all-powerful is actually weak? After all, he just let us kill him. Surely this means he is limited in his power."

My mother shook her head.

"It means just the opposite. Only the healer is powerful enough to conquer through suffering. His omnipotence works best through weakness. He uses his power to completely identify with the victims and suffers with them. Through his suffering with us comes the unleashing of an omnipotent love that will transform all of us who believe and all creation around us."

"But why didn't he reason with us?"

My mother smiled, even while the tears began.

As I write these words in my diary, her answer still makes me tremble. "He did not reason with us because the problem of evil cannot be answered by an argument. It is only answered by a story. And with a story you must wait for the ending before you can truly know the meaning."

Dealing with the Problem of Evil

The opening story wrestles with the problem of evil. We touched on this challenge earlier, but now we must take a closer look. Those on the road to spiritual intimacy with God can find the way ahead blocked by this issue. If we do not trust God or we feel that he is not good, then the closer we get to him, the more estranged we feel. As the Girl in our opening story said, "If God is so good, why does he allow so much suffering? If he is the King of the world, how come the world is in such a mess? Multiply these dying babies by millions and you have some of the reasons that are holding me back from following Jesus."

Some of the popular answers given for this problem are voiced in the opening story. The Girl decides that the best explanation is that God is good but not great. "I believe in God too, only I don't believe in an all-powerful God. I believe that God is good but that he is limited in his ability to overcome human sin and suffering. If he could he would, but he can't so he won't. That has helped me deal with the problem."

For many, God is too limited to stop evil in the world in all instances. Rabbi Harold Kushner, whose own faith was shaken by the death of his fourteen-year-old son, argued for this answer in his best-selling book, *When Bad Things Happen to Good People*. "How seriously would we take a person," Kushner wrote, who said, "'I have faith in Adolf Hitler, or in John Dillinger. I can't explain why they did the things they did, but I can't believe they would have done them without a good reason.' Yet people try to justify the deaths and tragedies God inflicts on innocent victims with almost these same words."[1] He argues that the Book of Job supports the idea that though God is good he is not all-powerful and therefore cannot always keep us from suffering. Millions of his readers seem to agree.

The Philosopher takes a second approach. He denies that evil exists except in our minds. "Evil was just a primitive way of thinking, he argued. He had developed a higher level of consciousness, he reported to me, that went beyond the infantile categories of good and evil. God just was, he told me. Whatever is, is right. True spirituality recognizes that evil is just an illusion." Deepak Chopra has defended this approach. He dislikes the Old Testament picture of God, calling him a "tyrant" and commending Adam and Eve for rebelling against his tyranny.[2] God was the real sinner in the story of the fall. "No amount of effort will totally appease this God. The courage to fight eventually must turn into courage to oppose him."[3] To this biblical God we must say, "I am tired of being afraid. You are not my God if I have to hide from your anger."[4] A higher view of God that moves beyond the biblical conception is that "God is in evil as much as in the good."[5] This is the path of "left hand spirituality." Chopra writes that on this path "a devotee shuns conventional virtue and goodness. Sexual abstinence is often replaced with sexual indulgence. . . . One might give up a loving home to live in a graveyard; some tantric devotees go so far as to sleep with corpses and eat the most repulsive decayed food."[6]

In between the Kushners and the Chopras are millions of spiritual seekers who do not feel comfortable with either option. They don't want to deny either the power of God or the reality of evil. What other options are available? Some turn to the freewill argument. They assert that free will accounts for the existence of wickedness and suffering in the world. Since God made us free, he can't control our behavior. He is therefore not responsible for our sin. Since our freedom limits God's power, evil is our problem not his. Others talk about the positive effects of evil, such as character building and the strengthening of faith, and seek to justify it in those terms.

What the African discovered in the opening story is that the death of Jesus Christ has something powerful to say about God's relationship to evil. When her mother appears to her, she attempts to explain this mystery.

"'The evil he permitted,' my mother explained, 'was the evil he saw in your hearts. He knew that allowing the evil would lead you to accuse him and kill him. And he also knew that by dying as an innocent man at the hand of those who accused him of being evil would be the way of cleansing each of you and all the world of evil. But that is not the best part. Once evil is washed away by his death, life in all its fullness returns.'"

It is this perspective on the problem of evil that I explore in this chapter. The death of Jesus is irrelevant to many models of spirituality. But to authentic Christian spirituality it is the key event that completes the homecoming experience for returning sons and daughters of God. The cross is the place of hope for those who have suffered or who wrestle with the problem of evil in our world or in our hearts.

The death of Christ, therefore, teaches a sixth homecoming truth that we need to experience: *True love conquers evil by becoming its victim.* Let me mention seven ways in which the death of Jesus on the cross overcomes evil in our world, beginning with the greatest evil of all.

1. The Death of Jesus Overcomes the Evil of His Own Unjust Death

The first evil that the death of Jesus must address is the death of Jesus himself. In the opening story, the African describes her anger at God in seeing his Son die such a horrible and humiliating death: "He looked to me like a limp scarecrow in a farmer's field. But scarecrows are supposed to scare evil away so that the crops can grow. This scarecrow seemed to gather evil around him. The crows of sin and death were pecking at him and eating his flesh. How could the God whom Jesus proclaimed, a God who had returned to be a loving Father to his people, allow this to happen? There was no solution to the problem of evil here, I thought."

Can the evil of killing an innocent man like Jesus be justified? We must travel back in time to deal with this first vindication of God and his goodness by understanding Jesus' own intentions for dying on the cross.

But before we look at Jesus' own intentions, we should recall why Rome and Judaism wanted him out of the way. Rome's reasons seem fairly straightforward. Rome's standing policy was to remove any potential threat to either her sovereignty or her famous peace. She would negotiate if she wanted to, but standing behind her official smile was also the ace up her sleeve—crucifixion. "Crucifixion was a powerful symbol throughout the Roman world," says N. T. Wright. "It was not just a means of liquidating undesirables; it did so with the maximum degradation and humiliation. It said, loud and clear: we are in charge here; you are our property; we can do what we like with you. It insisted, coldly and brutally, of the absolute sovereignty of Rome, and of Caesar."[7]

If Roman reasons for dealing with Jesus were cruelly simple, the Jewish reasons were slightly more complex. The strong claims made by Christ and recorded in the Gospel of John were scandalous enough to get Jesus killed by zealous heresy hunters. It is true that in Deuteronomy 13:1–5 Moses commanded Israel to treat false teachers severely. "That prophet or dreamer," Moses writes, "must be put to death." Yet in the case of Jesus, only certain Pharisees seemed to take the Deuteronomy command seriously. Theological rage, therefore, does not seem to be the Jewish leadership's real reason for wanting Jesus removed. What then was that real reason?

John 11:47–48 takes us to the heart of the matter. A special meeting of the Jewish Senate (or Sanhedrin) was called to decide what to do with Jesus and his growing popularity. If Jesus continued like this, some said, "the Romans will come and take away both our place [temple] and our nation." Caiaphas spoke up angrily that such a crisis of Jewish nationalism could be averted by having "one man die for the people" (John 11:50). Caiaphas becomes a key decision maker during the trial of Jesus (John 18:24). Militant Jewish nationalism, not religious purity or orthodoxy, was the real reason, from a Jewish perspective, why Jesus had to die.[8]

In contrast to Rome and Jerusalem, Jesus had different reasons for seeking the death penalty. How do we get at the personal reasons buried away in his heart and mind? The story of Jesus comes to our aid. The story climaxes with Christ's arrival in Jerusalem, which triggers six days that changed the world. The clue to his intentions are found on the day of the triumphal entry into Jerusalem and center on a certain young donkey.

The opening story begins with the triumphal entry into Jerusalem. Luke's account in 19:28–44 is full of the electricity of that moment. We hear the loud cries of "hosanna" from the crowd. We watch as the overenthusiastic faithful throw their cloaks on the road for the new Davidic King, the first in over five hundred years, as he enters Zion. Yet in reading this story I am immediately struck with an odd fact. The focus of Luke's story is not the triumphal entry itself but the donkey colt upon which Jesus rides. Luke, the careful historian, spends six verses on the donkey. He mentions the donkey directly or indirectly six times. No person or action receives this kind of attention in the narrative of the triumphal entry. Why the donkey? The donkey leads us back to Zechariah 9:9–17, where we discover much about what Jesus had in mind on Good Friday.

> Rejoice greatly, O Daughter of Zion!
>   Shout, Daughter of Jerusalem!
> See, your king comes to you,
>   righteous and having salvation,
>   gentle and riding on a donkey,
>   on a colt, the foal of a donkey.
> I will take away the chariots from Ephraim
>   and the war-horses from Jerusalem,
>   and the battle bow will be broken.
> He will proclaim peace to the nations.
>   His rule will extend from sea to sea
>   and from the River to the ends of the earth.
> As for you, because of the blood of my covenant with you,
>   I will free your prisoners from the waterless pit.
> Return to your fortress, O prisoners of hope;
>   even now I announce that I will restore twice as much to you.
> I will bend Judah as I bend my bow
>   and fill it with Ephraim.

I will rouse your sons, O Zion,
   against your sons, O Greece,
   and make you like a warrior's sword.
Then the LORD will appear over them;
   his arrow will flash like lightning.
The Sovereign LORD will sound the trumpet;
   he will march in the storms of the south,
   and the LORD Almighty will shield them.
They will destroy
   and overcome with slingstones.
They will drink and roar as with wine;
   they will be full like a bowl
   used for sprinkling the corners of the altar.
The LORD their God will save them on that day
   as the flock of his people.
They will sparkle in his land
   like jewels in a crown.
How attractive and beautiful they will be!
   Grain will make the young men thrive,
   and new wine the young women.

    The prophet Zechariah, writing around 500 B.C., prophesies in these verses about the coming of the messianic King to Jerusalem. He contrasts the coming of Israel's King with the violent coming of Alexander the Great on his great horses of war (Zech. 9:1–8). Just as Alexander's coming brought terror, so the coming of the messianic King will bring joy ("Rejoice greatly, O Daughter of Zion"). Zechariah explains why the daughters of Zion should rejoice by mentioning five blessings that the Davidic King will bring to the people of God.

    Blessing #1: The king will return to establish his rule nonviolently (9:9: "See, your king comes to you . . . riding on a donkey"). Jesus self-consciously, by the attention given to the colt, reveals that during his last six days (Sunday to Friday) his mind is on Zechariah 9. He sees his action as fulfilling the prophecy found there. He is unleashing his messianic rule in the way described in Zechariah. God will reign over Israel again. He will defend his people against his enemies. But how will he do this? Verses 9 and 10 make it clear that he will do this in a way that rejects militant nationalism. "I will take away the chariots from Ephraim and the war-horses from Jerusalem." The unridden colt symbolizes both gentleness and the rejection of violent militancy. Christ is riding into Jerusalem to do war, but it is war using different weapons than those of either Roman soldiers or Jewish revolutionaries. His war will be fought by acts of humble and sacrificial obedience to the Father's will.

Blessing #2: His kingdom will be established over all the earth: the gift of peace (9:10: "His rule will extend from sea to sea and . . . to the ends of the earth"). The Messiah will not just resume his kingship over Israel and the ancestral lands. All nations and all of the earth will now come under his dominion. When Jesus declares after his resurrection that "all authority in heaven and on earth has been given to me" (Matt. 28:18), another of Zechariah's blessings is fulfilled. This messianic authority of Jesus is the basis for his disciples to go into all the world to announce his rule and reign. This part of the prophecy also helps us explain why this essentially Jewish story about the return of its Davidic King has meaning for the world. This messianic King is also the King of all the nations, the Emperor of the earth. But how will he establish this global rule if he is committed to peaceful means?

Blessing #3: The new covenant will be established by a death (9:11: "The blood of my covenant with you"). The deliverance of Israel and all the earth will happen through the provisions of a new covenant that the Messiah will institute. The words of Jeremiah 31:33 come to mind: "I will be their God, and they will be my people." All the blessings of this reconciliation between an exiled people and their divine King are contained in this new covenant. But a death is needed in order to initiate the covenant ("blood of the covenant").

Jesus, during his last week, points to his covenant-making action. John 2:16–19 records the famous "temple tantrum." Jesus clears away the money changers, those who helped change idolatrous coinage (i.e., coins with Caesar's face) into coins the priests would accept for the purchase of animals for sacrifice. While abuses had crept into the practice of changing coins, it was nonetheless a necessary service, given the second commandment. Why then did Jesus focus his rage on them? Some have seen this action as merely an attempt by Jesus to reform the temple system of its corruption. Yet more seems to be going on than that. Jesus targets the money lenders not only because they represented the abuse of the system. He also targeted them because they represented the temple system itself. As John 2:19 makes clear ("Destroy this temple, and I will raise it again in three days"), Jesus was rejecting the temple system not just reforming it. His rejection was not based on its abuse but on what he was about to do through his death, a death that would bring to an end the efficacy of the temple and its sacrificial system. Jesus was about to offer a full and final sacrifice for sin, a sacrifice that would cover all sin forever.

Yet this new sacrifice would be outside the temple system, thereby rendering it unnecessary. In other words, Jesus was claiming "that in his work the Temple was being rebuilt."[9]

How does this relate to the blessing of Zechariah 9? Blessing three ("the blood of my covenant") is what Jesus has in mind. The sacrifice that he will offer to inaugurate this covenant will replace the temple system and redirect true worship to him. This action in the temple also sets the wheels in motion for his death. Challenge an idea and you can be rejected. Challenge a symbol and you can be killed. To attack the law was dangerous. To attack the temple was certain death. We are beginning to see that Jesus regarded this certain death at the hands of his enemies as crucial to the fulfillment of his own messianic role and to the unleashing of the messianic blessings of Zechariah.

The language of the Last Supper ("the new covenant in my blood") is yet another direct link between the intentions of Jesus and the blessings of Zechariah 9. We read in Luke 22:19–20 that on the night of the Last Supper, Jesus "took bread, gave thanks and broke it, and gave it to them, saying, 'This is my body given for you; do this in remembrance of me.' In the same way, after the supper he took the cup, saying, 'This cup is the new covenant in my blood, which is poured out for you.'" The mention of the shedding of blood brings to mind the Passover night in Egypt (Exodus 12), when the firstborn of Israel were spared from the angel of death by the blood of the lamb. Jesus was the new Passover Lamb whose blood would cover his new people. Jesus would be the new Moses leading his people into the freedom of the promised kingdom of God. Just as Jewish families complete their Passover celebrations with the words, "next year in Jerusalem," so Jesus completes his new Passover with the words, "I will not eat [the Passover meal] again until it finds fulfillment in the kingdom of God" (Luke 22:16). Jesus believed his death would deliver his new Israel from the judgment of God and lead them into the liberating covenant of the kingdom of God.

Blessing #4: The enemies of Israel will be defeated (9:15: "The LORD Almighty will shield them. They will destroy and overcome with sling-stones"). As we have seen in previous chapters, Jesus refused to identify Israel's enemy as either Rome or the Gentile nations. Just as David overcame Goliath with a sling, rejecting the armor of Saul, so Zechariah promises that God will enable Israel to overcome the nations of the world with unlikely weapons. When Jesus enters Jerusalem, it is to destroy the enemy behind all enemies, Satan himself. He will do this by rejecting and then foiling Satan's weapons of choice—violence and death. He will turn the ultimate symbol of violence and death itself, the cross, into a symbol of life and peace. The cross is Jesus' slingstone, the unlikely weapon that he, as new Israel, will use to defeat the new Goliath. This will be a total defeat of the enemy—defeating not only the enemy's ends (enslavement of people) but his means (violence and death).

Blessing #5: The people will return from their internal exile and enjoy the full favor of the Lord in all of life (9:16–17). Even though Israel was back in the Promised Land when Zechariah wrote his prophecy, they were still living in internal exile. The temple was not yet functioning, and the Davidic kingship had not been restored. What this meant for Jews is that their sins were still keeping them from enjoying God's full blessings. Zechariah envisioned the day when the people would no longer live under the cloud of their divine King's displeasure. The new covenant would so remove sins that God would save them completely and give them such total joy in their hearts that "they will sparkle in his land like jewels in a crown" (v. 16). There would be so much prosperity (the grain and new wine of verse 17) that the young men and women would be full of beauty and strength. The refusal of Jesus to engage in ritual fasting and his miracle at the wedding in Cana bear witness to the new end of exile and the new era of joy that his death would inaugurate.

Before Jesus' final week in Jerusalem is finished, Zechariah 9 will be fulfilled. Each of the five blessings will be unleashed: (1) The king will return to establish his rule nonviolently (v. 9). (2) His rule will be established over all the earth (v. 10). (3) The new covenant will be inaugurated by a sacrifice (v. 11). (4) Israel's enemies will be defeated (v. 15). (5) The people will return from exile and enjoy the favor of God (v. 16). Though future dimensions of this prophecy will remain, every blessing will be inaugurated by the death of Christ.

Christ's last words on the cross were, "It is finished" (John 19:30). The King has now returned to lift the curse from his creation and restore his rule and reign over all the earth. The death of Christ is the decisive act that fulfills all the promises and prophecies of God to Israel and to the world. The paradise predicted when the King returned to Zion has been inaugurated. God's people are now his treasured jewels. The exile has ended. This experience of homecoming has come about because Yahweh came back to earth as the scarecrow God—the almighty King who becomes the scapegoat in order to remove sin and restore creation. This act alone will usher in the future world so beautifully depicted in the dreamlike prose of the prophet Zechariah. The covenant is now fulfilled: "I will be their God, and they will be my people."

Why did Jesus die? The donkey helps us answer that question. It points us to the prophecy that dominated Jesus' words and actions throughout the climactic week in Jerusalem. Jesus believed his death would unleash the five blessings of Zechariah 9.

Was it a terrible thing that Jesus died? Yes. What is an evil thing? Though men meant it for evil, God meant it for good. The death of Jesus made it possible for all the benefits of the great homecoming of God to be unleashed to sinners. Jesus had lived within the wonder of those benefits and knew their power. By taking the place of sinners, he could put into effect the new covenant and make available the sonship experience to the whole earth.

2. The Death of Jesus Overcomes the Evil Human Heart, the Source of Sin and Suffering

Though the Philosopher in our opening story doubted whether the evil of human sin was real, the Theologian had no such hesitation. He believed that the source of evil was in fact the corruption of the human heart by sin. His only hope was in the temple and its sacrificial system. Centuries of sacrifice, however, had made little impact on human nature or the problems of sin and evil. In contrast, the writers of the New Testament believed that the single sacrifice of Jesus took care of the sin problem in a decisive way. How did his death overcome the evil of the human heart? Adrio König lists the many ways in which Jesus' death deals with sin. In biblical terms we are now restored to an eternal relationship with the living God through what Jesus did on the cross:

> In the apostolic preaching . . . reconciliation occupies an extraordinary position. Reconciliation is proclaimed as the fruit of Christ's cross (Rom. 5:10; Eph. 2:16). It is through the cross that our sins are "blotted out" or forgiven (2 Cor. 5:19; Gal. 1:4; Eph. 1:7; Col. 2:14) and our hostility is ended (Eph. 2:13, 19ff.). Our mutual antagonism and enmity toward God comes to an end (vv. 15–16). Through the cross, Christ has brought us into the right relationship with God (Rom. 3:24), and God has accepted us as his friends (2 Cor. 5:18–19 TEV) because Christ, by his crucifixion has made peace with God (Eph. 2:1). Through Christ's cross we become subjects of God's kingdom, members of his family (v. 19), members of Christ's body, and heirs of his Father (3:6). . . . Paul

puts it clearly: "when we were God's enemies . . . we were reconciled to him through the death of his Son" (Rom. 5:10). In fact, all the marvelous things Christ gained for us on the cross, he gained while we were still his foes. The reconciliation, the peace, the forgiveness, the status of God's children, all were actually gained, but still without us—only for us. This does not mean that real peace, forgiveness, and adoption did not fully come about. To suggest this would distort the preaching of the apostles. But it means that peace, forgiveness, and adoption must be realized in yet another way—in us—if we are really to accept our reconciliation (2 Cor. 5:20), begin to live in peace, and behave in this world as his children. But this is only attaining the same goal in another way.[10]

What we must understand is that whatever Jesus did on the cross he did for us, and whatever he did for us he must do in us. The often forgotten third dimension of the cross's eschatology is that whatever he does in me through his Spirit he will do with me in the future world. The cross thus points back (for us), down (in us), and ahead (with us). It can create these realities of peace with God and usher in the *shalom* of the kingdom because it brings us to God who has ended his exile and returned as our King.

Exactly how the cross accomplishes this reconciliation and homecoming has been the subject addressed by the many theories of atonement. Theologian Donald Bloesch surveys three theories—the dramatic theory with its emphasis on the defeat of evil powers, the mystical theory that sees the whole life of Jesus as re-creating human beings and infusing into us his new life, and the moral influence theory whereby human beings are inspired to follow Christ's example of self-giving sacrifice. While appreciating these various views as touching on aspects of the meaning of the cross, Bloesch focuses on the substitutionary sacrifice view as doing the most justice to the biblical writings. "A more biblical view would see both God's holiness and God's love as the ground of the atonement. Today we are prone to underplay the demands of God's holiness and depict God as exhaustively love."[11]

To believe that the death of Jesus is the return of Yahweh to Zion requires the forgiveness of sin. But there is no forgiveness of sin for the great God of Israel without a holy and acceptable sacrifice. The perfect Lamb of Yom Kippur, the Day of Atonement, is necessary to cover our sins. His blood must be sprinkled on the throne of God in order to cleanse it from his people's sins and make it possible to resume his seat as a God who now dwells on earth as well as in heaven.

This is what the substitutionary view is all about—not an invention of the legalistic West but the fulfillment of the Old Testament story and the exciting climax of the inbreaking of the King into history to become its beneficent ruler and the conqueror of all its enemies.

To make any real progress on resolving the question of God's goodness means that we need a change of heart leading to a changed perspective. Consider the words of John Frame: "The marvelous thing . . . is not that there is evil in the world, but that God has forgiven the evil in our own hearts for the sake of Christ. Without that new heart of faith, we are blind (1 Cor. 2:14; 2 Cor. 4:4). But Christ opens eyes that were blinded by sin and opens lips to sing his praise."[12]

He takes away our sin in several ways. He takes away first the guilt and condemnation we deserve by forgiving us. He then continues to work in us to take away the habits and attitudes of sin. How can we overcome the source of evil—sin in the human heart? This problem is overcome decisively in the death of Jesus.

3. The Death of Jesus Overcomes the Evil of an Indifferent God

In the story, the African's mother describes how the death of Jesus reveals the caring heart of God: "Only the healer is powerful enough to conquer through suffering. His omnipotence works best through weakness. He uses his power to completely identify with the victims and suffers with them. Through his suffering with us comes the unleashing of an omnipotent love that will transform all of us who believe and all creation around us."

The cross tells us that God is present in suffering not as an observer but as a victim. God came in the person of Jesus, not to flash around his glory but to enter into our misery in order to take it away. This is the message of Philippians 2:6–8, which speaks of Jesus, "Who, being in very nature God, did not consider equality with God something to be grasped, but made himself nothing, taking the very nature of a servant, being made in human likeness. And being found in appearance as a man, he humbled himself and became obedient to death—even death on a cross!"

The cross must change the way we view God. We can no longer charge God with indifference. He entered into the human condition and shared our sorrows. This does not mean that God is mortal, for God cannot be seen as finite and still be God. But we must see the

God whose perfection places him beyond suffering as willing to enter into our suffering.

> The death of God in the Christian sense means God with us and for us. God did not cease when he went to the cross in the person of Jesus; on the contrary, he demonstrated his deity in a way that only people under the cross can appreciate and understand. The death of God does not remove God from our lives but confirms his inescapable presence in our lives. The death of God means God triumphant over sin and death, and faith in this God as the key to overcoming the power of sin in our own Lives.[13]

"God was reconciling the world to himself in Christ," Paul reminds us in 2 Corinthians 5:19. What we must see in that act is that the great King Yahweh returned to Zion both to take sins away and then to bring about the *shalom* that the removal of sins unleashed. Yahweh returned from his holy exile of protest in order to enter into the exile of his sinful people. By taking their experience of exile upon himself and actually undergoing the exile from God within himself as God do we see that the death of God is not cessation of existence but separation from the source of life. Jesus shattered this separation on that Friday afternoon and in so doing conquered the evil idea of an indifferent God.

4. The Death of Jesus Overcomes the Evil of an Unjust God (Rom. 3:25–26)

From the perspective of the Theologian in the opening story, there was a greater evil than an indifferent God. That greater evil was an unjust God. From where the Theologian stood, the charge that God must answer is not why he punishes people as he does but why he is so merciful to them. Too many sins go unpunished. Too many human evils are passed over. From a biblical angle, given the holiness of God and his uncompromising hatred of sin and evil, the greatest evil of God is in being too merciful.

The biblical doctrine of sin teaches that it has damaged both our relationship with God as well our nature (Rom. 3:23; 5:17–19; 6:23). The Bible further teaches that there is nothing we can do, given our corrupted natures, to overcome sin. A just God, one might understandably conclude, should therefore punish us by destroying us. Why does he keep turning the other cheek and winking at sin? How can he be just if he lets the guilty go free? What kind of God permits a

Hitler or a Stalin to rise to power and get away with his crimes? Why does he show mercy to the undeserving and the criminal?

This is a great scandal for an educated conscience as are any of the other charges against God. All have sinned and therefore deserve to die as punishment for their sins. But God treats them unjustly by allowing them to live and often to continue in their sin and evil. In many cases he forgives them if they repent. Try asking a court to forgive you for robbing a bank or killing a child. How can God be just and not give us the punishment we deserve?

The answer the Bible gives to these questions is the death of Christ. The cross covers all sin and gives God the just and righteous basis to now lift the curse (Rom. 8:1; Gal. 3:13). Romans 3:25–26 states this truth boldly:

> God presented [Jesus] as a sacrifice of atonement, through faith in his blood. He did this to demonstrate his justice, because in his forbearance he had left the sins committed beforehand unpunished—he did it to demonstrate his justice at the present time, so as to be just and the one who justifies those who have faith in Jesus.

The truth here is that the death of Christ was necessary not only to justify sinners but also to justify God. He overlooked sins done in the past because he knew his Son's death would atone for those sins. He is merciful to fallen humanity today, even the most cruel of tyrants, because the blood of Jesus gives the Father a just basis for mercy and patience. How can a just God wink at sin? The death of Jesus the God-man on the cross vindicates the justice of God.

5. The Death of Jesus Overcomes the Evil of Meaninglessness

One of the great evils of our modern world is nihilism, the belief that life has no inherent meaning. Meaning must be imposed upon life by the human will. History is "an episode between two oblivions," Ernest Nagel once wrote.[14] Nihilism is a response to mortality. If death and ruin is the inevitable future for every human being, then life is meaningless. The grave swallows all. God must be blamed for this tragic tale "full of sound and fury, signifying nothing." But this bleak view of the future cannot hold up if the death of Jesus is properly understood. The cross changes the meaning of history by bringing one of Nagel's "oblivions" (death and its eternal consequences) into the middle of history and taking it away. The future judgment that we should have experienced has now fallen upon Jesus at the cross. Jesus thus experiences for us the great white throne judgment at the end of historical time. By being judged in our place, he also reverses the verdict that will be pronounced on us. No words of judgment remain, for the work of judgment has been accomplished already. The only words that can then be uttered is the invitation to "enter into the joys of the kingdom." A whole new positive way to look at history has opened up for those who believe.

Jürgen Moltmann comments on the new history created by Jesus. He notes how the scene of Good Friday is filled with the signs of the final judgment when "darkness descends on the earth, the veil in the temple is torn in two, the earth quakes, the rocks burst apart, the graves open, saints rise from the grave and appear." What this means, says Moltmann, is that the end of the old history has already happened in Jesus and a new plot for history has begun. "In the light of his messianic message about the kingdom of God and the new world aeon, the opposition Jesus experienced and the suffering and death he endured is apocalyptically interpreted as summing up and anticipation of the end-time suffering in which 'this world' will reach its end and the 'new world' will be born."[15]

This is Paul's testimony as well in Colossians 1: "For God was pleased to have all his fullness dwell in him, and through him to reconcile to himself all things, whether things on earth or things in heaven, by making peace through his blood, shed on the cross" (vv. 19–20). As one commentator observes: "We should therefore understand this statement to be a reference to the cosmic significance of Christ's work. . . . The disorder that has characterized creation will be done away and divine harmony restored. . . . All things eventually are to be decisively subdued to God's will and made to serve his purposes."[16]

The death of Christ is thus a new genesis. The declaration by Christ on the cross, "It is finished," must be seen as analogous to the commanding word of Genesis 1, "Let there be light"—for both commands, by the power inherent in God's Word, create new worlds. The commanding words of Genesis create the world of creation and culture. The commanding words of the cross, interpreting the commanding action of the cross, re-create the world, in a way analogous to the flood—not a world unlike the old but the old world made new, cleansed from sin, and now forever moving through time under the new rainbow of God's smile and favor. What is the true meaning of reconciliation? We must emphatically state that it means that in the death of Jesus the new covenant promises are now fulfilled (I will be your God, and you will be my people) and thus the new world order, which Jesus was already enjoying and embodying, is open to us.

6. The Death of Jesus Overcomes the Evil of Suffering

What about the problem of unjust suffering? I am not only a sinner, but I am also sinned against. Why does God allow "innocent" suffering? This question is substantially answered by much of what has been said above. We must always remember that the curse of sin has fallen not only on us but on all of life around us. That we would be stung by the fallenness of others and of our environment is to be expected given the facts of Genesis 3, which records humanity's original disobedience. The death on the cross has begun to address the curse of sin and to remove its effects one by one. The five blessings of Zechariah 9 are being unleashed. If these things are so, then why do believers have to suffer injustice? Doesn't the death of Jesus make all things new?

My first response to unjust suffering is 1 Peter 5:5–10. The apostle Peter is addressing the issue of innocent suffering. In 4:19 he wrote that "those who suffer according to God's will should commit themselves to their faithful Creator and continue to do good." Why? How can we overcome the disappointment and difficulties enough to do good and continue our commitment? Peter does not give the answer of stoicism—just grin and bear it. Rather, he gives the unique logic of the cross. We rise by dying. We are lifted up only by being made low. The pattern of the cross is duplicated in the life of the believing person. The death of Christ is therefore not only a way of salvation, it is also a way of seeing and a way of living. In Peter's own words: "Humble yourselves, therefore, under God's mighty hand, that he may lift you up in due time. Cast all your anxiety on him because he cares for you" (1 Peter 5:6–7). If we respond to suffering by seeing it as a Good Friday experience that will be followed by Easter joy, then suffering becomes a way of hope and of glory. Peter says as much in 1 Peter 4:14: "If you are insulted because of the name of Christ, you are blessed, for the Spirit of glory and of God rests on you." Because of the cross, the pattern of the Christian life now conforms to Easter weekend: We must go down in order to go up.

The second response to the problem of innocent suffering is actually a promise flowing from this pattern of the cross so celebrated by Peter. In Romans 8:28, 32, Paul echoes Peter when he explains that God will turn suffering into something that will issue in our good. The well-known promise of 8:28 states this truth: "In all things God works for the good of those who love him, who have been called according to his purpose." Evil and suffering are but the ugly prelude to all the beauty that God intends to do in us, for us, and through us.

But why is this so? Upon what basis does God promise to turn our tears into joy and our suffering into satisfactions of every kind? Romans 8:32 answers that question: "He who did not spare his own Son, but gave him up for us all—how will he not also, along with him, graciously give us all things?" Because of the death of Jesus, every good thing I need for the journey will be given. Suffering must be seen as part of the delivery system. The Puritan John Flavel saw this verse in that light:

> How is it imaginable that God should withhold, after this, spirituals or temporals from his people? How shall he not call them effectually, justify them freely, sanctify them thoroughly, and glorify them eternally? How shall he not clothe them, feed them, protect and deliver them? Surely if he would not spare his own Son one stroke, one tear, one groan, one sigh, one circumstance of misery, it can never be imagined that ever he should, after this, deny or withhold from his people, for whose sakes all this was suffered, any mercies, any comforts, any privilege, spiritual or temporal, which is good for them.[17]

The answer, then, to unjust suffering is to remember the story that we are in. We are not in a Promethean story in which God is the enemy and we must steal the fire of every good thing from him and pay the price of endless suffering because of it. We are not in the story of Narcissus, alone in the world with only ourselves to love, doomed to plunge into the pond of self-love, where we will be consumed forever. We are in the story of Jesus. We are living in and living out the story of the cross. Our suffering is neither Promethean (proving God is an enemy) nor narcissistic (providing an excuse for self-pity and self-indulgence). Our suffering is glorious and good because it unleashes every imaginable blessing that would be good for us. Our story, summarized by 8:32, is that "nothing will ever enter your experience as God's child that, by God's sovereign grace, will not turn out to be a benefit to you. This is what it means for God to be God, and for God to be *for* you, and for God to freely give you all things with Christ."[18]

The death of Christ overcomes the effects of evil and suffering by unleashing every imaginable good. Evil is not the last word. God uses evil for a greater good. This greater good is comprehensive in scope and eternal in duration. This is the greatest good that could be given to fallen mortals.

7. The Death of Jesus Overcomes the Evil of Death Itself

No greater evil confronts humanity than the evil of death. While there are many sources that feed the narratives of narcissism and Prometheanism, one of the most fundamental is the fear of death. This fear was analyzed by Paul Tillich in his classic study, *The Courage to Be*.[19] He spoke of anxiety about nonbeing—that is, the experience of becoming nonexistent. Death is the source of this anxiety. Death is the gateway to nonexistence or nonbeing. It produces three kinds of anxiety or dread. The first is physical anxiety—we dread the inescapable determinism of fate leading us to the grave. The second is existential anxiety—we dread the inescapable prospect of the meaninglessness and emptiness of life that death produces. All achievements and meaning are swallowed by the grave. The third anxiety is the moral dread of guilt and condemnation, which death itself may symbolize and to which it is a passageway. The inevitability of death is the source of this physical, existential, and moral anxiety. Fear is the attempt to find an object that we can blame for these anxieties. In that sense, fear is a diversion from the real issue. Despair occurs when one gives in to the realization that death is supreme over life. In Freud's classic struggle between love and death, anxiety is the tension in the struggle, courage is the action of love in the face of the struggle, and despair is giving up to the reality of death's power.

In the opening story, the death of Jesus is seen initially as but another victory for the grim reaper. Quite to everyone's surprise, however, the death of Jesus changes their lives in remarkable ways. Each of the main characters overcomes the dread and dark powers of death and finds new life and new power to love through the death of Jesus.

How does the cross of Christ remove the fear of death? Specifically, how does this life-giving cross help us to die to death itself and its shadows of anxiety? Consider Paul's answer to this question in 2 Corinthians 5:14–15:

> For Christ's love compels us, because we are convinced that one died for all, and therefore all died. And he died for all, that those who live should no longer live for themselves but for him who died for them and was raised again.

These verses are about the death of Christ but not only the death of Christ. They are also about what the Puritans called "the death of death" in the death of Christ. Our future death with its three fears of meaninglessness, condemnation, and physical suffering is dealt with by the death of Christ. He has already died that death for us. "We are convinced that one died for all, and therefore all died." His death was in our place. He died our death of meaninglessness, condemnation, and enduring pain. Because he died that death for us, a death that the sentence of sin imposed upon us, we cannot die that death. The death that awaits us now is the death of transformation, full intimacy with God, realization of ultimate purpose of history in general and our history in particular.

But what about the toll that our fear of eventual death takes on daily life? How does the cross help us lift the curse of death from daily attitudes and actions? Our living death, whereby we act out the three dimensions of our eventual death—daily feelings of meaninglessness, daily feelings of guilt and condemnation, and daily fear of pain and suffering—are addressed by this death of Jesus. He has died that death as well. The existential and psychological attacks of meaninglessness, alienation, guilt, and fear of suffering can be managed by the believer because of the death of Christ. Because he died for those daily attacks of death as well as the final attack, these assaults cannot mean destruction and ruin. That meaning has been absorbed by Jesus.

What do these attacks on the mind and emotions mean given the death of Jesus on our behalf? Jesus has already died this death. The experiences that give rise to these emotions are no longer testimonies of the supremacy of death but of the supremacy of the death of Christ. The daily attacks are now occasions to live by faith that no suffering is wasted, no dead end is meaningless, no attack of conscience and guilt can lead to condemnation. That attack of the forces of death upon the daily experience of the living has now been ended by the death of Jesus. He died this kind of death already, and therefore, the only daily pain that is left for us is the pain that is shared with Jesus and that he will use for good. The only daily guilt that is left for us is not the one that leads us to condemnation but one that we are to give to Jesus and one that has been covered by his blood. The daily attacks of anxiety, all three kinds, have only one intention now that Jesus has died. The Father, who has now brought us home, will use these little brushes with death to remind us that Christ has taken away all their destructive aspects and that the Spirit will turn these attacks into their opposite.

To make this even more explicit, the only death we can now die, even if it is the daily death brought on by anxiety, is the death of Jesus. His death of meaningfulness, his death of guilt removal, his painful death that would eventually take away all death—this is the only daily death we can now experience. We can only die a Zechariah 9 death—that which will lead to the enjoyment of all the blessings of the Messiah. Existential anxiety and despair need not be our daily portion. The rule of Narcissus or Prometheus is over. We can now live daily by the death of Christ, which reminds us moment by moment that God's wrath (meaningless living, endless suffering, the guilt that leads to condemnation) has already been appeased for us by God himself.

The life that emerges from living in and living out the death of Christ is the life described by Paul in 2 Corinthians 5:14: "Christ's love compels us." No more narcissism or Prometheanism, fueled by fear and anxiety to create a self-containing safety and security from pain, emptiness, and guilt, can be found. The love of God breaks through the defenses of these old stories and shows us the love of another, a crucified love that deals with all fears and takes away all anxieties. The Jesus story alone, climaxing on the cross, provides the narrative we need for a true spirituality, a truly effective spirituality that leads away from death to life.

Because of the death of Christ, guilt will become hope, fear of suffering that formerly led to a compulsive hedonism now leads to love, and the fear of meaninglessness is now turned into the focused life of faith. Death outside the death of Jesus was the source of daily despair. The death of death in the death of Jesus now is the source of daily joy. This is how the Christian lives in joy—because death itself has died and the only death we can now die either daily or ultimately is the life-giving death of Jesus. This is the seventh way in which the death of Jesus overcomes evil. It ends the evil reign of death.

Experiencing the Death of Jesus: Implications for Spirituality

How do we handle the problem of evil in our world? The search for spirituality will not get far until we get an answer to this question. The Kushners and the Chopras offer suggestions on the way forward but at a price. We must give up the biblical understanding of God.

In the opening story, a new answer to the problem of evil is presented. That answer is given at Skull Hill. After the world hurls accusations at the dying Jesus, something strange happens. Evil is overcome. Sorrow is taken away. Broken relationships are healed. Broken dreams are restored and fulfilled. The cross of the scarecrow God becomes a tree of life.

The death of Jesus is God's answer to the problem of evil. As the mother tells the African at the end of the opening story, "He did not reason with us because the problem of evil cannot be answered by an argument. It is only answered by a story. And with a story you must wait for the ending before you can truly know the meaning."

This is homecoming truth 5: True love conquers evil by becoming its victim. Getting used to this truth is a critical task for pilgrims on the road to spiritual fulfillment. What are some specific ways we can experience this truth and make it part of our personal reality? Let me suggest three applications.

1. *We must get excited about the cross as our tree of life—the key to every blessing of homecoming.* The passage that comes immediately to mind is Galatians 6:14: "May I never boast except in the cross of our Lord Jesus Christ, through which the world has been crucified to me, and I to the world." Paul saw something in the message of the death of Jesus that inspired the highest possible acclaim.

John Stott captures the heart of Paul's enthusiasm:

> There is no exact equivalent in English . . . to the Greek verb *kauchasthai*. It may be translated "to boast in," "to glory in," "to take pride in," "to revel in," even to "live for." In a word, our *kauchema* is our obsession. It engrosses our attention, it fills our horizons, it dominates our mind. . . . For Paul this was the cross. The cross of Christ was the centre of his faith, of his life and of his ministry; it should equally be the centre of ours. Let others be obsessed with money, success, fame, sex or power; those who follow Christ should be obsessed with him and with his cross.[20]

Martin Luther believed in boasting about the cross. So dazzled was he by the death of Jesus that he developed this insight into what he called a theology of the cross in which he contrasted prideful reason with Christ-centered faith. Luther once said that "the cross is our whole theology." By this he meant that the cross was not only a way of saving but it was also a way of seeing. It becomes our boast and our treasure. We must see that all the blessings of life, all the benefits of Zechariah 9, all the fullness of the love of God come to us because of the death of Jesus, which purchases these treasures.

If we are pursuing true spirituality, then we must learn to get excited about the cross, seeing it not only as the place of judgment but as the tree of life. Every spiritual benefit that we enjoy in life comes via the cross. Every aspect of the Father's love and the homecoming experience comes to us through the cross. It is the tree of life upon which all the fruits of grace grow.

2. *We must get used to the pattern of the cross.* We talked above about the Good Friday and Easter Sunday pattern of the Christian life. This pattern is established by the cross. If the cross is a tree of life and if every good fruit of life comes from that tree, then our entire life should be spent enlarging that harvest. The true quest that spiritual seekers should be on is how to live in and live out the death of Christ. We need to discover that following God moves us through the cycle of Good Friday emptiness to Easter fullness in varying ways. There are daily, weekly, monthly, annual, and lifetime patterns that we must get used to. Faith plays the key role in helping us to get used to the story of the cross, the pattern of Good Friday trials and Easter Sunday joys. Faith grows strong once we are educated about this circuitous path of joy. When we discover that the way to maximize pleasure and satisfaction in God is through suffering and trial, as demonstrated by the cross, we will run forward, leaving lust and unbelief behind. As John Piper has written:

> When faith has the upper hand in my heart I am satisfied with Christ and his promises. This is what Jesus meant when he said, "He who *believes* in Me shall never *thirst*" (John 6:35). When my thirst for joy and meaning and passion are satisfied by the presence and promises of Christ, the power of sin is broken. We do not yield to the offer of sandwich meat when we can smell the steak sizzling on the grill.[21]

Getting used to the story of the cross simply does not mean stoical resignation. It means a stallion-like surging of faith, champing at the bit for the joys set before us after we endure the crosses of life. The cross of Jesus purchased for us every good thing. Living in and living out the pattern of the cross enables us to pick up all that has been purchased. Faith is the state of mind and heart that gladly submits to this pattern in order to maximize its joy.

3. *We must realize that pride is the great enemy of authentic Christian spirituality.* For Deepak Chopra and to a lesser degree for Stephen Covey, personal pride is an ally in the pursuit of spirituality. We need to believe in ourselves. We need to see within ourselves nearly infinite resources for a meaningful and productive life. The story of Jesus sees pride in a completely different light, however.

Pride is dangerous in any walk of life, but it is particularly lethal in the pursuit of true spirituality. Os Guinness observes that pride has traditionally been viewed as the first, worst, and deadliest of the seven deadly sins. But the contemporary world has tried to transform this vice into a virtue—through changing the definition of pride into self-respect. So pride no longer "goeth before a fall," it cometh before a promotion, provided you have sufficient self-confidence and self-esteem. "Pride has always been one of my favorite virtues," actress Dame Edith Sitwell wrote. "I have never regarded it, except in certain cases, as a major sin. . . . I despise anything which reduces the pride of Man."[22]

Why is pride so deadly and so wrong? Guinness continues:

The sin of pride is wrong because it is inordinate and overweening. Consider its synonyms: egotism, arrogance, hubris, selfishness, vanity, haughtiness, presumption, boastfulness, big-headedness, self-satisfaction, self-centeredness, and the like. None of them is admirable and neither is the conceit that is the rotten fruit of calling. "The greatest curse in spiritual life," Oswald Chambers wrote, "is conceit."[23]

The cross reminds us that spirituality is a gift of grace purchased at an infinitely expensive price by the King of kings. The cross is the end of the Promethean conceit that I am the master of my fate. It is the end of the narcissistic presumption that the self is the source of life and happiness. The homecoming story smashes our prideful narratives as it reminds us that the only way to enjoy the riches of our Father's house is to humble ourselves at the foot of the cross. As Guinness advises:

Do we feel the wonder of being called? It is all a gift and all of grace. And contrary to expectations, grace is not a matter of God's welcoming the lawbreaker as well as the law-abiding, the disreputable along with the respectable, the prodigal son as well as the stay-at-home. Quite the reverse. Pride is the first and worst sin, so grace is most amazing when it embraces the fruits of pride rather than the fruits of gluttony or lust, when it reaches the Pharisee soul rather than the profligate Mary Magdalene, when it wins the proud person made prouder still by calling rather than the sinner feeling unworthy to be addressed. Only grace can dissolve the hard, solitary, vaunting "I" of the sin of pride in each of us. But the good news is that it Does.[24]

The death on the cross is a death that covers not only our failures but also our successes. Christ died not only for prodigals but for Prometheans alike. "Let him who boasts," says 1 Corinthians 1:31, "boast in the Lord."

Following the Way of Aslan

One of the great children's books of all time is C. S. Lewis's *The Lion, the Witch and the Wardrobe*. It tells the story of a magical land called Narnia, which is ruled by a wicked witch. The sign that her rule has cursed the land of Narnia is that it is "always winter and never Christmas." Life in all its variety is frozen into stone and chilled into lifelessness. Her touch is a killing frost. Into this frozen tragedy comes the great lion, Aslan, true ruler of Narnia. He enters into a conspiracy with some children from our own world who have stumbled into Narnia through a magic wardrobe, which acts as a portal between the world of everyday reality and the higher world of spiritual reality. But treason and sin destroy the conspiracy. Aslan himself is a great disappointment to the children because instead of conquering the witch, he is captured by her and tied to a great stone, where he is butchered to death. The reign of the great witch never appeared more triumphant than at the hour of Aslan's apparent defeat.

Yet the story has one more surprise. The death of Aslan releases untold power. Not only does he rise from the dead, but he is empowered with life-giving breath. As he breathes upon all the frozen wasteland of Narnia, the snow melts and the animals and humans who had been reduced to stone come back to life. The spirit of life in Aslan is released into Narnia through his death. Through his death all things become alive again and are filled with color and richness. The killing reign of the witch is broken, and paradise is restored. The children become kings and queens in the new world order created by the death of Aslan and the power that emanated from that death.

In our own pursuit of Narnia, of heaven on earth, the death of Jesus is the key we need. Spirituality is not only getting used to the story of Jesus. It is at heart getting used to the death of Jesus. We must get used to it not in the sense of taking it for granted and getting bored by its familiarity. We must get used to treasuring it. We must get used to it as the tree of life, the fountain of every joy and treasure. We must get used to the cross in a Galatians 6:14 way, so we can say with Paul, "May I never boast except in the cross of our Lord Jesus Christ, through which the world has been crucified to me, and I to the world."

7

THE LOCKED ROOM

EXPERIENCING
THE RESURRECTION
AND MISSION OF JESUS

Are you in trouble? How did you get in trouble? If you are in trouble, have you sought help? If you did, did help come? If it did, did you accept it? Are you out of trouble? . . . Do you know who you are? Do you know what you are doing? Do you love? Do you know how to love? Are you loved? Do you hate? Come back. Repeat. Come back. Come back. Come back.

Radio message from outer space, Walker Percy, *Lost in the Cosmos*

Since the children have flesh and blood, he too shared in their human-ity so that by his death he might destroy him who holds the power of death—that is, the devil—and free those who all their lives were held in slavery by their fear of death.

Hebrews 2:14–15

The Story: The Locked Room

On the evening of the first day of the week, the disciples were together with the doors locked for fear of the Jews. Everyone was getting on one another's nerves, and there was fierce debate among them about the report from the Girl, the Philosopher, the Theologian, the African, and some of the women. The first four had told the disciples about the miracles that had happened at the cross. The disciples had listened with great interest. When the four friends told them about their visit to the tomb that very morning, however, the reaction of the disciples was different. The Girl described excitedly how they arrived at the tomb at the crack of dawn and found the stone rolled away and the tomb empty. They also saw Jesus a few yards away—alive. The others confirmed her story.

Thomas spoke.

"We've got to keep our heads. This is no time to talk about who saw what, when. I know only two things. I know Jesus died, and until I feel a warm body, I must assume that he has stayed dead. I also know that his death was by order of the Jews and the Romans, and therefore, our names are probably on a list somewhere as well. My plan is this: We stay together for two or three more days until the heat dies down. Then we sneak out of Jerusalem, blend into the countryside, and start our lives all over again. What do you say to that, Peter?"

Peter said nothing at first because he was confused about what to say. Earlier that day he had heard the story from Mary and her four companions. Without thinking, he had run to the tomb and on the way had seen something he couldn't explain. It was just a hallucination. Unfortunately, the hallucination had spoken to him. Peter had not stayed to chat but had run in terror back to this hiding place. The door was bolted and locked now but not just to keep out the priests and the police.

"What do you say to that, Peter?" Thomas asked again.

"Whatever you say, Thomas. Whatever you say. You're the one with the level head. Whatever you say."

Peter was slumped near the door. In his hand he held a bottle in a brown bag. He took a big drink. He glanced around the room and noticed the African glaring at him. She had been following them, off and on, since that day in Capernaum. Peter disliked her. She was different from the rest of them. She came from a different place, and she was a Gentile. But the Master had wanted her to join them after she told her story about being sold into slavery by her father. The Master always had a soft spot for charity cases like the African. But Peter had been against the decision.

"She'll be trouble, Master. She's not one of us. She's different."

The Master had rebuked Peter and had allowed her to join the group. But Peter had been right. She was trouble, always contradicting him and questioning his judgments. Now she spoke of seeing miracles at Skull Hill on Friday and of dead people walking around on Sunday. She was just the kind of person who might blow the whistle on them all. He stood to his feet and yelled at her.

"What are you looking at? Can't a man take a drink in peace?"

"You can drink as much as you want, Peter. Don't let me bother you. We should in fact all take a drink in honor of Peter, our bold and courageous leader. In fact, I propose a toast. Join me in a drink, a toast to a great friend of Jesus Christ who when he hears that Christ is alive does what any bold and courageous friend and leader would do. He refuses to believe our eyewitness report. When he does check it out for himself, he comes back doubting his own eyes. Poor Peter, suffering from a chronic case of 'skepticitis.' This fever of unbelief is running so high that the only way he can cool it down is by hiding in a locked room like a coward and guzzling cheap wine. I propose a toast. A toast to our hero—Peter the great."

"Shut up," Peter yelled, determined to attack the African. The Theologian and the Philosopher rushed to stop him. But before they made contact, a noise from the corner of the room made them freeze where they stood.

"Peace" said a voice from the shadows. The greeting sounded more like a command. "Peace be with you."

Peter jerked his head to look toward the voice and then lowered his hand and let the bottle drop noisily to the floor. The voice moved from the shadows into the light. The disciples moved away because it was obviously a ghost who was speaking. It was obviously a ghost because it was obviously Jesus.

"Why are you so terrified? Why so full of disbelief? Take a good look at me. Touch my hands and feet. It's not a ghost who stands before you. It's really me."

Jesus moved closer to them. The African, the Girl, the Philosopher, the Theologian, and most of the disciples all fell before him, grasping his warm hand and kissing his dusty feet. Peter and Thomas moved farther away.

"What?" asked the African, wondering what a resuscitated corpse was like.

"How?" asked the Girl, wondering how a corpse returns to life.

"Why?" asked the Philosopher, wondering what this event meant.

"What now?" asked the Theologian, wondering what impact this event would have on the future.

"So many questions," Jesus replied with a laugh. "Let me start with the 'what.' Come and touch this 'resuscitated corpse.'"

The African reluctantly obeyed. The hands were warm. The face familiar. She hugged Jesus and said, "My Lord and my God."

"I am not a resuscitated corpse," he said to the African. "Through the power of the Holy Spirit that my Father gave to me, I have a completely new kind of body that will never grow old or die. Someday you will all have a body exactly like mine," he said and laughed like they had never heard him laugh before. "This body is for you. For all of you, if you follow me."

The African bowed, her tears dropping to the floor.

Jesus turned to the Girl. "How, you ask? How did I come back to life? I was raised by the power of God. That same power I now give to you. He will be in you and will not only raise you up on the last day, but he will raise you up every day. When you are empty, he will fill you. When you are frightened, he will comfort you. When you are alone, he will communicate my presence and power to you."

At that moment Jesus breathed on them all and said, "Receive the Holy Spirit. Now you can be my witnesses."

The Girl also bowed but took Jesus' hand and kissed it. He smiled and touched her head with affection.

Jesus then turned to the Philosopher.

"You ask why, wanting to know what this victory over death means. It means everything. It means that Zechariah 9 and the return of the King to rule and bless the earth has all happened. It means the new covenant has begun. It means the days of exile have ended. Most importantly it means that the Spirit that raised me from the dead has now been unleashed to make all things new. Don't you remember when I was with you that I told you all of this would happen? This is part of the master plan of the kingdom. Everything must be fulfilled that is written about me in the law of Moses and the prophets."

Then Jesus ordered that more lamps be lit. He called for the scrolls of the Jewish Scriptures. He opened them one by one and showed them the many places in the Bible that made it clear that the Christ must suffer and rise from the dead on the third day.

Jesus then turned toward the Theologian.

"You, my dear friend, have asked what happens now." Jesus went over to the window and parted the closed curtains. He went over to the locked door and unlocked it. He swung it open wide.

"What I want you to do now is to pack your bags and get out of this tomb. Roll back your stones. Get out of here and tell everyone you meet from Jerusalem to the farthest corner of this good earth that I am alive and because of that the kingdom of God has been inaugurated. Tell them that the Zechariah 9 program will now be launched in all the nations and civilizations of the world. Membership in the New Israel is now open to all people. Tell them that the Father has returned to earth and that the road that leads back home is open to prodigals and Pharisees alike. Know that all power is given to me in heaven and on earth. Know that I now make that power available to you in order to accomplish this global mission. The same Spirit of homecoming that shaped my story and raised me to life will now be at work in you and in the world to do the same. As the Father sent me so I am sending you."

Jesus then embraced the disciples one by one. Thomas remained in the back next to Peter.

"I don't believe in ghosts," Thomas blurted out. "I don't believe in resurrections or life after death or . . ."

"Put your finger in my side, Thomas," commanded Jesus. Thomas obeyed. "Stop doubting and start believing. I am the resurrection and the life. Blessed are those who have not seen and yet have believed."

"My Lord and my God," said Thomas, giving Jesus a bear hug. "My Lord and my God."

Then Jesus stood before Peter and repeated his command about going to the far corners of the earth. Peter refused to look at Jesus and said, "Lord, I am not worthy to go. I'm an unclean man."

Jesus raised Peter's chin. "Don't ever call anything unclean that I have died to purify." Peter smiled for the first time in four days. He was about to thank Jesus when he saw that Jesus was looking at the African and then at him.

"Lord, you know I love you, but you can't ask me to go there, to live with Gentiles."

Jesus spoke a second time. "Don't ever call anything unclean that I have died to purify."

Then Jesus turned to the African. "I want you to go back to your people. Go back to your father and tell him everything you have seen."

The African protested. "But you know what they did to me, Lord. They rejected me; they sold me into slavery. I can never go back. I will never forgive them for what they did to me."

Jesus said a third time, "Don't ever call anything unclean that I have died to purify."

Many more things were said that night and over the next five weeks before Jesus left the earth to sit at the right hand of the Father and carry on his kingdom work from that place of power.

Peter was there when Jesus ascended into heaven, as was Thomas, the African, the Girl, the Philosopher, and the Theologian. They were there on the day of Pentecost when the Spirit of Jesus came upon them in power just as he had come upon Jesus at the Jordan. They were also there the day the African packed her bags and announced that she was returning to Africa to tell the good news to her enemies. Thomas hugged her and wished her well. The disciples gave her a royal send-off as one by one they kissed her cheek and squeezed gifts into her hand. They all said their good-byes and dried their eyes, but none of them squeezed the African as tightly nor wept as hard as Peter. (Based on John 20; Luke 24.)

Forgetting How to Love

Into the locked room came the resurrected Christ. The impact of his presence changed his disciples, turning fearful failures into dynamic witnesses. The impact on Peter was especially powerful. He is transformed, in the story, into an agent of mission whose hatred for the African dissolves and turns into a deep and committed love.

In the same way, when we grasp anew the significance of Easter Sunday, our hearts and minds are altered and enlarged. The resurrection of the mediator gives meaning to everything else in the story of Jesus. When we speak of the cross as our whole theology, we do not mean the cross divorced from the resurrection but rather the cross in light of the resurrection. Without the resurrection our faith is vain. The entire story unravels, and Christian spirituality becomes a poor joke. If the resurrection is true, then the entire Christian story and its model of spirituality have been validated.

Experiencing the resurrection of Jesus can help us deal with an important life issue: the loss of the power to love. Earlier I quoted

Douglas Coupland in *Life after God:* "I need God to help me give, because I no longer seem capable of giving; to help me be kind, as I no longer seem capable of kindness; to help me love, as I seem beyond being able to love."[1]

In a world of hate crimes, ethnic cleansing, and cold indifference, learning how to love others is a major need. New Age spirituality claims to have an answer. Much of what Deepak Chopra writes, for example, addresses the issue of how to regain the power to love. He agrees with Christian spirituality that finding the power to love is one of the most important goals in life: "The desire to love and be loved is too powerful ever to be extinguished, and fortunately a spiritual path exists based upon this unquenchable longing."[2] What is this path? Chopra believes that all spiritual masters, including Christ, have taught the secret of where to find the power to love.

This path to love requires a change in the way we understand ourselves. Chopra describes that change: "Restoring the spiritual dimension to love means abandoning the notion of a limited self with its limited ability to love and regaining the Self with its unbounded ability to love."[3] This entails recovering the idea that God is within us. The great enemy of this new consciousness, according to Chopra, is duality, the idea that I am a separate self and not simply an expression of the one infinite self. "The mask of matter," says Chopra, "disguises our true nature, which is pure awareness, pure creativity, pure spirit. . . . When you perceive yourself as spirit, you will not simply feel love—you will be love."[4] Learning to love, therefore, means giving up an identity that is tied to our bodies and individual self-perceptions. We must discover the infinite self inside us.

Can this infinite and unlimited love conquer death? Not in a time-space way according to Chopra. Death is simply our passageway to the journey back to the infinite self.

> The Vedic seers say, "The real you cannot be squeezed into the volume of a body or the span of a lifetime." Just as reality flows from the virtual to the quantum to the material level, so do you. Whether we call this reincarnation or not almost doesn't matter. The package of body and mind that came before is a stranger to you now, and the one that might arise after your death is equally alien.[5]

Chopra is addressing one of the most important issues of our time. How can we regain the power to love? Walker Percy, in his whimsical *Lost in the Cosmos: The Last Self-Help Book*, ends his searching discussion of human lostness and powerlessness to love with an imaginary scenario. Humankind receives a message from an extraterrestrial intelligence, "the first after hundreds of years of monitoring." What will that message contain? Will it reveal the secrets of the universe? The message reads:

> Are you in trouble? How did you get in trouble? If you are in trouble, have you sought help? If you did, did help come? If it did, did you accept it? Are you out of trouble? . . . Do you know who you are? Do you know what you are doing? Do you love? Do you know how to love? Are you loved? Do you hate? Come back. Repeat. Come back. Come back. Come back.[6]

Percy's message from outer space provides no answers, just more questions. Yet his thrice repeated last line, "come back," is ambiguous. Is the universe simply asking us to respond to their great questions about salvation and love? Or is the universe suggesting the way to find salvation and love? Is "coming back" the way forward?

In light of the resurrection of Jesus, I have no doubt that the way forward is to "come back." It is by going back to the story of Jesus that the power to love can be regained. Once someone has experienced the power of the resurrection of Jesus, he or she can no longer accept the answers of a Chopra. The resurrection of Jesus gives us a very different answer to Coupland's cry of powerlessness. What comes out strongly in the opening story is not only that Jesus rose from the dead but also that he gives the power of the resurrection, the power of the Spirit, to those who believe in him. Christian spirituality cannot be understood without some grasp of the Holy Spirit and his role. We should not equate this Holy Spirit with the human spirit, as Chopra does. The Holy Spirit is the Third Person of the Triune God. But it is with his work, not his identity, that we are concerned in this chapter. We want to discover the Spirit as the great secret of love. He is the one who completes the homecoming experience in Jesus and in us. This is the heart of homecoming truth 7 and the Christian response to powerlessness in life: *The love that is stronger than death is the greatest power in the world.*

In this chapter, I'd like to look at three dimensions of the Spirit's resurrection power. I want to point out his role (1) in the resurrected life of Jesus after Easter Sunday, (2) in our resurrected life in Jesus as believers, and (3) in the resurrected life being unleashed around the world. What I trust will come through strongly is that spirituality without the Holy Spirit, who alone raises all things to new life, is no spirituality at all. Let's begin with the experience of Jesus.

The Spirit and the Resurrection of Jesus

In the opening story, Jesus gives the Holy Spirit the credit for raising him from the dead.

"'I am not a resuscitated corpse,' he said to the African. 'Through the power of the Holy Spirit that my Father gave to me, I have a completely new kind of body that will never grow old or die. Someday you will all have a body exactly like mine,' he said and laughed like they had never heard him laugh before."

While the New Testament writers sometimes speak of the resurrection as caused by the Father or the Son, a number of key texts point to the Spirit as the key agent on Easter Sunday. Romans 1:4 states that it was "through the Spirit of holiness" that Jesus was shown to be the Son of God because of "his resurrection from the dead." In Romans 8:11, Paul repeats this truth with even more force: "And if the Spirit of him who raised Jesus from the dead is living in you, he who raised Christ from the dead will also give life to your mortal bodies through his Spirit, who lives in you." What is Paul affirming about the resurrection of Jesus? I hear him declaring three important points.

First, the resurrection of Jesus by the Spirit is a fact of history. Paul faced some skepticism in his day about the resurrection. He created quite a buzz on Mars Hill in Athens by teaching about the resurrection of Jesus (Acts 17:31–32). Even some of the Corinthian Christians denied that such a thing could happen (1 Cor. 15:12). Paul, however, had ample reasons for believing that the Spirit of God had indeed raised Jesus from the dead. In 1 Corinthians 15:4–8 he lists the evidence:

> He was raised on the third day according to the Scriptures, and that he appeared to Peter, and then to the Twelve. After that, he appeared to more than five hundred of the brothers at the same time, most of whom are still living, though some have fallen asleep. Then he appeared to James, then to all the apostles, and last of all he appeared to me also, as to one abnormally born.

Paul believes that the resurrection was a fact of history. Supporting this belief were hundreds of eyewitnesses. Since Jewish law said that the truth could be established on the basis of two or three witnesses, Paul with his hundreds of witnesses is on safe ground.

As in the cases of Thomas and Peter in the opening story, however, even eyewitness testimony may not be enough to convince someone who is precommitted to unbelief. In our own time, the fact of the resurrection has been vigorously denied and alternative explanations offered to explain what people "really" saw. Some argue that the real resurrection was not of the body of Jesus but the faith of the disciples. Another view suggests that Jesus emerged from the tomb but only because he never really died. He had only "swooned" and was thought to be dead. A third view is that the Spirit of God was so real to the early church that it was as though Jesus were alive even though everyone knew he really wasn't.

Against such skepticism both ancient and modern we must affirm with Paul that the resurrection is a fact of history. The tomb was empty. Even Jewish critics who lied about how the body disappeared admitted as much. Hundreds saw him. The faith of the disillusioned disciples was transformed not by an idea but by a death-conquering person. The Word of God, which cannot lie, asserts the truth of this event. In summary, this cloud of witnesses points to the resurrection as (1) an objective, historical event (meaning one could take pictures of it); (2) a physical event (real flesh and blood, Luke 24:39); and (3) a transforming event in which the body of Christ is changed from a mortal one (subject to death and decay) to a glorified one (beyond the possibility of death and decay).

Why then the modern "skepticitis" about the raising of Jesus? The problem has to do with presuppositions. We must recognize that even scholars are controlled by their master narratives. A controlling story that does not allow for miracles will dismiss the case of Jesus even before weighing the evidence. Most people admit that presuppositions *of others* can keep them from accepting even obvious truth. The man who believes he is a chicken will find a way to deny the abundant evidence to the contrary, so deeply ingrained is his belief (absurd, though it is). What most of us have trouble accepting is that *our* presuppositions sometimes cause us to suppress good evidence and screen out the truth. Hostile presuppositions play a major role in denying the fact of the resurrection of Jesus.

But don't take my word for it. Take the word of a modern Jewish rabbi. Pinchas Lapide, formerly of the American College in Jerusalem, is an orthodox Jew who rejects the Christian claim that Jesus is the Messiah. "Christianity is a who-religion," Lapide writes. "Judaism is a what-religion. Or, if you will, Judaism is a religion of redemption; Christianity, one with a redeemer." Lapide rejects the Christian concept of individual salvation apart from the salvation of the world. He also rejects Jesus as the Messiah. But does that mean he rejects Jesus' resurrection? Not at all. Though theologically closed to Jesus as the Messiah, he is intellectually open to the possibility of resurrection. "I accept the resurrection of Easter Sunday not as an invention of the community of disciples, but as a historical event."[7] Why does he accept the historical fact of the resurrection? "If [the disciples], through such a concrete historical event as the crucifixion, were so totally in despair and crushed, as all the four evangelists report to us, then no less concrete a historical event was needed in order to bring them out of the deep valley of their despair and within a short time to transform them into a community of salvation rejoicing to the high heavens."[8]

With Paul, then, we must agree that to understand the meaning of the resurrection we must first accept that it is a historical fact based on reliable evidence.

Second, the resurrection is not just a random miracle but part of the connected story of Jesus. In the opening story, Jesus answers the Philosopher's question about what his resurrection from the dead really means.

"You ask why, wanting to know what this victory over death means. It means everything. It means that Zechariah 9 and the return of the King to rule and bless the earth has all happened. It means the new covenant has begun. It means the days of exile have ended. Most importantly it means that the Spirit that raised me from the dead has now been unleashed to make all things new. Don't you remember that when I was with you I told you all of this would happen? This is part of the master plan of the kingdom."

Seen from the perspective of the Old Testament story, God defeated Satan, sin, and death through the death and resurrection of his beloved Son. The resurrection itself is a dramatic and bold demonstration of God's return to earth to lift the curse and restore paradise. If he raises the dead, then who could doubt that all the other promises of Zechariah 9 (God's rule, defeat of enemies, new covenant, peace, and beauty and blessing in all of life) will be fulfilled.

In the death and resurrection of his Son, the Father fights for his people. The victory of the Messiah over death had been predicted in one of the earliest Old Testament messianic prophecies—Psalm 110:1: "Sit at my right hand until I make your enemies a footstool for your feet." The great story of homecoming whereby God returns to earth as the royal Father ruling through his royal Son is not just a story of heartwarming reunion. It is a story of war. The kingship of Jesus and the restoration of his people and kingdom will be accomplished and demonstrated by the subjugation of his enemies. As Gregory Boyd writes:

> Through Jesus' death and resurrection, the former "ruler of the world" had been "driven out" (John 12:31) and a new "Leader," a legitimate ruler, has been enthroned in his place. Whereas the former ruler held humanity in misery, sin and bondage, this Leader offers "repentance and forgiveness of sins" at no cost. Christ becomes our "Savior" because he has become our "Leader" by ousting the old "ruler of the world" through his death and resurrection.[9]

Jesus defeats his enemies by the power of the Spirit through both Good Friday sufferings as well as Easter Sunday glory.

With his enemies defeated, Jesus now appears to his disciples prior to his formal ascension to the throne of universal rule to announce his victory and to complete the story of homecoming. All of his work as a *prophet* (teaching the truth about the kingdom story), all of his work as a *priest* (paying for sins on the cross and unleashing the new covenant and its blessings), and all of his work as a *king* (defeating his people's enemies and inaugurating the new world order of life in the Spirit freed from the law of sin and death) has now been validated, vindicated, and established. The new covenant blessings of life in the Spirit (Jer. 31:33) purchased by the death of Jesus have now been unleashed. The promises of God rise from the empty tomb along with Jesus and begin their long and transforming journey around the world.

Third, the resurrection of Jesus unleashes the Spirit to bring the new life of homecoming to us. In Romans 8:11, Paul is confident that the Spirit will bring new life to the believer because the Spirit brought new life to Christ. Why would Paul logically conclude that Jesus' resurrection by the Spirit would mean a similar ministry in the life of the believer? The answer is that Jesus is a *mediator*, a middleman. Whatever he does, he does for us. If by the Spirit he overcame Satan, sin, and death in his own person, then he will make sure his Spirit shares the benefits of his victory with us.

Because Jesus is our mediator, Peter could stand up on the day of Pentecost and announce that the resurrection of Jesus was more than a miracle in the life of a single Jewish man. In Acts 2:34, Peter sees the resurrection as the fulfillment of the messianic promise of Psalm 110:1 ("Sit at my right hand until I make your enemies a footstool for your feet"). He draws two conclusions from this fact. The first is that a new world order has begun under the leadership of a new Lord and Savior, Jesus the Messiah. During his earthly ministry, Jesus was the only beneficiary of the new order of the kingdom returned to earth. Now these privileges of sonship and Spirit endowment can be shared with the world. The second conclusion Peter draws is that anyone who wants these blessings of new life in Jesus can have them for the asking. In Acts 2:38, he announces this great development: "Repent and be baptized, every one of you, in the name of Jesus Christ for the forgiveness of your sins. And you will receive the gift of the Holy Spirit." The Spirit that gave life to Jesus, kingly life, lordship life, new world order life, has now been loosed by Jesus to give new life to believers.

In summary, the resurrection is a fact of history. The great agent of this event was the Holy Spirit. Through the power of the Spirit, Jesus was not only raised but the power of his homecoming story was unleashed for all who would believe.

The Spirit and the New Life of the Believer

In the opening story, Jesus answers a question about the resurrection asked by the Girl: "How, you ask? How did I come back to life? I was raised by the power of God. That same power I now give to you. He will be in you and will not only raise you up on the last day, but he will raise you up every day. When you are empty, he will fill you. When you are frightened, he will comfort you. When you are alone, he will communicate my presence and power to you."

He elaborates on these services of the Spirit to the believer by answering the Theologian's question about the meaning of this event: "It means everything. . . . It means the days of exile have ended. Most importantly it means that the Spirit that raised me from the dead has now been unleashed to make all things new."

The Spirit that raised Jesus from the dead is now at work to do the same work of resurrection in our lives. That work of resurrection begins now. That is the further truth taught by Romans 8:11. What does this mean? How does the Spirit give new life to us? Let me make some general comments on the role of the Spirit in the life of the believer and then focus on some of the specific aspects of the believer's new life in the Spirit mentioned in Romans 8.

The pattern of spirituality already established by Jesus at the Jordan was composed of two elements: sonship and Spirit empowerment. These two elements are linked in that they both come from Jesus' relationship with God as an all-sufficient and all-loving Father. Sonship is the name we give the full intimacy and standing that Jesus enjoyed with the Father. Spirit empowerment is the sign of the generosity and fullness of the Father's bounty, which filled Jesus' life and which he graciously shared with others. As James Dunn observes, "Spirit and sonship, sonship and Spirit, are but two aspects of the one experience of God out of which Jesus lived and ministered."[10] This experience of God makes up the heart of the new world order that the coming of the kingdom of God ushers in. Jesus experiences this new order of things first and then through his sacrificial death removes the stain of sin, enabling sinners to enter into this kingdom spirituality with him.

When we look at the Epistles of the New Testament to see what this kingdom spirituality looked like for believers, we see both sonship and Spirit empowerment. One of the best places to see this new life of sonship and power described is Romans 8. In this famous chapter, which climaxes Paul's greatest letter, nine benefits of new life in the Spirit are described. They range from the gift of freedom from judgment ("no condemnation" in 8:1) to freedom from any fear about the future ("no separation" in 8:38–39). Each of these gifts is an expression of the power of the resurrection now at work in our lives, power that will one day culminate in our bodily resurrection from the dead.

Benefit #1: No Condemnation—Freedom from the Curse of Sin (Rom. 8:1–4: We Are Forgiven and Accepted)

Romans 8 begins with the declaration that because of our union with Christ Jesus as the head of a new creation, we can now enjoy a host of benefits, the first of which is "no condemnation." The verdict of "no condemnation" that the Gospel pronounces on the repentant sinner is equivalent to the statement made by God to his Son at the Jordan River: "This is my beloved Son in whom I am well pleased." The favor of the Father rests on us because of Jesus. The wrath of an exiled God upon his exiled people has ended and has been replaced with the homecoming experience of sonship. Theologians call this benefit justification by faith. Paul's explanation of it goes something like this.

Because of the death and resurrection of Jesus Christ, we have entered a new order of existence. The old order Paul calls "the law of sin and death" (8:2). The new order is called "the law of the Spirit of life." This change of kingdoms or shift of controlling laws or narratives is the beginning of the Spirit's work of resurrecting the dead. Paul describes sinners as "dead in your transgressions and sins" (Eph. 2:1). By the power of the Spirit that raised Jesus from the dead, we were made alive in Christ (Eph. 2:4–5). Now that we have been raised spiritually, our lives are on the path that will lead to total resurrection from death.

This life in the Spirit is life freed not from God's righteous law but from the powerlessness of our fallen human nature. By covering our sins, the Father can now bring us into his kingdom and share its riches with us. The greatest power and wealth he possesses is the power of the Spirit, who can make all things new. This enrichment and empowerment by the Spirit makes possible the other benefits mentioned in Romans 8. These benefits are aspects of the resurrected life infused within us once we are in union with Christ. Because of this gift of new life in the Spirit, "the whole of Christian life is a matter of Spirit."[11]

Benefit #2: No Bondage—Freedom from Sin (Rom. 8:5–14: We Are Controlled by the Spirit of Life Not the Mind of Death)

Life in the Spirit carries with it ethical benefits. In the old order of things, when we were dead in our spiritual exile, we were hostile to God's law. Under the life-giving influence of the Spirit, we can break the control of the sinful nature and be responsive to God's holy desires. Gordon Fee describes the ethical freedom and power now available to those enjoying the Spirit of sonship. Fee explains, "The reason for [Christian law-keeping] lies with the gift of the eschatological Spirit, who has rendered Torah observance obsolete, but who has at the same time made possible the 'fulfillment of the righteous requirement of Torah.'"[12]

Because of this gift of freedom from bondage to sin, believers have a new love for the law of God. Those who deny that Christians are in any way obligated to obey the moral law of God are out of step with the New Testament "because for Paul there is no such thing as 'salvation in Christ' that does not also include righteousness on the part of God's people."[13]

Life in the Spirit becomes a rich and full-orbed life of living in obedience to the law of God. The ethical dimensions of this life include: "(1) the purpose (or basis) of Christian ethics is the glory of God (1 Cor. 10:31); (2) the pattern for such ethics is Christ (1 Cor. 4:16–17; 11:1; Eph. 4:20); (3) the principle is love, precisely because love alone reflects God's character; (4) and the power is the Spirit. Hence the crucial role of the Spirit."[14]

The Christian life is therefore a life of "walking in the Spirit" (Gal. 5:13–6:10). About this expression Fee comments that "Paul adopted it as his most common metaphor for ethical conduct (17 occurrences in all). All other imperatives proceed from this one."

What does it mean to walk in the Spirit?

> For Paul "holiness," i.e., walking by means of the *Holy* Spirit, was two-dimensional. On the one hand it meant abstaining from certain sins—absolutely. . . . On the other hand, "holiness" also (especially) means the *Holy* Spirit living in believers, reproducing the life of Christ within/among them, especially in their communal relationships. To do otherwise is to "grieve the Holy Spirit of God" (Eph. 4:30).[15]

This does not imply a life of sinless perfection, but it does imply a life that persistently pursues righteousness. That is the second benefit—no bondage to sin. It is another element of the resurrected life given to us by the Spirit of Jesus.

Benefit #3: No Fear—Freedom from Alienation and Exile (Rom. 8:15–17: We Are Sons Not Slaves)

In Romans 8:15, Paul talks the language of sonship. "For you did not receive a spirit that makes you a slave again to fear, but you received the Spirit of sonship. And by him we cry, 'Abba, Father.'" Jesus lived his entire life in the sheer joy of this reality, and now we can as well. This means that we are "God's children" and heirs of all things. We have come home to the Father, who has received us into a sonship relationship. Through the Spirit he fills our lives with the fullness that comes from living in our Father's house and belonging to his family.

Sinclair Ferguson comments on this third benefit of homecoming. "The Spirit whom believers have received is not a spirit of bondage, but the, 'Spirit of sonship.' The evidence of this is that in the Spirit 'we cry "Abba, Father,"' the implication being that the Christian participates in a communion with God first experienced by Jesus himself, hence the echo of Jesus' own prayer-language in the prayer life of the church."[16] What this means in more everyday terms is that "although he may be broken and bruised, tossed about by fears and doubts, the child of God nevertheless in his need cries out, 'Father!' as instinctively as a child who has fallen and been hurt calls out in similar language, 'Daddy, help me.'"[17]

Our cry to our Father in the hour of need is not a cry from the wilderness of exile nor a cry from a frightened child to an angry and distant father. Our cry is heard by a loving Father, ever at hand, through the Spirit of Jesus, who comforts and supplies what is needed. There is no need to fear life as we did in our days of exile. We have been raised with Christ from the inner deadness of unbelief into the fearless freedom of the sons of God.

Benefit #4: No Despair—Freedom from Decay and Death (Rom. 8:18–25: A Future Resurrection Awaits)

New life in the Spirit piles treasure upon treasure for the child who has returned home. Besides the sandals, ring, and beautiful robe, we are also given the gift of future transformation. Romans 8:22–23 describes this future benefit: "We know that the whole creation has been groaning as in the pains of childbirth right up to the present time. Not only so, but we ourselves, who have the firstfruits of the Spirit, groan inwardly as we wait eagerly for our adoption as sons, the redemption of our bodies." This promise of future liberation from death and decay is not just an existential victory over anxiety. It is not just a promise of shedding duality and becoming one with the universe. The new age of life in the Spirit means that we will be physically raised from the dead just as Jesus was (8:11). It means that the bodies we shall be given will be like the glorified body of Jesus (1 Cor. 15:52–55). Death need hold no terror for us now. We, in our glorified bodies, will one day awake in a world transformed by the same Spirit who raised Jesus to life.

Though I will have more to say about this transformed world in the next chapter, let me mention here that Romans 8:23 is a standing reminder that the homecoming story we have entered through faith in Jesus means more than empty tombs and continuing personal existence. Paradise will be restored. The Spirit raises us from despair over death and decay by pointing out the glistening peaks of future glory.

Benefit #5: No Silence—Freedom from Broken Communication with God (Rom. 8:26–27: The Spirit Helps Us Pray)

But how do we manage the time between the "already" aspects of our resurrection and the "not yet" aspects described above? The Spirit has already thought about this problem for us: "In the same way, the Spirit helps us in our weakness. We do not know what we ought to pray for, but the Spirit himself intercedes for us with groans that words cannot express" (Rom. 8:26).

The Spirit keeps us from despair about the slow progress of change while we await the day of glory and resurrection. The Spirit enables us to pray as Jesus taught us to pray in the Sermon on the Mount. He takes our wandering requests and infuses them with God's kingdom agenda. He knits our personal concerns with that divine agenda and produces powerful prayer. From the daily death of worry, we are raised to the new life of kingdom prayer.

Benefit #6: No Mistakes—Freedom from Chance (Rom. 8:28: God Doesn't Make Mistakes with His Children)

But what if after we have prayed, things still don't seem to be going right? Another benefit of life in the Spirit is how God turns things into their opposite. "And we know that in all things God works for the good of those who love him, who have been called according to his purpose" (Rom. 8:28). As the following verses make clear, the path that leads to the full and final homecoming experience of glorification is not subject to chance and contingency. Romans 8:29–30 takes care of this fear: "For those God foreknew he also predestined to be conformed to the likeness of his Son, that he might be the firstborn among many brothers. And those he predestined, he also called; those he called, he also justified; those he justified, he also glorified."

John Piper comments on the force of these verses:

> What's the point of a chain of statements like this? The point is certainty and confidence and assurance and security. The fact is that God is the one who saves his people, really saves them. He does not just offer salvation, he saves them. From beginning to end he is the One who decisively and infallibly acts so that not one of his own is lost. The point is that the chain cannot be broken: all the foreknown are predestined; all the predestined are called; all the called are justified; and all the justified are glorified.[18]

One of the amazing things about these verses is that a future reality such as being "glorified" is in the past tense. This implies that because of God's decision to return to Zion, to his whole inhabited world to save a people for his great name, nothing will thwart his saving purpose. It is as good as done. None of his children will be lost. Each one will find his or her way home. That is yet another benefit of life in the new order of the Spirit. Because of the Jesus story and the power of the Spirit operating in that story, there will be no mistakes. All his children will make it all the way home.

Benefit #7: No Limits—Freedom from Want (Rom. 8:32: God Will Give Us Every Good Thing Because of Jesus)

But what about the resources we will need for this journey through life, this odyssey to the future? In our old Promethean stories, we could grab what we needed. Now what do we do? Romans 8:32 is one of the great promises of the Bible and addresses the resources question squarely: "He who did not spare his own Son, but gave him up for us all—how will he not also, along with him, graciously give us all things?"

I talked about this great promise in the previous chapter. God will give us everything we need to finish the journey and finish it well. The Spirit of sonship assures us of that. Our intimate and unbreakable relationship with the God who owns all things guarantees this future provision. If the Father has already given us the most costly of gifts, his Son, then there can be no question about either his ability or his willingness to give us everything else. The Spirit makes the story of Jesus a source of unlimited provision for those who live in that story and are committed to living it out as well.

Benefit #8: No Guilt—Freedom from Accusation (Rom. 8:33–37: Jesus Will Protect Us from the Accuser)

The above benefits of life in the Spirit seem to cover most of the bases. One more thing, however, is needed. We need to get our heads straight. We need to *believe* that these treasures are ours. What good is it to have a million dollars in the bank if you don't really believe it is there? We need protection from the accusations of the evil one that will otherwise convince us that we are miserable beggars with no claims to divine wealth and love.

What happens when the enemy attacks our conscience and tries to rob us of our sense of freedom from condemnation, the first benefit of the Spirit mentioned in Romans 8? Another benefit of the Spirit kicks in. He quiets our conscience by communicating to us the current intercessory work of Jesus, who defends us before the Father. The Spirit not only conveys to us all the riches of Jesus. He also guards those treasures for us by reminding us of Jesus' intercession.

"Who is he that condemns? Christ Jesus, who died—more than that, who was raised to life—is at the right hand of God and is also interceding for us" (Rom. 8:34). The resurrected Jesus continues to do what he did in his earlier phase of ministry—conquer our enemies. Just as his death and resurrection conquered Satan, death, and sin, so too his living intercession continues to win victories on our behalf. He who did not fail to win those earlier victories cannot fail to win these additional victories on our behalf. The Spirit applies this action of Jesus to us as he does all other actions. Consequently, our conscience is secure from the enemy's attacks. No false guilt can creep in and rob us of our joy. We are free from the accuser and his lies.

Benefit #9: No Separation—Freedom from Falling Away (Rom. 8:38–39: God's Love Will Keep Us Close)

The final benefit of life in the Spirit is described in Romans 8:38–39: "For I am convinced that neither death nor life, neither angels nor demons, neither the present nor the future, nor any powers, neither height nor depth, nor anything else in all creation, will be able to separate us from the love of God that is in Christ Jesus our Lord."

This conviction of the inexhaustible love of God is the climactic benefit of life in the Spirit. The resurrection power of the Spirit is such that it overcomes death, demons, and every barrier to the maximum enjoyment of the full love of God our Father through his Son. The Spirit of sonship delivers this maximum enjoyment of the Father's love in this final benefit—the assurance of God's unfailing love. Of the inner conviction of this assurance, the great Puritan theologian John Owen wrote with rapture:

> Of this joy there is no account to be given, but that the Spirit worketh it when and how he will; he secretly infuseth and distils it into the soul, prevailing against all fears and sorrows, filling it with gladness, exaltations; and sometimes with unspeakable raptures of mind.[19]

This is the highest level of faith, the "full assurance of faith," when the spiritual beauty of God and his love fills the souls and binds him to us. True faith, according to John Piper, is full of the sense of this spiritual beauty of the love of the Father for us in Christ: "Spiritual beauty is the beauty of God diffused in all his works and words. Embracing this, or delighting in it, or being satisfied with it, is the heart of saving faith."[20]

Through the power of the Spirit, sinners in exile can achieve a homecoming so deep that their sense of intimacy and connection with the Father excludes the possibility of separation by anything in time or eternity. This is the highest level of life in the Spirit and, like all the other benefits he bestows, is a result of the application of the resurrection of Jesus to the life of the believer.

The Spirit and the New Life of the World

At the end of the opening story, Jesus turns to his disciples and mentions an even wider implication of his resurrection.

"What I want you to do now is to pack your bags and get out of this tomb. Roll back your stones. Get out of here and tell everyone you meet from Jerusalem to the farthest corner of this good earth that I am alive and because of that the kingdom of God has been inaugurated. Tell them that the Zechariah 9 program will now be launched in all the nations and civilizations of the world. Membership in the New Israel is now open to all people. Tell them that the Father has returned to earth and that the road that leads back home is open to prodigals and Pharisees alike. Know that all power is given to me in heaven and on earth. Know that I now make that power available to you in order to accomplish this global mission. The same Spirit of homecoming that shaped my story and raised me to life will now be at work in you and in the world to do the same. As the Father sent me so I am sending you."

The wider mission of his disciples had a large place in the teaching of Jesus. In Matthew 24:14, Christ told his disciples that "this gospel of the kingdom will be preached in the whole world as a testimony to all nations, and then the end will come." After his resurrection he reiterated this commission in Matthew 28:19: "Therefore go and make disciples of all nations." The Pentecost experience in Acts 2 was the outpouring of the Spirit of mission that would make possible the fulfillment of the Matthew commands. The Spirit of Jesus seeks to raise not only individuals but also the nations from the grip of death.

I'd like to make four observations about the Spirit and missions. These observations will hopefully answer the question about the shape that the Spirit's resurrection power takes as it seeks to roll away the stones that are holding back the nations from experiencing the full freedom of sons of God.

First, the new life that the Spirit wants to bring to the nations is not just spiritual. Just as the resurrection of Jesus by the Spirit was bodily, so also is the ministry of the Spirit among the nations. We are to take the homecoming story to the nations. God is moving through our world to raise our civilizations from the dead. This raising means the renewal of all things in culture. Personal salvation must be expected but so should public transformation. The work of the Spirit should produce a renaissance on many levels. He is after all the Spirit of new life. The biblical basis for this broader view of missions stems partly from taking seriously the need to see the Bible's two great commissions as interconnected. Genesis 1:28 is the great commission of creation ("Be fruitful and . . . rule"), and Matthew 28:18–19 is the great commission of re-creation ("Make disciples"). Both are God's will, and both are needed by a world dead in trespasses and sins. Individuals lie in spiritual death. Cultures also feel the dust of death settling softly on their theaters, parliaments, and academies. The mission of God (the transformation of all things in Matt. 19:28) must be the wider context for the mission of the church.

The great Dutch missiologist of an earlier generation, J. H. Bavinck, wrote with wisdom on the need to end the dualism so characteristic of Western missions: "It is therefore necessary above all else that our entire life be presented as a fundamental unity in which faith in God, love to God and obedience to God controls our every activity."[21] Rediscovering the Jesus story as a comprehensive narrative that unlocks the meaning of the past, present, and future, for individuals as well as civilizations, is part of achieving that "fundamental unity." The missionary or the church that sends him or her may be so captured by an exile mentality that there is no hope of a unity of life built around the homecoming story. We can achieve this fundamental unity "only if the missionary himself has conquered the dualism of our culture" by experiencing "all of life in a fellowship with God in Jesus Christ." Until this unitive vision is achieved, "the great problem of the mission field is and remains the missionary and the sending congregation."[22]

Christianity's goal in world history, therefore, is not just conversion and church planting as ends in themselves, central though these may be. Such a view of missions betrays the lingering frost of a killing dualism in the vision of life under God. The larger goal of missions is the redirecting of creation and culture for God's glory.

Second, the aim of kingdom missions is taking possession of cultures for Christ. When the Spirit begins to release his resurrection power among the nations, we should expect to see all the results that we see in the Gospels. What Jesus began to preach and to do on earth he continues to do in his resurrected and ascended state. The blind will see, the deaf will hear, the dead will rise, the unbelieving will be given faith and salvation. As the power of the risen Christ increases in a culture, the aim of missions draws closer—to glorify God by redirecting all civilizations toward his worship, service, and sonship. Bavinck elaborates on this task of redirection, a task that he calls the *possessio* ("taking possession"):

> Within the framework of the non-Christian life, customs and practices serve idolatrous tendencies and drive a person away from God. The Christian takes them in hand and turns them in an entirely different direction; they acquire an entirely different content. Even though in external form there is much that resembles past practices, in reality everything has become new, the old has in essence passed away and the new has come. Christ takes the life of a people in his hands, he renews and reestablishes the distorted and the deteriorated; he fills each thing, each word, and each practice with a new meaning and gives it a new direction. Such is neither "adaptation," nor accommodation; it is in essence the legitimate taking possession of something by him to whom all power is given in heaven and earth.[23]

This inward redirection of a culture is done only by the power of the Spirit. This is not a call for the cultural domination of the nations by a Constantinian Church. This is a call to realize that the power that raised Jesus from the dead is at work among the nations, filling "each thing, each word, and each practice with a new meaning." The aim of missions is to glorify God by partnering with the Spirit and to watch as the old passes away and the new comes.

Third, the delay of the consummation of the kingdom of God can be explained by the mission of God. Between Good Friday and Easter Sunday was Silent Saturday. That Saturday of passion weekend was a time of delay and of waiting. It is a reminder that we as followers of Jesus and participants in the Jesus story live between the times.

We live between the kingdom come but not consummated, between the "already here" and the "not yet arrived." We are Saturday people in many ways, waiting for the fireworks to go off and for the silence of the tombs to be broken.

But there is a purpose for the Silent Saturdays of the Christian life. That purpose is missions. The global mission of the church is in fact the key explanation for the delay in the coming of the kingdom in glory. The reason why Jesus only inaugurated the kingdom in the first century and did not bring it into full realization was so that the blessings of homecoming could be extended to the nations. Bavinck explores this mystery by recounting Old Testament expectations for the Messiah and his work:

> Old Testament prophecy regards Messianic salvation as including both the spiritual renewing and glorification of Israel, and also the spontaneous coming of the heathen and the radical transformation of the world order. And this Messianic salvation has arrived in principle in the coming of Jesus Christ. . . . The new era has begun, the parousia is here, the kingdom of God is at hand. In the unfolding or disclosure, however, various other elements now come to the fore. The wonders Jesus performed were indeed mighty signs of the great salvation, but they did not immediately become the great Messianic miracle, the transformation of the world order, so that the wolf may lie down with the lamb. The spiritual renewal of Israel has indeed set in, but it has not yet broken through in power.[24]

Why the delay? Why the signs of the messianic miracle without the arrival of the full messianic transformation? Bavinck continues to explore the mystery of the delay:

> Salvation is indeed present in principle but its unfolding cannot at once come about in all its fulness. Missions thus developed from the great Messianic salvation foretold by the prophets, as the element which will mark the delay. The delay is necessary since the kingdom must now be given to another people. And when that has come about, when this gospel of the kingdom shall have been preached in the whole world, then shall the end come.[25]

The mission of God and of his church thus explains the delay of the kingdom's consummation. We are Saturday people. But we need not be idle and anxious as we wait for the full resurrection power of Easter to be revealed. We can work on Saturday. We can use this time of delay to tell, in word and deed, the great story of homecoming to the entire world.

Fourth, the major means to the renewal of all of life is the translating and unleashing of the Jesus story of homecoming into all civilizations. What we will find as we move through civilizations is the dominance of rival narratives. Prodigal master stories dominate some cultures. Pharisaic narratives dominate others. The story of homecoming that we will bring with us will interact with these dominant narratives in the new civilization in a way very similar to the ways Jesus' homecoming teaching and actions interacted with the Judaism of his day. We will face disinterested prodigals bored with their traditional culture and the old view of religion associated with that tradition. We will face fundamentalist Hindus, Muslims, Buddhists, animists, confucionists, and other religious variants. Our task will be to translate the Jesus story into the civilizations of the world.[26] The power of that story is incalculable (Rom. 1:16).

Given that task and the resistance of cultural prodigals and elder brothers to our best efforts, how are we effectively to bring the story of homecoming into these cultures in exile? John 20:21 gives us the key: "As the Father has sent me, I am sending you."

When this verse is mined for missiological principles, the emphasis is usually on incarnation. Jesus entered our world and became human, became a servant, and became a sacrifice. We must express an incarnational mission that is characterized by those three levels of incarnation. While I have no desire to quibble with the valid insight contained in this understanding of John 20:21, I feel a major thrust of these words has been missed. If we take the Jesus story seriously, then the principles of Jesus' mission are found not primarily in the Christmas event but in the baptism event. It was at his baptism that Jesus began his mission to the world in a formal sense and embraced two powers that enabled him to be successful in his work. As we have seen and emphasized repeatedly, the two gifts given to Jesus at his baptism were (1) a new sense of his sonship and the homecoming heart of the Father as well as (2) the full empowerment of the Spirit for all of his work. These two gifts of his homecoming encounter at Jordan need to be seen as the key to our own success in missions. Only as I allow the Spirit to raise my exiled soul from its death to the various levels of homecoming life described in Romans 8 will I be able to communicate the Jesus story in a powerful and life-changing way. Only as I operate as a satisfied son of God in Christ will I have the staying power and the divine connection to both persevere and triumph over the many obstacles produced by the younger brothers and elder brothers of the world's cultures.

What is needed then for the global mission of the church to go forward in the twenty-first century is a new spirituality of missions built around the kingdom spirituality of the Jesus story. Only this spirituality of sonship and Spirit empowerment is sufficient to overcome the challenges before us.

Only as we bring this strong homecoming mentality to the mission task before us will we be able to overcome the dualism described above. We will avoid the one-dimensional exile mentality that reduces people to souls to save. We will also avoid the one-dimensional exile mentality that reduces people to sociological units only valuable on social, economic, or political levels. In other words, a one-dimensional liberation theology is as destructive to true missions as is a one-dimensional pietism. Missions, in an attempt to be holistic, can neglect the need to win individuals through persuasive means to personal loyalty to the Jesus of the homecoming story. For all of our talk of the scope of the *missio Dei,* we must not forget the heart of it: finding the sons who were dead and are becoming alive again (Luke 15:32). This is the great homecoming flowing from the Jesus story that the Spirit seeks to spread globally. Once the Spirit that raised Jesus finishes with the nations, the power to love will have been restored around the world.

Experiencing the Resurrection: Lessons on Living in the Spirit

The opening story begins with a frightened group in a locked room and ends with a bold mission to the nations. What happened? The experience of the resurrected Jesus unleashed a new attitude and direction. We have focused on this new power that was unleashed by Jesus in his resurrection and in the Pentecost experience. By experiencing the resurrected Jesus, the disciples were empowered to unlock their doors and to move back into their world as agents of light and life.

Not all spiritual writers today believe that the Spirit of the resurrected Jesus is what we need. As we saw at the beginning of the chapter, Deepak Chopra argues that we ourselves are the "holy spirit," expressions of the one infinite spirit from whom all things flow. "The mask of matter," says Chopra, "disguises our true nature, which is pure awareness, pure creativity, pure spirit. . . . When you perceive yourself as spirit, you will not simply feel love—you will be love."[27]

I have suggested a different path to love from the one of Chopra. It is the path hinted at by Walker Percy's communication from outer space: "Do you know who you are? Do you know what you are doing? Do you love? Do you know how to love? Are you loved? Do you hate? Come back. Repeat. Come back. Come back. Come back."[28]

To what must we "come back" in order to answer these questions? We must come back to the story of Jesus. Experiencing the power that raised him from the dead is the path to love. This is the insight found in homecoming truth 7: *The love that is stronger than death is the greatest power in the world.* This power to love is found in and through the Holy Spirit of God, the Spirit of homecoming, who fills us with this death-defeating power and equips us to move out into our personal worlds in love and service. How then can we deepen our experience of the Spirit and enjoy more his resurrection power in our lives? Let me mention two very personal ways we can experience the resurrection of Jesus in our lives.

1. *Depend on the Spirit daily.* As Romans 8 reminded us, the power of the Spirit is sufficient to meet all our needs including the need to grow in grace and godliness. As we depend on the Spirit of God (or "keep in step with the Spirit" in the language of Gal. 5:25), two things will happen. First, we will find ourselves becoming dead to sin. This is the daily killing of sin within us. Indwelling sin remains a problem for believers because we are not yet glorified and perfected. But by depending on the power of the Spirit, we can experience victory in the lifelong fight against sin. As John Calvin wrote, it is only "through continual and sometimes even slow advances [that] God wipes out in his elect the corruptions of the flesh, cleanses them of guilt, consecrates them to himself as temples renewing all their minds to true purity."[29] Though this warfare against the flesh may end only at death, it is nonetheless the good fight of faith to be enjoined daily.

The second purifying work of the Spirit on which we must depend involves becoming alive to godliness. This work of the Spirit is based on the believers' union with the resurrection of Christ. The infusion of new life within us "comes to pass when the Spirit of God so imbues our souls, steeped in his holiness, with both new thoughts and feelings, that they can be rightly considered new."[30]

Wilhelm Niesel summarizes this principle of dependence on the Spirit in dying to sin and becoming alive to godliness and righteousness:

Christ is the crucified and Risen One not in and for Himself. He does not remain aloof from us but He who once-for-all has experienced death and resurrection meets us today and really communicates to us those benefits which for our sakes He has obtained. Our old man is seized upon and crucified by the power of the death of Jesus Christ. We are awakened into a new life by the power of His resurrection. This happens through the Spirit of Christ which binds us to Him and evokes in us faith and obedience.[31]

Since the Spirit is the power that brings life out of death, I must trust him, through prayer and the Word of God, to raise me, with Jesus, out of my sin and into the new life of the Jesus story.

2. *Seek the regeneration of the Spirit.* Experiencing the resurrection of Jesus is impossible without the experience of new birth by the Spirit. In John 3, Jesus told Nicodemus that he needed to be "born again." For all the baggage the term has acquired in recent decades, the importance of this directive remains undiminished. Only the Spirit can produce that faith in the Jesus story that truly saves. John Calvin called the new birth experience the "principal work of the Holy Spirit." Only the Spirit can produce the faith that is "a firm and certain knowledge of God's benevolence toward us, founded upon the truth of the freely given promise in Christ, both revealed to our minds and sealed upon our hearts by the Holy Spirit."[32]

When I first entered the Jesus story as a boy, it meant more than simply private confession of sin. For me, to repent and follow Jesus was more than walking down the aisle in a revival meeting. It meant a total realignment of values and dreams and action. It meant embracing a new story with Jesus at the center and abandoning the exile stories that placed the self or the nation at the center. It meant experiencing the Spirit's work of regeneration.

One of the greatest jazz musicians in history was the saxophonist John Coltrane. "Trane," as he was known, played with such jazz greats as Dizzy Gillespie and Miles Davis. Despite his genius as a musician, Coltrane was running on empty as a human being. In 1957, he nearly died in San Francisco from a drug overdose. He hit bottom. But in his hour of need, he met the Jesus of the biblical story and came to profound personal faith in Christ. Christ rebuilt his life and restored his music. Coltrane went on to record some of his greatest music in the years that remained but none greater than his famous jazz composition "A Love Supreme"—a thirty-two-minute jazz composition that became his hymn of praise to his Savior for showing him the truth about God, humanity, sin, and salvation. What did Coltrane need that his money, fame, talent, and success couldn't give him? He needed Jesus. He encountered the Jesus story and it shattered the rival stories that had been controlling his life. Encountering the historical Jesus restored Coltrane's humanity, which the sin and alienation of his exile from God had damaged. Experiencing the death and resurrection of Jesus through the power of the Spirit cleansed Coltrane of his own sin and produced a saving faith in him that changed his life. Coltrane rediscovered the power to love by being born again through the Spirit. We would expect the power to love to return after such an experience because, as the resurrection of Jesus shows, love conquers death and is the greatest power in the world.

"IS IT WORTH IT?"

EXPERIENCING THE FUTURE OF JESUS

That man is the product of causes which had no prevision of the end they were achieving; that his origin, his growth, his hopes and fears, his loves and his beliefs, are but the outcome of accidental collocations of atoms; that no fire, no heroism, no intensity of thought and feeling, can preserve an individual life beyond the grave; that all the labor of the ages, all the devotion, all the inspiration, all the noonday brightness of human genius, are destined to extinction in the vast death of the solar system, and that the whole temple of man's achievement must inevitably be buried beneath the debris of a universe of ruins. . . . Only within the scaffolding of these truths, only on the firm foundation of unyielding despair, can the soul's habitation henceforth be safely built.

Bertrand Russell, "A Free Man's Worship"

Then the angel showed me the river of the water of life, as clear as crystal, flowing from the throne of God and of the Lamb down the middle of the great street of the city. On each side of the river stood the tree of life, bearing twelve crops of fruit, yielding its fruit every month. And the leaves of the tree are for the healing of the nations. No longer will there be any curse. The throne of God and of the Lamb will be in the city, and his servants will serve him. They will see his face, and his name will be on their foreheads. There will be no more night. They will not need the light of a lamp or the light of the sun, for the Lord God will give them light. And they will reign for ever and ever.

Revelation 22:1–5

Story: "Is It Worth It?"

Some time after the ascension of Jesus Christ and the miracle of Pentecost, King Herod arrested some who belonged to the church. He had James, the brother of John, put to death by the sword. When Herod saw that this action pleased the Jews, he seized Peter also. He threw Peter in prison and had him bound with chains between two soldiers. The waiting was tough, but Peter did get a few encouraging postcards from Christian friends.

The Girl sent him a postcard from Spain, where she was working with university students. As she wrote on the card, she enjoyed the task of "contending for the Jesus story against the challenge of Prometheanism and narcissism raging for control of these young minds."

The Theologian had moved to Alexandria, Egypt, to be near the Great Library. He was working on his multivolume history of the Jesus movement. The message on his card was short and sweet: "Can't believe how much there is to the story of homecoming. Five volumes in the planning stage. Could be more."

The Philosopher had gone to India. He was now a Jesus guru, wandering the countryside with his disciples much like Jesus had done in Palestine. In his postcard he wrote how "easily translatable the Jesus story is into the cultures of the East."

The African also dropped him a postcard. Her father had repented and embraced the Jesus story as the new master narrative of his life and the life of his people. There was a great response in her native village to her teaching about homecoming.

"I love the work of missions most of the time," she wrote, "but I have my down days also."

Peter kept rereading the last sentence of her message. "On those down days, as I wait impatiently for the return of the Master, I find myself asking, 'Is it worth it?'"

Peter wondered about these words. He was afraid to ask himself the question on the postcard. He was not sure what his answer might be.

The night before he was to stand trial, Peter fell into a deep sleep and had a dream.

In his dream he was still in jail, but Jesus was there. They were talking together.

"Is it worth it, Peter?" Jesus asked.

"Is what worth it, Master?" Peter replied, pretending not to understand the question.

"Is following me worth it? Tomorrow you stand trial and you may be sentenced to death for my name. Is it worth it?"

"It's not what I expected, Master," Peter said in his dream. He was shocked by his honesty.

"What did you expect?" Jesus asked.

It all came pouring out then. The dreams about the kingdom, the personal aspirations, the expected rewards. "A chicken in every pot, two cars in every garage, no more death and taxes—all these things would be true when the Messiah came. Angels would descend on Jacob's ladder, and the glories of heaven would come spilling out like fish from a full net. That's what I expected, Master."

"And instead of the chicken, the cars, and the descent of angels, you get Herod, a set of chains, and two snoring soldiers."

"Exactly," replied Peter.

Jesus paused for a moment and then put his hand on Peter's shoulder and spoke.

"I tell you the truth: No one who has left home or brothers or sisters or mother or father or children or fields for me and the gospel will fail to receive a hundred times as much in this present age (homes, brothers, sisters, mothers, children, and fields—and with them, persecutions) and in the age to come, eternal life."

Peter looked at Jesus, trying to process this astounding statement. He couldn't, so he changed the subject.

"What will happen at the end, Master?" he asked Jesus. "Who really wins? The ones like Herod or the ones like you?"

"I'll tell you who really wins," Jesus replied. "When the Son of Man comes in his glory, and all the angels with him, he will conquer the nations, bring an end to sin and death, and sit upon his throne in heavenly glory. All the nations will be gathered before him, and he will separate the people one from another as a shepherd separates the sheep from the goats. He will put the sheep on his right and the goats on his left.

"In that day of judgment I will rise from my throne and look at all of those gathered on my right. Many of them will be from the poor and wretched of the earth. There will be single moms, widows, the aged, the infirm, and many children. There will be men and women and young ones from every tribe and ethnic group on earth. There will be Wall Street brokers and Vietnamese boat people. The African will be there. So will the Girl, the Theologian, and the Philosopher. And you will be there too, Peter. James, who died for my name, will be there also.

"I will say to you all, 'Come, you who are blessed by my Father, take your inheritance, purchased with my own blood, for you have inherited the kingdom of God, the new world order, a world of justice and mercy, a world without sin and death and suffering, a world prepared for you since the time of creation.

"I will say to you, 'Come into the joys of my kingdom because when I was hungry, you gave me something to eat, when I was naked, you clothed me, when I was thirsty, you gave me something to drink, when I was a stranger, you invited me in, when I was sick, you looked after me, and when I was in prison, you visited me.'

"On that day of judgment you will say to me with one voice: 'But Lord, when did we do all of these things for you? We don't remember you as hungry, thirsty, naked, or in prison.'

"My reply on that great day will be this: 'Whatever you did for the least of these my brothers, you did for me.'

"Then I will lead you through the gates of the new Jerusalem. I will lead you to the river of life that flows from my throne down the middle of the great street of the city. And you, who have suffered for my name in this life, will walk among the trees of life that line the banks of the great river. The leaves of those trees have enough power to heal all the sufferings and injustices of all the nations. In my eternal city there will be no curse of sin or pain. All tears will be wiped from your eyes.

"But the main attraction of the city will be the love between me and my people. I will be their light. I will be their joy. I will be their greatest treasure and pleasure. And the best part will be this: My reign over the whole world will never, never end. And you will reign with me forever and ever."

Peter, in his dream, was overcome by these words. Tears came. But then a puzzled look came across his face.

"But what about the Herods, Master? What about the Pilates and the Caiaphases and all those who despise your church, your gospel, and your name? What about them?"

Jesus answered, "Peter, on that day of judgment I will also turn to those on my left. There before me will be the proud of the earth: the wealthy who despised the poor, the rich who rejected the orphans, the learned who rejected my Word. The presidents of the nations and the captains of industry will be there, as will the CEOs of the world's multinational corporations and the gangster politicians who raped their citizens of their wealth and resources.

"On that day I will say to them, 'Depart from me, you who are cursed, into the eternal fire prepared for the devil and his angels. For I was hungry and you gave me nothing to eat. I was thirsty and you gave me nothing to drink. I was naked and you refused to clothe me. I was sick and in prison and you never came.'

"Then the unbelieving rich, the self-sufficient powerful, the mocking proud, and the skeptical learned will act indignantly. They will take offense at my words and protest among themselves. They will say, 'Lord, when did we see you hungry or thirsty or a stranger or needing clothes or sick or in prison and didn't help you?'

"My answer will be simple: 'Whatever you did not do for one of the least of these, you did not do for me.' And then, while you and my followers are walking into the paradise of the new Jerusalem, the proud and the unbelieving will go away to eternal punishment, but the righteous to eternal life."

Peter seemed satisfied by these words of Jesus. Then he looked at his chains, at the snoring soldiers, and at the bleak prison walls. He lifted his eyes to the Master and asked, "How long, Lord? How long until the end will come?"

"I'll tell you the sign of my coming in glory. The gospel of the kingdom will be preached in the whole world as a testimony to the nations, and then the end will come."

Then Jesus asked Peter a final time, "Is it worth it, Peter?"

"Yes, it's worth it, Master."

Suddenly, as Peter uttered those words, he awoke from his dream. His face was stinging. Someone had slapped him on the cheek. Peter woke up with a stinging cheek into the world of Herod, snoring soldiers, and chains anchored to prison walls. In that real world, full of the symbols of Herod's power and hate, Peter heard the real words, "Quick, get up! Put on your clothes and sandals. Your work is not yet done." And Peter, glancing at the postcard from the African, obeyed the angel of the Lord and walked out into the world a free man. (Based on Acts 12; Matthew 25:31–46.)

Hunting for Hope

Peter was in bad shape. Even after the years with Jesus, the teachings about the kingdom, the conviction that Jesus was the Messiah, the witness to the resurrection, and the empowering by the Spirit, he could still get discouraged. Many mature Christians today can identify with Peter. When hard times come, they are tempted to ask with Peter, "Is it worth it?"

What caused the discouragement in Peter's life? For Peter, it was a momentary eclipse of his future hope. The vision in the dream renewed his sense of the future and restored his resolve and joy. His brush with hopelessness was real, however, and something that modern disciples, like ancient ones, sometimes wrestle with.

The issue of hopelessness touches many of the life issues we have looked at in previous chapters. If life has no ultimate hope, then no wonder we wrestle with a chronic sense of dullness, emptiness, loneliness, homelessness, powerlessness, and meaninglessness. In many ways the force of our stories comes from the vision of the future. We must explore, then, how one can find hope and vision in a world that is uncertain about the future.

This sense of hopelessness is not just a personal issue. Our modern master narratives have let us down in this area. When we turn our backs on the biblical narrative, a very different story of reality emerges. The philosopher and atheist Bertrand Russell was painfully honest about the only story that he found believable on the basis of his atheism:

> That man is the product of causes which had no prevision of the end they were achieving; that his origin, his growth, his hopes and fears, his loves and his beliefs, are but the outcome of accidental collocations of atoms; that no fire, no heroism, no intensity of thought and feeling, can preserve an individual life beyond the grave; that all the labor of the ages, all the devotion, all the inspiration, all the noonday brightness of human genius, are destined to extinction in the vast death of the solar system, and that the whole temple of man's achievement must inevitably be buried beneath the debris of a universe in ruins. . . . Only within the scaffolding of these truths, only on the firm foundation of unyielding despair, can the soul's habitation henceforth be safely built.[1]

By beginning with some non-Christian versions of the story of reality, human beings are led to this bleak and tragic tale of ruined dreams and endless despair.

Writers such as Deepak Chopra have little more to offer seekers searching for hope. What is Chopra's vision of the future? Death and dark night fill the pages of *How to Know God*. Consider the following sample. In "Hinduism the forces of light and darkness will battle eternally, the balance of power shifting in cycles that last thousands of years." This struggle is never ending because "the demons . . . never give up. They can't, in fact, since they are built into the structure of nature, where death and decay are inevitable." What about heaven? Chopra quotes a Vedic master with approval: "If you got your fantasy of living forever, you would be condemning yourself to eternal senility." Is there any hope for material reality? Not really says Chopra since "the body breaks down over time, and even the galaxies are heading toward 'heat death' when the stars burn out their supply of energy."[2] The mechanism for renewal in the universe is death. Our one hope is to break out of the endless battle of death and life through an enlightenment that allows us to escape to the void that is God.

The story of Jesus rejects the views of a Russell or a Chopra. It further rejects the implication that God is either too helpless or too angry to do anything about the coming disaster. In dramatic contrast to these scenarios of despair, the Jesus story presents homecoming truth 8: *We overcome hopelessness with a love that will never end and will one day fill the world.*

Christian spirituality differs with the modern world on this issue as on many others. Hope is our stock and trade. "We are people of the future," Tertullian once wrote. I can't think of a better description of the Christian church or Christian spirituality. Jesus was future oriented. He taught his disciples to look beyond the cross and the empty tomb to a bright new day of glory and gladness—his second coming.

We want to look at the future of Jesus Christ—his visible and glorious second appearing. We will examine six affirmations about the second coming of Jesus drawn from Christ's speech about the sheep and goats in Matthew 25. This famous declaration about the future is not a parable but a prophecy. By listening carefully to these words about the future, we will hopefully discover for ourselves what Peter eventually discovered. When we look ahead to the future grace and glory that Christ will display at his appearing, then we can say with certainty in the midst of life's little and big disappointments, "Yes, it's worth it, Master."

Affirmation #1: The King Will Return (the Fact of His Coming)

As the story opened, Peter, while in prison, heard from some of his old friends. Each of the four main characters sent him a postcard with an update on their work. The postcard from the African touched Peter in a special way, possibly because she put into words some of his own unspoken feelings: "I love the work of missions most of the time," she wrote, "but I have my down days also. On those down days, as I wait impatiently for the return of the Master, I find myself asking, 'Is it worth it?'"

The phrase that deserves a closer look is "as I wait impatiently for the return of the Master." One reason why the story of Jesus fails to grip and transform his disciples more deeply is the doubt born of apparent delay.

Jesus speaks to this issue of doubt about his future in Matthew 25:31–46, which contains the parable about the sheep and the goats, featured in the opening story. Most of the important points concerning the future of his story are addressed in this parable, including the issue of the certainty of his return.

Consider verses 31–32: "When the Son of Man comes in his glory, and all the angels with him, he will sit on his throne in heavenly glory. All the nations will be gathered before him, and he will separate the people one from another as a shepherd separates the sheep from the goats." Why is Jesus so certain about this future event?

First, Jesus believes in the power of the Word of God. The certainty with which Jesus declares the future reality of his glorious rule and reign on earth comes not because Jesus is psychic but because he believes in Scripture. His words reflect the prophecy of Zechariah 14, which describes God's renewed rule over the earth and the dividing of the world's plunder. "A day of the LORD is coming when your plunder will be divided among you" (v. 1) writes the prophet. How will it be divided? "I will gather all the nations to Jerusalem" (v. 2). There will be a great conflict, and the Lord will punish those who have attacked Jerusalem and reward those who defended her.

As a faithful Jew, Jesus believed that this word of God, as all words of God, would be literally fulfilled. As a radical Jew, Jesus believed that Zechariah was talking about him. As he utters these words about his future, three days before his death on Skull Hill, he believes that this event is as certain as his death and resurrection. He believes it is certain because the Word of God creates what it commands and is the prime shaper of history.

Second, Jesus is certain of his future appearing because he isn't really going anywhere. The apostles follow their Master in speaking with bold conviction about the certainty of the future glorious return of Jesus. They refer to the coming of Jesus by using three key words.

Each of the key words gives us a strong hint as to why both Jesus and the early church were so certain about the future coming of Jesus.

The key terms for the future coming of Jesus are *parousia* ("coming," "arrival," "presence"), *apokalypsis* ("revelation"), and *epiphaneia* ("appearing" or "manifestation"). These three terms dominate the New Testament discussion about the second coming of Christ. What seems strange is that none of these most commonly used terms really means "second coming" or "return." They all more or less refer to the unveiling of something already there but not necessarily visible. The image that comes to mind is the unveiling of a painting at a museum. The painting is there on the wall. Everyone can see its size and shape. But a cloth covers the painting, blocking its full "appearance." The "unveiling" (or *parousia,* or *apokalypsis,* or *epiphaneia*) of the work of art does not involve bringing the painting in from outside but merely removing the covering. This is apparently the concept the New Testament writers were trying to convey.

Why would Jesus himself and his disciples use these terms to refer to Jesus' return? I believe the answer is that Jesus, even in his ascended glory, is never that far away. Jesus, through his Spirit, is still "with" his disciples. The veil of time and space separate us from the next dimension, where Jesus reigns in glory, but that dimension is right next to our own. His farewell speech to his disciples in John 14–16 may sound like it is from someone who is going on a long trip, but it is also possible to interpret the words of Jesus as referring to his death. After the resurrection, he will "be with them always, even unto the end of the world."

Jesus was regarded as temporally near because he was spatially near. Adrio König expands on this idea:

> Since Jesus' ascension in no way implies that he has gone far away but rather that he will forever be very close (spatially) to his disciples, they expect his return in the near future. They reason along precisely the same lines as people did in the Old Testament [where God's future coming was anticipated by many inbreakings of his glory and presence]. The nearness of the second advent is thus directly related to Christ's presence in the interim period.[3]

In other words, the presence and closeness of Jesus was so real for Paul and the disciples that the word *return* was strangely inappropriate. Jesus was still in the theater. The performance was still going on. Though he was not visible on stage, he was there behind the curtain, waiting for his next "appearance" in act 3.

With the theater analogy we are once again in the realm of story. Ben Witherington III explains how the Jesus story gave the disciples such a strong sense of the Lord's nearness in time and space:

> Behind all of Paul's theologizing stands the christological narrative of faith about one Jesus who came, died, rose and would return. For Paul the performance of this narrative on the stage of history is still [in act 2]. Paul cannot conclude the drama prematurely, for the main actor must first return to the stage for a final act.[4]

Thus, the Jesus story, as a master narrative, opened the apostles' eyes to the new reality of the ascended and coming King, who was nonetheless only an arm's length away in the dimension behind space and time. This helps explain why there was constant talk in the early church about his imminent return. The fellowship and contact with the living Jesus was so real every day that Jesus' followers were confident that at any moment he could take that one last giant step from behind the curtain and stride into their world. Christ does not become Lord at his parousia, but his lordship will then be shown. What is real and hidden will one day be real and revealed. The curtains of heaven will be drawn back and the greatness of our Savior will be on global display. Jesus was certain of his coming and so were his disciples. He was certain of his return because he had already come home to an earth being reunited to heaven. When God comes home to us in Jesus, he never goes away.

Affirmation #2: The King Will Return in Glory (the Nature of His Coming)

In Peter's dream, he sees the Lord coming in glory. In his dream, he asks about who will win in the end. Jesus replies in direct terms. "I'll tell you who really wins. When the Son of Man comes in his glory, and all the angels with him, he will conquer the nations, bring an end to sin and death, and sit upon his throne in heavenly glory."

This is almost a direct quotation from Matthew 25:31. I'd like to comment on what this passage and other New Testament passages say about the *nature* of his coming. What *kind* of coming will it be? In Matthew 25:31–46, three characteristics help describe what his coming will be like. Jesus' reappearance on the stage of history will be glorious, decisive, and sudden.

First, his coming will be glorious. In Matthew 25:31, Jesus uses the term *glory* twice in describing his future appearing. He speaks of angels coming with him. At his word of command, the nations will gather obediently before him (v. 32). What is clear from these phrases is that one day Jesus will let his full splendor be displayed. We may then speak of the coming of Jesus as being both visible and cosmic. This future coming is not just for the eyes of Israel. It is not just for the eyes of the church. It will be visible to the entire world.

Jesus is not skulking in heaven licking his wounds. He is enthroned. All power is already his in heaven and on earth. The nations are already his footstool. He controls the direction of history like a driver controls an automobile. What difference will the future coming make if Jesus already enjoys such powers? We will get to see it. Unlike his first coming, as a servant and sacrifice for sin, at his second coming he will display his glory as the Davidic King and the divine Son of God.

Second, his coming will be decisive. In Matthew 25, Jesus not only gathers the nations, but he also divides them, judges them, and then gives each their due. The clear implication is that his future appearance is the "end of history" as we know it. But caution needs to be exercised. Popular language makes us think of the end of history as a doomsday that will bring the world to a screeching halt. That is not what the Bible teaches. History will enter a new stage. Jesus' return is decisive in that it will usher in the end of current world history. Jesus will judge all people and end all enmity. He will then open up the next glorious era in history in a redeemed world. This seems to be the idea Paul expresses in 1 Corinthians 15:24: "Then the end will come, when he hands over the kingdom to God the Father after he has destroyed all dominion, authority and power."

Third, his coming will be sudden. Matthew 25 implies that Jesus' reappearance on the stage of history will be sudden, but we must go back one chapter in Matthew to get more light on the subject. Matthew 24:42–44 reads:

> Therefore keep watch, because you do not know on what day your Lord will come. But understand this: If the owner of the house had known at what time of night the thief was coming, he would have kept watch and would not have let his house be broken into. So you also must be ready, because the Son of Man will come at an hour when you do not expect him.

This speaks of a sudden and unexpected coming. Jesus eliminates the possibility of gradual progressive unveiling. He who is near will walk onto the world stage in a single bold step. Yet, we will talk about the signs of his coming below. If there are signs signaling Christ's reentry, how can it then be sudden and unexpected?

Suddenness is opposed to calculation. What is sudden cannot be carefully and accurately predicted. Jesus uses the imagery of lightning in Matthew 24:27: "For as lightning that comes from the east is visible even in the west, so will be the coming of the Son of Man." As Adrio König writes:

> Unlike the thunderclap, for which we may be prepared, the lightning flash comes without warning. That is how we must expect the coming of Jesus. . . . We must see in this a further indication that the signs of the times are not given to warn the faithful in advance about when he will come, but to call them to be ready at every moment for his sudden and unexpected coming.[5]

While there are signs of his coming, the moment of his coming is not known. There is a difference between "imminence" ("at any moment" without signs) and suddenness (though there will be signs, the exact moment or date cannot be predicted, and therefore, we must carefully watch for it). We may believe both. What we should not believe is that we can bottle this lightning and put a date on it. What will his appearing at the end of current history be like? It will be stunning, for it will be glorious, decisive, and sudden.

Affirmation #3: The King Will Return with a Purpose (the Reasons for His Coming)

One could read Matthew 25:31–46 and conclude that the purpose of Christ's future appearance is judgment. That reading would not be wrong. But more reflection on Matthew 25 opens up a wider picture of the main reason for his coming: to finish the story that he started. Just as Jesus inaugurated the story of the kingdom, of Yahweh's return to rule his people, during his first coming, so his second coming will complete that story. Jesus in his ascended state is continuing his story now, but there are at least four specific things in the homecoming narrative that he will complete "when he comes in his glory."

First, he will complete the work of redemption. Jesus has already saved his people from their sins and has already unleashed new life upon them. But additional dimensions of this salvation and life are mentioned in the New Testament (cf. Rom. 8:18–21; 1 Cor. 15:22–28;

Rev. 12:7–11). He will finish this great work of redemption. As Bruce Milne says, "It is important to maintain the essential links between the second advent and the first. It is not that the first advent was inadequate and needs the second to do the job properly. Rather the work of Christ in his second advent is to implement the conquest and victory won decisively in his first."[6] The homecoming to the Father's fullness will be made complete.

Second, he will resurrect the dead. John 5:28–29 announces this reason for his coming: "Do not be amazed at this, for a time is coming when all who are in their graves will hear his voice and come out— those who have done good will rise to life, and those who have done evil will rise to be condemned." Jesus will finish the story of history by maximizing life for those who entered his story and lived it out. He will also raise those outside his story so that they can experience the full future consequences of their Promethean and narcissistic narratives, narratives they freely chose in life.

Third, he will judge all people. This is the most prominent feature in Matthew 25:31–46, but it is also mentioned throughout the New Testament (Acts 17:31; 2 Tim. 4:1). The act of judgment in the future will be a reflection of the decisions we have made in life. To reject Christ, says John 3:18, means that one is "condemned already because he has not believed in the name of God's one and only Son."

Fourth, he will deliver his church. The purpose of the homecoming story is, of course, to bring God's children home. This does not mean simply "going to heaven" but living eternally with him in a reunited heaven and earth. Revelation 21:1–3 describes this final homecoming for the new people of God:

> Then I saw a new heaven and a new earth, for the first heaven and the first earth had passed away, and there was no longer any sea. I saw the Holy City, the new Jerusalem, coming down out of heaven from God, prepared as a bride beautifully dressed for her husband. And I heard a loud voice from the throne saying, "Now the dwelling of God is with men, and he will live with them. They will be his people, and God himself will be with them and be their God."

This is the climax of the new covenant that Jesus purchased with his blood. This is the ultimate fulfillment of the blessings promised in Zechariah 9. Why is Christ coming again? Certainly to accomplish the individual purposes mentioned above, but they all add up to a single grand design: to complete the story he started.

Affirmation #4: The King Will Return in Time (the Signs of His Coming)

Peter in prison asks the Lord about signs that might help him know when to expect the Master's return.

"He lifted his eyes to the Master and asked, 'How long, Lord? How long until the end will come?'"

Jesus' reply was straight to the point: "I'll tell you the sign of my coming in glory. The gospel of the kingdom will be preached in the whole world as a testimony to the nations, and then the end will come."

Is there but one sign of Jesus' return? The context of Matthew 25 would seem to disagree with the opening story. Consider some of the signs mentioned in Matthew 24:

- *Religious persecution.* "Then you will be handed over to be persecuted and put to death, and you will be hated by all nations because of me" (Matt. 24:9).
- *Wars.* "You will hear of wars and rumors of wars, but see to it that you are not alarmed. Such things must happen, but the end is still to come" (Matt. 24:6).
- *Natural disasters.* "Nation will rise against nation, and kingdom against kingdom. There will be famines and earthquakes in various places" (Matt. 24:7).

These signs are deceptive, however. Jesus is not telling us about *unique* signs that clearly mark his return. Rather, he is giving us *chronic* signs that should put us in a state of continuous readiness in every generation. The one sign, if not an exception to the above rule of readiness, is the sign of missions: The worldwide proclamation of the gospel mentioned in Matthew 24:14. "And this gospel of the kingdom will be preached in the whole world as a testimony to all nations, and then the end will come."

Paul speaks of this sign in Romans 11:25–26:

I do not want you to be ignorant of this mystery, brothers, so that you may not be conceited: Israel has experienced a hardening in part until the full number of the Gentiles has come in. And so all Israel will be saved, as it is written: "The deliverer will come from Zion; he will turn godlessness away from Jacob."

This is the sign of signs. The worldwide spread of the gospel is certainly a unique sign compared to all the others because it is the only sign Jesus mentions that speaks of the success and growth of his king-dom. All the other signs are negative and belong to the old word order: persecution, wars, false prophets, natural disasters. Rising like a man from a grave is this sign of the gospel spreading around the world. But like the other signs, it also keeps us in a state of readiness. We will see revivals in our respective times in history. We will see missions forge ahead after persecution and setback. Anyone who has even glanced at the outline of mission historian K. S. Latourrette's seven-volume *History of the Expansion of Christianity* will see this pattern of retreat and advance. The very rhythms of this expansion keep the church expectant, ready, and watching.

We conclude, then, that the signs are not intended to show us the "times and seasons." Christ condemned this in Acts 1:7: "It is not for you to know the times or dates the Father has set by his own authority." They are, however, intended to keep us in a state of continual readiness, enjoying the nearness of the Lord and expecting his breakthrough at any moment.

Affirmation #5: The King Will Return for Our Good (the Power of His Coming)

Halfway through the opening story and in the middle of Peter's dream, Jesus asks Peter a question: "Is following me worth it? Tomorrow you stand trial and you may be sentenced to death for my name. Is it worth it?"

"It's not what I expected, Master," Peter said in his dream. He was shocked by his honesty.

"What did you expect?" Jesus asked.

It all came pouring out then. The dreams about the kingdom, the personal aspirations, the expected rewards. "A chicken in every pot, two cars in every garage, no more death and taxes—all these things would be true when the Messiah came. Angels would descend on Jacob's ladder, and the glories of heaven would come spilling out like fish from a full net. That's what I expected, Master."

"And instead of the chicken, the cars, and the descent of angels, you get Herod, a set of chains, and two snoring soldiers."

"Exactly," replied Peter.

The African also suggested that she too was wondering if the return of Jesus would sufficiently reward her for all her suffering for his cause. Jesus did not rebuke such sentiments. Instead, he responded by laying out a picture of glorious reward: "I tell you the truth . . . no one who has left home or brothers or sisters or mother or father or children or fields for me and the gospel will fail to receive a hundred times as much in this present age (homes, brothers, sisters, mothers, children and fields—and with them, persecutions) and in the age to come, eternal life" (Mark 10:29–30).

In Jesus' sermon in Matthew 25, he refers to this blessing. "Come, you who are blessed by my Father; take your inheritance, the kingdom prepared for you since the creation of the world" (v. 34). Jesus will not be stingy in rewarding his sons. Just as the father in the parable of Luke 15 spared no expense to celebrate the return of the prodigal, so our Lord will celebrate the final reunion with us with unimaginable bounty. Let me mention a few treasures included in our kingdom inheritance.

First, we shall receive transformed bodies. Philippians 3:20–21 reminds us that "our citizenship is in heaven. And we eagerly await a Savior from there, the Lord Jesus Christ, who, by the power that enables him to bring everything under his control, will transform our lowly bodies so that they will be like his glorious body." The resurrection of Jesus, as we saw in the last chapter, is the model of the new body that we each shall inherit. It will not be subject to death and decay. It will provide "a greater capacity to enjoy God, to pursue the pleasure of his company and service without heaviness, sickness or fatigue."[7]

When Jesus, in Matthew 22:32, declares that the almighty Father was "not the God of the dead but of the living," he was underscoring the certainty of this future treasure. I agree with John Piper that "the point here is that if God is your God, you must be raised."[8]

Second, we shall receive transformed hearts. This promise is made in 1 John 3:2: "Dear friends, now we are children of God, and what we will be has not yet been made known. But we know that when he appears, we shall be like him, for we shall see him as he is." Now our hearts are full of corruption. Then they shall be pure and unalloyed. Now our hearts are full of the dark designs that lead to the works of the flesh. Then they shall be full of the fruit of the Spirit. Now our hearts are drawn like a magnet to the far country of indulgence or the frozen fields of arrogant service. Then they shall rejoice that they have found their true home in our Father's house.

In C. S. Lewis's *The Last Battle,* the land of Narnia is made new by the power of the lion king, Aslan. The unicorn approaches the boundaries of this new world transformed by Aslan and hesitates. Is it really what he wants? What about his love for the old Narnia? At last the unicorn speaks: "I have come home at last! This is my real country! I belong here. This is the land I have been looking for all my life, though I never knew it till now."[9] This is the language of a transformed heart.

Third, we shall be given transformed minds. "Now we see but a poor reflection as in a mirror," says Paul in 1 Corinthians 13:12, "then we shall see face to face. Now I know in part; then I shall know fully, even as I am fully known." The words of praise that I grope for, the clichés that I fall back on to capture without success the mountain range of his excellencies—all these will be replaced by a renewed and transformed mind. As Jonathan Edwards says, "There shall be no want . . . of words wherewith to praise the object of their affection. Nothing shall hinder them from communing with God, and praising and serving him just as their love inclines them to do."[10]

Fourth, we shall enjoy transformed relationships. Commenting on 1 Corinthians 13:13 ("And now these three remain: faith, hope and love. But the greatest of these is love"), Edwards describes the relationship with God that makes up this future "world of love."

> In heaven there shall be no remaining enmity, or distaste, or coldness, or deadness of heart towards God. . . . As the saints will love God with an inconceivable ardency of heart and to the utmost of their capacity, so they will know that he has loved them from all eternity, and still loves them, and will continue to love them forever.

What about our relationships with one another?

> Heavenly lovers will have no doubt of the love of each other. They shall have no fear that the declarations and professions of love are hypocritical; but shall be perfectly satisfied of the sincerity and strength of each other's affection, as much as if there were a window in every breast, so that everything in the heart could be seen. . . . Everyone will be just what he seems to be, and will really have all the love that he seems to have.[11]

We will not wonder what others *really* think of us on that day because there will be perfect transparency of heart and words. We will not grow weary of community because there will be abundant energy to embrace any number of relationships. We will not fear intimacy because there will be no duplicity or selfishness to hide. Love pure and unconstrained will flow between one another. So shall it be on that day when the Son comes in glory.

Fifth, we shall live forever in a transformed world. Jesus' vision of the future is usually based on words from the past. When he imagines the new world that he will enjoy with his transformed people, he draws the images from places in the prophets such as Isaiah 11:6–9:

> The wolf will live with the lamb,
>   the leopard will lie down with the goat,
> the calf and the lion and the yearling together;
>   and a little child will lead them.
> The cow will feed with the bear,
>   their young will lie down together,
>   and the lion will eat straw like the ox.
> The infant will play near the hole of the cobra,
>   and the young child put his hand into the viper's nest.
> They will neither harm nor destroy
>   on all my holy mountain,
> for the earth will be full of the knowledge of the LORD
>   as the waters cover the sea.

These words describe a world transformed. How do they square with the idea of the destruction of the heavens and the earth after the return of Jesus? Romans 8:20–21 answers this question. In Romans 8:20, Paul talks about the current "frustration" that creation suffers under. But according to verse 21, the frustration is temporary. There is a great hope whispered through creation that it "will be liberated from its bondage to decay" (v. 21). John Piper comments on this text:

> The creation is not destined for annihilation. It is destined for liberation. It will be set free from the "slavery to corruption"—the futility that God subjected it to *in hope.* This is the clearest statement that the earth and the heavens will not "pass away" or be "destroyed" *in the sense of going out of existence.* Paul says plainly, *they will be set free from corruption.* The futility will be destroyed. The bondage to corruption will be consumed in the purifying, liberating fire of God's judgment. But the earth will remain. And there will be no more corruption. No more futility. No more sin or pain or death or crying.[12]

Dallas Willard supports this conclusion. When the Son returns, "the physical universe, vast and dark from the merely human point of view, of dreadful dimensions and terrifying powers is then recognized as God's place."[13] Will we be annihilated? No, says Willard:

Our experience will not be fundamentally different in character from what it is now, though it will change in significant details. *The life we now have as the person we now are will continue and continue in the universe in which we now exist.* Our experience will be much clearer, richer, and deeper, of course, because it will be unrestrained by the limitations now imposed upon us by our dependence on our body. It will, instead, be rooted in the broader and more fundamental reality of God's kingdom and will accordingly have far greater scope and power.[14]

As if all of these treasures of future transformation were not enough, one more promise must be mentioned. Mark 10:29 reminds us that the Father takes the seasoning of this glorious future and sprinkles these riches on our current experience in ways that give joy to the ordinary. This is our future, a future that enriches our present. We do not know what this new heaven and new earth will really be like, but we know that the beauty awaiting us there will be beyond that which we have found in this life.

Affirmation #6: The King Will Return for the Compassionate (the Test of Practical Love)

I can imagine someone raising an old objection at this point. The objection goes like this. To deal with hopelessness now by imagining a perfect hope in the future doesn't help a person immediately. This is one of the longest-standing criticisms of Christ's second coming. Sure, he's going to come and set everything right, but that is too far in the future. What about now?

Our opening story suggests an answer to this objection. By experiencing the future of Jesus, we can live compassionate lives now. The actions of future-oriented believers can help alleviate the corruption and pain of modern life. The future shapes Christians. Christians reshape the present.

This is what Matthew 25 says. Jesus teaches as much in verse 40: "The King will reply, 'I tell you the truth, whatever you did for one of the least of these brothers of mine, you did for me.'" To live in and live out the Jesus story means to live a life of loving action. This is the command Jesus gave in John 13:34: "Love one another." This is the heart of Christian ethics according to Paul in Galatians 5:14: "The entire law is summed up in a single command: 'Love your neighbor as yourself.'" This is the great work of the Holy Spirit according to Romans 5:5: "And hope does not disappoint us, because God has poured out his love into our hearts by the Holy Spirit, whom he has given us." And from the word of command and the empowerment of the Holy Spirit comes a life that is filled with loving action. This life is described in Ephesians 5:1–2: "Be imitators of God, therefore, as dearly loved children and live a life of love, just as Christ loved us and gave himself up for us as a fragrant offering and sacrifice to God." Love produces sacrificial action of compassion for others.

By entering the Jesus story and following its movement into the future, we are changed. Love for others begins to shape our lives. The power of the future liberates us from the "grab and guard" mentality that produces so much hate and so much strife in our world today. This vision of the future of Jesus deepens the life-giving, love-producing attitudes of sonship and glad surrender that we have discussed previously.

Jonathan Edwards in his classic on true spirituality, *The Religious Affections,* speaks of this practical love as the most reliable sign of authentic godliness. In the age of Ben Franklin, when the maxim seemed to be "the great business of America is business," Edwards begged to differ. The great business of America, at least of American Christians, should be compassionate action. After describing eleven other reliable signs of a true work of the Spirit of God, Edwards comes to number twelve: "Gracious and holy affections have their exercise and fruit in Christian practice." Here is his description of the Christian committed to compassion.

> This implies three things: (1) That his behaviour or practice in the world, be universally conformed to, and directed by, Christian rules. (2) That he makes a business of such a holy practice above all things; that it be a business which he is chiefly engaged in, and devoted to, and pursues with highest earnestness and diligence; so that he may be said to make this practice of religion eminently his work and business. And, (3) That he persists in it to the end of life; so that it may be said, not only to be his business at certain seasons, the business of Sabbath days, or certain extraordinary times, or the business of a month, or a year, or of seven years, or his business under certain circumstances; but the business of his life; it being that business which he perseveres in through all changes, and under all trials as long as he lives.[15]

When the sweep of the homecoming story is grasped from humble beginning to bright end, it will produce the compassionate action that Jesus will commend and reward upon his glorious reappearance on the stage of history.

Experiencing the Future of Jesus: Preparing for His Coming

How do we address the issue of hopelessness in our world? The future of Jesus has something to say. What is the future of Jesus? Will his story go the way of the scientists with burnt-out stars or the way of Chopra with his cosmic cycles of spiritual struggle lasting for thousands of years? The opening story presents a third scenario.

"Then I will lead you through the gates of the new Jerusalem. I will lead you to the river of life that flows from my throne down the middle of the great street of the city. And you, who have suffered for my name in this life, will walk among the trees of life that line the banks of the great river. The leaves of those trees have enough power to heal all the sufferings and injustices of all the nations. In my eternal city there will be no curse of sin or pain. All tears will be wiped from your eyes.

"But the main attraction of the city will be the love between me and my people. I will be their light. I will be their joy. I will be their greatest treasure and pleasure. And the best part will be this: My reign over the whole world will never, never end. And you will reign with me forever and ever."

It would be difficult to imagine a future of greater beauty or greater joy. In dramatic contrast to scenarios of despair, the Jesus story presents homecoming truth 8: *We overcome hopelessness with a love that will never end and will one day fill the world.* What lessons on spirituality can we draw from such a truth? Two come to mind.

1. *Pursue the discipline of simplicity.* Though we have talked little about spiritual disciplines, one discipline demands comment as a response to the truths about the future of Jesus: the discipline of simplicity. This discipline is not only about living on little. At its heart is the practice of "willing one thing."

First John 3:3 is a verse that connects the future of Jesus with the discipline of simplicity: "Everyone who has this hope in him purifies himself, just as he is pure." The purity of which John speaks is a single-minded focus on the coming kingdom and its coming King. It sees the present as the hidden but indomitable march of the ascended Lord to his appointed glory. We need to tap the power inherent in visionary goal setting in order to deepen our experience of the future of Jesus.

This discipline is greatly needed by modern Christians. As Os Guinness writes, "The trouble is that, as modern people, we have too much to live with and too little to live for." What is needed is a sense of calling. We need to know "the purpose for which we were created and to which we are called."[16] Guinness defines this calling as follows: "the truth that God calls us to himself so decisively that everything we are, everything we do, and everything we have is invested with a special devotion and dynamism lived out as a response to his summons and service."[17]

The Puritan William Perkins in the 1590s wrote an important book on calling called *On Vocation*. He made the important distinction between a *general* and a *particular* call. A general call is all-encompassing and focuses on relationships not work. A particular call is more work-related or ministry-related.

This distinction is critical. Many of us have vision statements for our work but not our life. Our first calling is not to do something but to be with Someone. God must become our highest pleasure and treasure. Through Christ and the story he has inaugurated, this is now possible. We need to identify a general calling that can make the experience of God more important than anything else in life.

I learned this lesson the hard way. Some years ago ministry was everything to me. My whole reason for being was tied up with what I could do for the Lord. I had a vision statement, but it was too much geared toward ministry. The Lord permitted me to go through a crisis in my place of ministry that shook me to my foundations. I realized that my purpose needed to change. I needed a sense of calling that transcended my job. I needed a life purpose that I could pursue even after retirement, even into eternity. I found some practical wisdom in Stephen Covey's writings on effective habits. I developed the discipline of simplicity in which I identified my general and more ultimate purpose for living. I learned to plan my week around this higher calling. It has held me in good stead.

We all need a sense that we are in this Jesus story and heading toward a glorious future. We could develop exile-type purpose statements, full of arrogant Prometheanism or indulgent prodigality. But if the Jesus story makes its mark, we will give up lesser visions.

Only by winning a personal victory in this area of focusing on the call to come home daily to enjoy the Father's love can we go into our work with the inner resources we need. The Jesus story with its future orientation can help us to simplify our lives and pursue the most important things.

2. *Reject the way of despair by exercising faith in future grace.* This single-minded focus on the present and future triumphs of Christ can

be aided by another discipline of the Christian life—"faith in future grace." This is John Piper's phrase for the confident faith that looks ahead to all that God wants to do for us and be for us in Jesus. Why do we need this future-oriented faith? I agree with the diagnosis of Dallas Willard:

> To love strongly and creatively in the kingdom of the heavens, we need to have firmly fixed in our minds what our future is to be like. We want to live fully in the kingdom now, and for that purpose our future must make sense to us. It must be something we can now plan or make decisions in terms of, with clarity and joyful anticipation. In this way our future can be incorporated into our life now and our life now can be incorporated into our future.[18]

But many Christians are obsessed with the losses of the past not the treasures of the future. Willard continues:

> I meet many faithful Christians who, in spite of their faith, are deeply disappointed in how their lives have turned out. Sometimes it is simply a matter of how they experience aging, which they take to mean they no longer *have* a future. But often, due to circumstances or wrongful decisions and actions by others, what they had hoped to accomplish in life they did not.[19]

What is the hope for such people?

> Much of the distress of these good people comes from a failure to realize that their life lies before them. . . . What is of significance is the kind of person they have become. Circumstances and other people are not in control of an individual's character or of the life that lies endlessly before us in the kingdom of God.[20]

The lesson of Matthew 25 is that we cannot live without faith in future grace. This is the great antidote to the despair implied in Peter's question, "Is it worth it?" Piper is convinced that "radical, free obedience to Jesus Christ comes only through the channel of faith in future grace. And that channel is the embracing and cherishing and trusting and enjoying of all that God promises to be for us in Jesus."[21]

Meditating on the personal return of Christ and all the benefits that he will give his church on that day (not speculating on the arcana of Bible prophecy) should have a transforming impact on our lives. As Piper elaborates:

> When we rely on God who raises the dead (2 Cor. 1:9), and revel in the hope of the glory of God (Rom. 5:2), we don't yield to the sinful pleasures of the moment. We are not suckered in by advertising that says the one with the most toys wins. We don't devote our best energies to laying up treasures on earth. We don't dream our most exciting dreams about accomplishments and relationships that perish. We don't fret over what this life fails to give us. Instead we savor the wonder that the Owner and Ruler of the universe loves us, and has destined us for the enjoyment of his glory, and is working infallibly to bring us to his eternal kingdom. So we live to meet the needs of others, because God is living to meet our needs (Isa. 64:4; 41:10; 2 Chron. 16:9; Ps. 23:6).[22]

This faith in future grace should alter our personal landscapes. It should make us answer with Peter, "Yes, Lord, it's worth it."

The Last Battle

Augustine, at the end of his epic interpretation of history, *The City of God,* envisioned what our future will be because of the power of the Jesus story: "There we shall rest and see, see and love, love and praise. This is what shall be in the end without end. For what other end do we propose to ourselves than to attain to the kingdom of which there is no end?"[23]

Commenting on this vision, Dallas Willard adds one significant addition:

> And yet for all their beauty and goodness, these words do not seem to me to capture the blessed condition of the restoration of all things—of the kingdom come in its utter fullness. Repose, yes. But not as quiescence, passivity, eternal fixity. It is, instead, peace as wholeness, as fullness of function, as the restful but unending creativity involved in a cosmos wide, cooperative pursuit of a created order that continuously approaches but never reaches the limitless goodness and greatness of the triune personality of God its source.[24]

Perhaps, then, better than the benediction to history given by Augustine is the one given by C. S. Lewis in *The Last Battle:*

And for us this is the end of all the stories and we can most truly say that they all lived happily ever after. But for them it was only the beginning of the real story. All their life in this world and all their adventures in Narnia had only been the cover and the title page: now at last they were beginning Chapter One of the Great Story, which no one on earth has read: which goes on for ever: in which every chapter is better than the ones before.[25]

THE STORY OF MY LIFE

RESPONDING TO JESUS

We are not our own: let not our reason and will, therefore, sway our plans and deeds. We are not our own: let us not see it as our goal to seek what is expedient for us according to the flesh. We are not our own: in so far as we can, let us forget ourselves and all that is ours.

John Calvin, *Institutes of the Christian Religion*

Then he said to them all: "If anyone would come after me, he must deny himself and take up his cross daily and follow me."

Luke 9:23

The Story of My Life

"Tell me the story about the woman," the Girl asked Peter. "You know, Peter, the one about the woman at the well." Peter nodded. He remembered the story. Jesus had told him all about the episode. Many years had passed since Jesus had ascended to heaven. The followers of Jesus had gathered in Jerusalem around Passover to find out how everyone was doing and to share stories about what the risen Christ was continuing to do in their midst. The Philosopher and the Theologian both reported on progress in India and Egypt respectively. The African was encouraged by signs and wonders going on in her continent. The Girl's work with university students was going well.

Peter was also doing well. But no one really wanted to hear his report. What they all wanted was one more story about Jesus. Peter, like some of the other apostles, thought about getting a ghostwriter to help him write down some of the stories. Until that happened, however, the movement demanded more stories to feed its faith and fan its devotion. For some reason the Girl loved the story about the woman at the well, a story she had heard a dozen times.

"One day," Peter began, and everyone eased back into their chairs, "as Jesus and his disciples were passing through Samaria . . ."

They came to the village of Sychar, which was near the plot of ground Jacob had given to his son Joseph. Jesus was tired and hot when they reached an old well near the town. It was about noon, and Jesus sent his disciples into Sychar to buy some food.

As he sat on the edge of the well, a woman came to draw water. She was attractive, and though it was midday, the woman was dressed to kill. Her hair was freshly curled, and the heavy red gloss on her lips sparkled in the Samaritan sun. Her dress was low cut. She carried the water jar on her shoulder like it was a prop in a fashion show in which she was the featured model.

She glanced at Jesus but said nothing as she lowered her jar by a rope into the old well. After pulling the jar up again, she placed it on the edge of the well near Jesus.

"Excuse me," Jesus said. "Would you give me some of that water, please? I'm very thirsty."

"Don't ask me for water, Rabbi," she replied. "You are obviously some Jewish holy man. And as we have all heard ad nauseam, one drop of water from my jar would make you unclean before your so-called God. So much for Jewish spirituality." With an indignant air, the woman turned to leave. Jesus spoke again.

"If you knew all that the 'so-called' God wanted to do for you and if you knew who I was, you would be asking me for a drink—not of water from this well but living water that gives incredible satisfaction."

She did not answer at first. She knew most of the slick clichés men used to manipulate women, but this didn't sound like a line. She didn't like his tone, however, and his air of self-confidence.

"So you're an expert on water. I suppose you know a better place to get water than our father Jacob. And I can see you really came prepared to get this great water of yours. You don't even have a jar."

"I'm not trying to insult Jacob or the water in this well," replied Jesus with a smile. "My point is simply that everyone who drinks this well water will thirst again. But whoever drinks the water I give him will never thirst again. In fact, once you drink my living water it becomes a bubbling spring inside you. Every day you live, it will flow through your heart and soul and satisfy like nothing else in life."

"Sure it will, and I bet you have some land in Tel Aviv that you'd like to sell me," she said with sarcasm.

"No land in Tel Aviv. Just living water."

"I come to the well and I get a lecture on water. But I understand your riddles. You're trying to give me some kind of God sales pitch so I'll clean up my life. Let me tell you something about religion. I have my religion and you have yours. I believe in spirituality too, you know. But I believe in laissez-faire spirituality, where everybody gets to do his or her own thing. You know what I mean?"

Jesus answered by saying, "I am the way, the truth, and the life. No man comes to the Father but by me."

"You're not supposed to say things like that," the woman said with anger. "In this day and age it's not spiritually correct. It's arrogant, it's divisive, it's . . ."

". . . true," said Jesus.

"I'll tell you what's true," the woman replied. "Love is true. It's the only thing I believe in. I hate to go home to an empty house, an empty bed. Love is the way, the truth, and the life."

"Does your husband share your convictions that sexual love is the path of life?"

"I'm not married," the woman answered, tossing back her curls and smoothing her dress.

"Not married at this moment, you mean. You have, in fact, had five husbands, and the man you are currently living with is not your husband."

The woman was shaken by these words for they were true, yet Jesus was a perfect stranger to her. She tried to regroup.

"Who told you about my personal life?" asked the woman.

"I know your old story. I also know there is another story you could enter and enjoy."

"You've got your story and I've got mine. We all play the cards we've been dealt. I've tried changing a million times. It never works. But I make the best of it."

"Making the best of an old story is not good enough," Jesus said softly, still sitting on the edge of the well.

The woman was beginning to perspire. She continued.

"One of my husbands, number three I think, was a psychiatrist. He used to tell me that people like you suffer from delusions of grandeur. He also believed that religion is just a crutch, an illusion of wishful thinking. So I don't need to listen to anything you have to say. I know what you must think of me, but why should I care about the opinion of a lunatic?"

"I tell you the truth, whoever hears my word and believes him who sent me has eternal life and will not be condemned; he has crossed over from death to life," Jesus replied.

"You're crazy," screamed the woman. She waved wildly at him as if to tell him to go away. Her arm knocked the water jar over and it smashed on the ground.

"Look what you made me do," the woman shouted, bursting into tears.

"What about my offer?" Jesus said to the woman.

"What offer?"

"The living water. If you're thirsty, come to me and drink. If you believe in me, then out of your innermost being will flow living water. Drink that water and a whole new story will open up."

She stood motionless and silent, staring at the ground.

Jesus moved from the well's edge and knelt on the ground. He began gathering the pieces of the jar.

"Why are you doing that?" asked the woman, still sobbing. "It's no good now. It's broken."

"I'm very good at picking up broken pieces and putting them back together," Jesus said, continuing to collect the pieces.

They talked for several more hours. The woman poured out her whole life story to Jesus, and the parts she left out Jesus filled in. He knew more about her than she knew about herself. Halfway through the conversation, the woman felt that Jesus not only knew the story of her life but that somehow, in a way she could not understand, he was a part of her story. By the end of the conversation, she was convinced that she was a part of *his* story—a story so different from the love stories and power stories of her day that it struck her as a brand-new script for her life. She began to believe that she could be part of this new story for the rest of her life.

Many more things happened that day. The disciples returned, wondering what Jesus was doing with such a floozy. He never explained.

The woman herself rounded up most of the villagers and told them that the Messiah had come and was sitting on Jacob's well. One by one, as they spoke with him, doubts vanished, old wounds were healed, and they found themselves responding to Jesus. The woman watched as others told Jesus stories like her own, stories of bitterness, skepticism, sin, and doubt. She saw Jesus take those stories and turn them into stories of new beginnings, new kinds of love, and new faith. She felt good. She felt new.

Jesus was right about the water too. She never did go back to the well. She never went back to Sychar for that matter. She followed Jesus that day and all the days that followed. One day someone asked her whatever happened to her convictions about New Age spirituality and romantic love as the greatest thing in life. Her response that day was puzzling. She no longer believed those things she said. Why not, she was asked. She smiled and said, "Because he told me the story of my life." (Based on John 4:1–38.)

The Revenge of God: Evaluating the Modern Quest for Spiritual Life

The obituary in the British newsmagazine *The Economist* caught me by surprise. In their millennial issue they had an obituary for God. But as Mark Twain once said, the reports of his death have been greatly exaggerated. Harvard political scientist Samuel Huntington has documented that one of the most surprising features of the post–cold war world is the return of religion. *La Revanche le Deux*, he calls it—the revenge of God. So best-sellers on spirituality abound. The great search for God is on.

In the opening story, the search for God takes place beside a village well. Jesus strikes up a conversation with a femme fatale from Sychar, and sparks begin to fly. The sparks ignite new ideas and new narratives, however, and by the end of the story, the woman has not only a new address (as a roving disciple of Jesus) but also a new script. Her old story is left behind. A new plot for her future is discovered. She never looks back.

Spirituality, we have said, is not so much about states as it is about stories. We will never get closer to God than our stories allow. Choose an exile story in which pleasant thoughts of God obscure deeper enmity against him and your spirituality is doomed before you start. Choose the homecoming story that Jesus came to tell and God comes running down the road like a father meeting his lost but greatly loved child. After that reunion comes celebration and a life of sonship.

But does the homecoming story of Jesus deal with the issues? We have looked at a number of life issues so far. We have insisted that any spirituality worth taking seriously needs to provide answers for these issues. Let me mention the key issues for contemporary spirituality one more time:

1. The issue of dullness: How do I find life and enthusiasm in a world grown dull and bored?
2. The issue of emptiness: How do I find love in a world that has forgotten how to love?
3. The issue of loneliness: How do I find community and peace in a world of diversity and differences?
4. The issue of homelessness: How do I find a place to belong in a world of enmity and alienation?
5. The issue of fatherlessness: How do I find truth and wisdom in a world of confusing ideologies and competing theories?
6. The issue of evil: How do I find comfort and justice in a world of evil and suffering?
7. The issue of powerlessness: How do I find the power to love and live in a world that overwhelms me and saps my strength and energy?
8. The issue of hopelessness: How do I find hope and vision in a world that is uncertain about the future?
9. The issue of aimlessness: How do I find direction and purpose in a world that has no direction?

We've taken a look at how new models of spirituality, such as Deepak Chopra's mystic model, deal with these issues. To a lesser degree we've made passing reference to how moral models of spirituality, represented by Stephen Covey, might respond. Their answer to most of the nine challenges is to "go up." We need to raise our consciousness higher says Chopra. We need to raise our habits higher says Covey. While there is truth in both of their models, something very important is being overlooked.

In contrast to these models that point *up*, the model of Jesus points *back*. History rather than the heavens is the transformation zone where lives can be changed and God can be found. Only by going back to the story of Jesus can we go forward into the future with the spiritual resources needed to face the challenges of life.

So we have spent our time cruising through the first-century sources on the life of Christ, scrutinizing the Jesus story, and measuring its potential for effective spirituality. What discoveries have we made? Let me mention two.

First, the Jesus story as a whole responds to the issues of life. The overall response to each of the issues is that the Jesus story is a comprehensive answer to the challenges of life and the search for spirituality. I have argued in the previous pages that the greatest relevance of Jesus for our day and the greatest power to transform our lives is the story that he has to tell, a story in which he is the main character. In contrast to the exile stories that most of us live by, the Jesus story is a story of a double homecoming. Through the life, death, resurrection, and ascension of Jesus, the God who created the world has returned to us in favor and in blessing. At the same time, by entering and experiencing the Jesus story, we can return to this God, who wants to call us his children and whom we can call Father. This master narrative can lead to an authentic spirituality in which the true and living God is not only encountered but also enjoyed. True spirituality, therefore, in light of the Jesus story, is learning to live in and live out the story of Jesus.

Second, the Jesus story in its various stages responds to specific life issues. How does the Jesus story provide specific answers to the challenges we all face? To the eight issues we have looked at so far, the story of Jesus is a story of great promise:

1. How do I restore color to my life when everything has gone gray? This addresses the problem of boredom and dullness in life. Only by going back to the Jesus story do I experience the *love that turns water into wine.*
2. How do I find love and the ability to love in a world that has forgotten how to love? Human sin has driven so much real love

from our midst that the effects may seem irreparable. Most of our attempts to find love are made impotent by the exile stories that limit growth and real intimacy with God. Only by going back to the homecoming story of Jesus can I go forward to receive the love of God and others. Faith in him, fueled by his story, opens up my future because it teaches me that *love's power is unleashed by a story that leads us home.*

3. How do I find community and peace in a world of diversity and differences? Because of the Jesus story, I know that *love comes to me as a stranger from a strange land.* By going back to experience the birth of Jesus, I can go forward with a God who breaks into our world to build unity amid diversity.

4. How do I find a place to belong in a world of enmity and alienation? Utopian visions try to meet this need, but they disappoint in the end. The Jesus story teaches me that *love brings in the new world order by first becoming the new world order.* By going back to experience the baptism and temptation of Jesus, I can go forward with God as my Father and this world as my Father's house.

5. How do I find truth and wisdom in a world of confusing ideologies and competing theories? Into this world without fathers, without sources of wisdom and guidance, Jesus comes. The Jesus story overcomes confusion and competing claims on truth by teaching me the heart of wisdom: *Love is found only by those who lose it.* By going back to the kingdom vision of Jesus, I can go forward with a new master narrative that lights the path ahead.

6. How do I find comfort and justice in a world of evil and suffering? The Jesus story teaches me that *love conquers evil by becoming its victim.* By going back to the death of Jesus, I can go forward into a future confident that evil and suffering are not the last word but have been dealt with decisively by Jesus.

7. How do I find the power to love and live in a world that overwhelms me and saps my strength and energy? The Jesus story teaches me that the *love that is stronger than death is the greatest power in the world.* By going back to the resurrection of Jesus, I can go forward with the same power that raised him from the dead.

8. How do I find hope and vision in a world that is uncertain about the future? The Jesus story teaches me that *love will never end and will one day fill the world.* By going back to the future of Jesus, I can go forward into a future with Jesus.

These are the homecoming truths that shape the lives of those who experience the story of Jesus for themselves.

But one more life issue remains to be addressed. It is an issue raised in the opening story by the aimless life of the woman at the well. How do I find direction and purpose in a world that has no direction? For the woman, her personal answer involved serial marriages and various affairs. Seasoning her selfism was a heavy dash of laissez-faire spirituality.

In this closing chapter, I want to suggest another way forward. How do I find direction and purpose in a world that has no direction? The Jesus story teaches a final homecoming truth: *Love demands all and gives what it demands.* By going back to the demands of Jesus, I can go forward in union with him.

In Luke 9:23, Jesus made the following demands: "If anyone would come after me, he must deny himself and take up his cross daily and follow me." These three demands of Luke 9:23, if taken together, make up the proper response to the Jesus story we have been telling. They are also the path to experiencing the story of Jesus in a transforming way.

Response #1: Deny Yourself by Rejecting Your Old Story

In the opening story, the woman shares with Jesus her belief that love is all there is. At first she defends her belief in eroticism, but then it becomes clear that she doesn't know how to break its slavish hold on her.

"I've tried changing a million times. It never works. But I make the best of it." With these words she brushes off the bondage that she feels helpless to break. Jesus isn't so easily brushed off, however.

"Making the best of an old story is not good enough," he tells the woman, and in so doing hints at the starting point of true spirituality. To go forward with the Jesus story, we must first reject our old stories.

What does this involve? When Jesus in Luke 9:23 commanded us to deny ourselves, he wasn't thinking of giving up chocolate for Lent or going on a new diet. He had something more radical and comprehensive in mind.

John Calvin, in his classic exposition of Luke 9:23, moves us closer to a proper understanding of self-denial. "We are not our own: let not our reason and will, therefore, sway our plans and deeds. We are not our own: let us not see it as our goal to seek what is expedient for us according to the flesh. We are not our own: in so far as we can, let us forget ourselves and all that is ours."[1]

If we are not our own, then who do we belong to? If we are not the author of our own story, then who is the author to whose plot we must submit? Calvin continues.

> Conversely, we are God's: let us therefore live for him and die for him. We are God's: let all the parts of our life accordingly strive toward him as our only lawful goal. O, how much has that man profited who, having been taught that he is not his own, has taken away dominion and rule from his own reason that he may yield it to God.[2]

Calvin correctly senses that the real issues of spirituality are ownership and authorship: Who runs my life? Whose story am I living out?

In Philippians 2:3, Paul picks up these issues of ownership and authorship. He reminds the new Christians of Philippi what the old story of their lives looks like and what they need to do with that old story. "Do nothing out of selfish ambition or vain conceit," he writes. Selfish ambition and vain conceit are the watchwords of Promethean plots and narcissistic narratives. They lead to a lifestyle that Jesus rejected during his experience of temptation in the wilderness: seizure and selfism. Selfish ambition speaks of a master narrative of grabbing. Vain conceit echoes the narcissistic voice of self-worship.

As I have insisted throughout this book, our actions flow from a certain kind of story. We have deeply internalized the stories of exile from God and rebellion from God captured in Luke 15. We have become elder brothers of enmity and arrogance. We have become prodigal sons absorbed by the pursuit of pleasure. We are a cast of characters. Our soul is a theater upon whose stage the angry story of these two sons is daily performed. We are the arrogant and angry Pharisee one day and the indulgent prodigal the next.

Our lives are vicious circles spent in the service of an all-consuming selfism that teaches us to seize what we want because God cannot be trusted to give us the good we desire. I am the prodigal. I am the elder brother. What both these lost sons have in common is a low view of the father. He is a drag and a bore to the prodigal. He is a hard taskmaster who cannot be trusted to the elder brother. I have these attitudes in my heart. I am allergic to God. I sometimes view sin as the path of joy that God's law prevents me from following. That is perverse. I sometimes view God as cruel and uncaring.

This pattern of seizure and selfism is ugly and unsatisfying. The story that our lives follow when elder brothers and far country prodigals are writing the script is a story of exile. The issue is not to try to make our exile story as pretty as possible or as comfortable as we can. That's what the woman at the well tried to do. She was powerless to change her story because she never fully rejected the master narratives of Prometheanism and narcissism upon which her life was based.

Do you feel like your life is a soap opera of vain conceit and selfish ambition? Are you sick of the soap opera, the miserable story line of seizure and selfism? Good. Daily homecoming involves rejecting the old story. I don't want to live there anymore. I want a father. I want a home. I want another story. That's step one in experiencing the story of Jesus—rejecting the old story of seizure and selfism. To grow spiritually, we must reject this old story every day.

Response #2: Take Up Your Cross Daily by Entering the Jesus Story

In the opening story, Jesus ruffled the feathers of the woman by declaring, "I am the way, the truth, and the life." Even though this was a politically incorrect statement in her eyes, she eventually came to accept it as true.

Jesus promised the woman that there was another story she could follow—his own story. Taking up the cross means entering each day into the Jesus story of which the cross is the center. Taking up the cross does not simply mean suffering. It means following the pattern of Good Friday and Easter Sunday in the life of Jesus. When we enter the Jesus story by believing in his death and resurrection, we make a surprising discovery. That pattern of death and resurrection becomes the pattern of our lives.

Philippians 2:5–11 describes the great script that characterizes not only the life of Christ but the lives of all who follow Christ:

> Your attitude should be the same as that of Christ Jesus: Who, being in very nature God, did not consider equality with God something to be grasped, but made himself nothing, taking the very nature of a servant, being made in human likeness. And being found in appearance as a man, he humbled himself and became obedient to death—even death on a cross! Therefore God exalted him to the highest place and gave him the name that is above every name, that at the name of Jesus

every knee should bow, in heaven and on earth and under the earth, and every tongue confess that Jesus Christ is Lord, to the glory of God the Father.

After we turn our backs on the old story daily, what alternative story should we enter? The great answer to this question is the story of Jesus. There is a story so powerful, so liberating, so transforming that it acts as a bridge to carry us away from the old story into the powerful experience of the new story we want.

We see many things in Philippians 2:5–11: We see Jesus' equality with God, yet his voluntary act of emptying his divine glory while on earth. We see the servanthood, the humility, the suffering, and finally the death. Then amazingly we see exaltation and victory and glory coming from the ashes of his humiliation.

How did he live in and live out this pattern of humiliation and exaltation? Let me mention two key elements of the Jesus story, referred to in previous chapters, that explain why this pattern of the cross is so powerful both for him and for us. The two main elements underlying this pattern are *sonship* and *surrender*. Unlike the elder son in the parable of Luke 15, and unlike the prodigal who rejected the goodness of the father, Jesus gladly surrenders to the Father's will. He never gets angry at the Father or doubts his goodness. Even his cry of forsakenness from the cross is not a Promethean cry of defiance. Just a moment later he says to the Father, "Into your hands I commend my spirit." Why? Why can he do this? What gives him the ability to trust God so radically that he can surrender every right and every privilege and endure every outrage with patience? How did Jesus surrender so willingly to the pattern of the cross?

The answer is sonship. This is the reason for his glad and patient surrender in verses 5–11. Jesus was convinced that his Father was the fountain and source of life in all areas. He knew that the riches of his Father's love would restore his divine glory and privileges. By verse 11 the Father had done exactly that. At his baptism in Matthew 3:17, Jesus had been so filled with a powerful sense of sonship through the Spirit that he never doubted his Father's heart. He could endure suffering in faith and joy. In the temptation in the wilderness, the enemy attacked the goodness of the Father, implying that if Jesus' sonship experience was so great, why was he hungry, unknown, and uncrowned? Jesus resisted the temptation by surrendering to the Father's good story. The best things in life, Christ believed, are given not seized.

What does this mean for us? The way to leave behind the old story and gain the new story of life in the Spirit is by embracing the Jesus story. We are on one bank of the river in bondage to our old story. We see across the river to the new life we want, the story of life in the Spirit. How do we get across? The Jesus story of humiliation and exaltation is the bridge that takes us from one side to the other. Like Jesus we must believe in the reality of sonship and the power of surrender.

This is the path of life, this is the story that liberates—the story of sonship and surrender to the truth of sonship. When we daily renew that sonship relationship with God as our all-powerful and all-sufficient Father, we will stop our habit of seizure and selfism and enter into the joys of sonship and surrender. This kind of crossbearing spirituality looks dirty, gritty, and even secular sometimes. But it involves being a follower after the historical Jesus (not just the risen Lord) in his state of humility—that is, when his glory was veiled. If we go down with him to the cross, we will also rise with him in triumph and in power.

That is exactly our situation today. Jesus, though risen, moves through the world with his glory hidden. Newspapers can't see him. TV cameras don't pick up his travels. But the eyes of faith can follow his movements. We detect Jesus heading off to Samaria, or the slums, or the shop, or the market. He calls us to go with him. Spirituality involves smelling the scent of first-century sandal dust in the air. The one who did his most spiritual work in tax offices or marketplaces is leading us through every event of every day. He leads us along this crooked path that goes down into the grave before rising in new life.

True spirituality is a matter of getting used to the gospel. It means living in and living out the pattern of the cross and the resurrection. We must renew our commitment to this pattern of the cross daily. This is the second demand of Jesus.

Response #3: Follow Jesus into the New Story of Life in the Spirit

Jesus, in his conversation with the woman, makes constant reference to life in the Spirit using the imagery of living water. "If you're thirsty, come to me and drink. If you believe in me, then out of your innermost being will flow living water. Drink that water and a whole new story will open up."

By the end of the story, the woman at the well has changed. She discovered something in the words of Jesus that gave her new direction. When she told others about her discovery, they seemed to change too: "The woman watched as others told Jesus stories like her own, stories of bitterness, skepticism, sin, and doubt. She saw Jesus take those stories and turn them into stories of new beginnings, new kinds of love, and new faith. She felt good. She felt new."

This is the third demand of Jesus—that we follow him into this new life in the Spirit. After rejecting the old story and entering the Jesus story comes the enjoyment of the new story of Spirit-controlled living.

In Philippians 2:1–2, Paul describes the new story that Jesus' followers can enjoy. Once we are in union with Christ and have entered his story, we can expect a life like his. What is the new story that Jesus calls us to? Listen to Paul outline the possibilities: "If you have any encouragement from being united with Christ, if any comfort from his love, if any fellowship with the Spirit, if any tenderness and compassion, then make my joy complete by being like-minded, having the same love, being one in spirit and purpose." Life in the Spirit is filled with these benefits of encouragement, comfort, love, and purpose.

The pattern of the cross is the means of spirituality. Becoming like Christ is the goal of spirituality. By faith we enter into a strong bond of union with him that nothing can break. The pattern of the cross precedes this third step. It leads to the experience of the power of the resurrection.

Colossians 3:1 describes this third step: "Since, then, you have been raised with Christ, set your hearts on things above, where Christ is seated at the right hand of God." What the homecoming story of the Gospels tells us is not how far away the right hand of God is but rather how close it is. His throne room lies just behind the veil of visible reality. It is so close that the Spirit-filled believer can taste it. By drawing down his gifts and grace each day, we can live a life characterized by the nine fruits of the Spirit mentioned in Galatians 5:22–23: love, joy, peace, patience, kindness, goodness, faithfulness, gentleness, and self-control. Who wouldn't want to live this way? Who wouldn't want to have a marriage, family life, job relationships, friendships, and church fellowship filled to the brim and beyond with such quality and greatness?

This new story is life in the Spirit as described in Romans 8. Recall the benefits of this life mentioned previously:

- Benefit #1: No condemnation—freedom from the curse of sin (Rom. 8:1–4)
- Benefit #2: No bondage—freedom from sin (8:5–14)
- Benefit #3: No fear—freedom from alienation and exile (8:15–17)
- Benefit #4: No despair—freedom from decay and death (8:18–25)
- Benefit #5: No silence—freedom from broken communication with God (8:26–27)
- Benefit #6: No mistakes—freedom from chance (8:28)
- Benefit #7: No limits—freedom from want (8:32)
- Benefit #8: No guilt—freedom from accusation (8:33–37)
- Benefit #9: No separation—freedom from falling away (8:38–39)

Embracing the new story means believing in the Father and in his fullness. "How much more will your Father in heaven give good gifts to those who ask him!" (Matt. 7:11). The greatest gift of all is the Spirit himself, who now infuses this resurrected life within us. So we must ask, How big is our Father's house? How much does he own?

When I was young, my father was a giant and my home was a vast country. As I grew up, my sense of my father's size and my home's vastness shriveled. I lost a sense of wonder. Only in these last years have I really begun to realize the values and deep faithfulness to God that have characterized my father's life. I have grown to appreciate the wealth of character and quality that define who he is. When I return to the place where my parents live, I realize that it has a beauty and a depth that I could never exhaust.

Similarly, after decades of overly small thoughts of God, I am learning that my Father's bounty and his area of control are as big in scope as all of life, as all of my longings, and as all of my heart. I am learning to hear the Father whisper to me each day the words of Luke 15:31: "You are always with me, and everything I have is yours." All my inner and outer needs can be met by such a Father.

To unleash the Jesus story, we must do more than reject our old stories and embrace the story of the cross. For true spirituality to blossom, we must want the fullness that is in our Father and our Father's house. We must want life in the Spirit. We must want the new story of homecoming. This is the third direction of Luke 9:23: following Jesus into the fullness of the homecoming experience. This is the way, the truth, and the life.

The Legions of Cleopas

G. K. Chesterton once said that we continue to read *The Iliad* because it reminds us that life is a battle; the *Odyssey* because life is a journey; and the Book of Job because life is a riddle. I would add that we continue to read the Gospels because life is a story of hope and salvation. Because of the Jesus story we can change the stories of our lives. We don't need to live out Homer's *Iliad* or *Odyssey*. We don't need to get stuck in the riddle of Job. We have a new plot for our lives, a new path out of the battles, the trials, the riddles.

This is what the woman at the well discovered. It is the final homecoming truth: Love demands all and gives what it demands. By going back to the demands of Jesus, we can go forward in union with him. We have looked at the three demands that will help us to both go back and go forward: (1) Deny the self by daily rejecting our old stories; (2) take up the cross by reentering daily into the Jesus story of Good Friday and Easter Sunday; and (3) follow Jesus by wanting the new story of life in the Spirit. These three demands show us how to experience the Jesus story for ourselves. They show us the way to true spirituality: living in and living out the story of Jesus.

Let me end our meditations on the story of Jesus and its implications for spirituality by relating one final story from the Gospel of Luke—the story of Cleopas found in Luke 24:13–35. The focus of this last chapter of Luke's history of the Messiah is not about Peter or Christ's Cape Canaveral–like launch into outer space. Mary is mentioned, but the focus is not on her. The final face that Luke illuminates in the fireworks of his grand finale is the obscure face of an obscure character who goes by the name of Cleopas.

Cleopas, you may recall, is the one who while walking with a friend on the road to his home in Emmaus encounters a stranger who seems uninformed about the dramatic events of Good Friday. With a great sadness he tells the stranger that though "we had hoped" Jesus was the Messiah, the agent of homecoming, his death destroyed that possibility. Rumors were flying, he admits, that Christ was alive, but who could believe such things? So Cleopas is trudging home to pick up his old story of life. But the stranger accompanies him home, opens the Scriptures to him, breaks bread with him, and changes his life by revealing his true identity. The mysterious stranger is none other than Jesus risen from the dead. It is a moving story of faith reborn, but it leaves me with a question. Why would Luke give the bulk of the last chapter of his Gospel to Cleopas the obscure? The answer is threefold.

246

The first reason is Luke's vision of the kind of risen Lord Jesus is.
The Jesus about whom he writes is alive and doing in the world today
what he did in the world then. Luke does not write about a cosmic
Christ who rises and becomes the untouchable and unapproachable
pantocrater of the universe—although he is all that. The Jesus moving through the world today is the same Jesus who moved through
the world then. And he comes for the same kind of people now as he
did then. He came for the little guy then. He comes for the little guy
now. He sought the marginalized then. He seeks the marginalized
now. He was a sacred shoulder to cry on then in that weeping century. He continues to comfort now. Why Cleopas? Luke wants to
remind us that Jesus hasn't really changed. He's only expanded the
business of serving the little guy.

The second reason is Luke's vision of who we are. Who are we? What
does it mean to be a twenty-first-century disciple of Jesus who like
Cleopas bears a Gentile name? Cleopas is a snapshot of ourselves.
We, like him, are walking away from Jerusalem, our backs to its history, its events, and its messianic mysteries. We are walking back
toward our obscure homes, disappointed at God, furious at the
church, snapping at strangers who pretend to be naive about life,
about death, and about the disappointments that both bring. We are
the ones who, like Cleo, have heard the reports of good news in the
cemetery but who struggle with too much unbelief and too many dead
dreams to let it change our lives too much. But it is to us that Jesus
comes, slipping in alongside us like a purring sports car in a traffic
jam. He speaks to us from Luke 24 as we inch forward on our express-
ways, making little progress, fighting the road rage of those whose
whole lives seem to be stuck in that oxymoron we call rush hour.

We don't have two heads or blind eyes or legions of demons. We
are not freaks or even unique. We are simply the vast legions of the
world's disappointed, disheartened, and disillusioned. We are the
legions of Cleopas. And it is to us that the risen One comes to set our
hearts on fire, to make sense of the story that alone makes sense of
life, and to show us his risen beauty. We are the ones, pilgrims march-
ing numbly down the great ruts of life, who will open up the bread
and break out the soda water only to have our water turned into wine,
our bread become the shape of someone from long ago, and our
kitchens become the empty tomb. We are the sons and daughters of
Adam the fool and Cleopas the downcast. And yet it is to us that the
glory of the new age in the Spirit, the new age of the risen Lord, comes
in quietness and in meekness but still in power.

The third reason is Luke's vision of what the real story of life is all about. The story of Cleopas illustrates the daily journey of true spirituality. Cleopas and his friend were walking toward home, doubting the Jesus story. With each step they were slipping back into the old exile story of Israel. Jesus meets them on the well-traveled road of disappointment. He walks with them all the way to their home. He joins them at the supper table. And as he walks with Cleopas and dines with him, Jesus retells his story of homecoming. The true and living God has returned to begin the new world order. Jesus is proof of that. His birth, life, death, and resurrection tell the story of the inbreaking of the kingdom of God.

By rediscovering the Jesus story that he already knew but had trouble believing, Cleopas is changed. This is not the change of a Covey or a Chopra. Cleopas is not practicing either mysticism or moralism. What changes the familiar is the presence of the past. The story of Jesus breaks out of time and space. It reenters Cleopas's story and changes his life. Swept up in this new story, Cleopas meets the demands of Jesus. He gives up his old exile story of dashed hopes and unbelief. He walks with Jesus along the road of life, experiencing the pattern of humiliation and resurrection. He follows Jesus into new life in the Spirit. The light dawns. A mini-resurrection of faith, hope, and love occurs in Cleopas's mind and heart. His unspectacular Emmaus flat is transformed into a room in his Father's house. All this comes from meeting Jesus through stories and Scripture. From such encounters, Cleopas finds the power to deny himself, to take up his cross, and to follow the risen One.

So thank you, Father, for such journeys of rediscovery. Thank you for the chance to leave the shores of our old stories of exile. Thank you for the chance to walk out on the waves with you and ride the peaks and valleys of humiliation and exaltation. Thank you for the new story of Jesus that guides us back to our familiar shore and opens our eyes to the kingdom of God around us and opens our ears to the transforming whisper, "I am always with you, and everything I have is yours."

NOTES

CHAPTER 1

1. Douglas Coupland, *Life after God* (New York: Pocket Books, 1994), 359.

2. Philip Zalesky, Amazon spirituality e-mail newsletter, 30 November 1991, 1.

3. Ibid.

4. Ibid.

5. Eugene Peterson, *Subversive Spirituality* (Grand Rapids: Eerdmans, 1997), 34–35.

6. The Dalai Lama and Howard Cutler, M.D., *The Art of Happiness: Handbook for Living* (London: Hodder & Stoughton, 1998).

7. Lama Surya Das, *Awakening to the Sacred: Creating a Spiritual Life from Scratch* (London: Bantam, 1999), 371.

8. Leslie Kenton, *Journey to Freedom: Thirteen Quantum Leaps for the Soul* (London: HarperCollins, 1998), 8.

9. Ibid.

10. Deepak Chopra, *How to Know God* (London: Harmony Press, 2000); *The Path to Love: Spiritual Lessons for Creating the Love You Need* (London: Rider, 1997).

11. Comment on John 10:10 in Frank Gaebelein and J. D. Douglas, eds., *Expositor's Bible Commentary* (Grand Rapids: Zondervan, 1989–1998).

12. Dallas Willard, *The Divine Conspiracy* (San Francisco: HarperSanFrancisco, 1998), 41.

13. Compare the discussion of these three categories as they relate to spirituality during the time of the sixteenth-century Reformation in Alister McGrath, *Roots That Refresh: A Celebration of Reformation Spirituality* (London: Hodder & Stoughton, 1991), 120ff.

14. Alister McGrath, *Christian Spirituality* (Oxford: Blackwell, 1999), 39.

15. McGrath, *Roots That Refresh*, 125.

16. John Piper, *Desiring God: Meditations of a Christian Hedonist* (Portland, Ore.: Multnomah, 1986), 18.

17. Ibid.

18. Lawrence Crabb, *Inside Out* (Colorado Springs: NavPress, 1988), 83–84.

19. Coupland, *Life after God*, 359.

NOTES

CHAPTER 2

1. Milan Kundera, *The Book of Laughter and Forgetting* (London: Faber & Faber, 1996), 124–25.

2. Quoted in Bernard Scott, *Hollywood Dreams and Biblical Stories* (Minneapolis: Fortress, 1994), 259.

3. Diogenes Allen, *Spiritual Theology* (Boston: Cowley, 1997), 22.

4. Ibid., 23.

5. Ibid.

6. Peterson, *Subversive Spirituality*, 37.

7. Henri Nouwen, *Wounded Healer* (New York: Image Books, 1972), 28.

8. Ibid., 30.

9. G. K. Chesterton, *Orthodoxy* (London: The Bodley Head, 1957), 22.

CHAPTER 3

1. McGrath, *Christian Spirituality*, 59.

2. Deepak Chopra, *The Path to Love: Spiritual Lessons for Creating the Love That You Need* (London: Rider, 1997), 3.

3. Ibid., 13.

4. Ibid., 27.

5. John Hick, "Whatever Path Men Choose Is Mine," in *Christianity and Other Religions*, ed. J. Hick and B. Hebblethwaite (London: Collins, 1980), 174.

6. Ibid., 180.

7. Ibid., 182.

8. Paul Knitter, *No Other Name: A Critical Survey of Christian Attitudes toward the World Religions* (Maryknoll, N.Y.: Orbis Books, 1985).

9. The discussion of Matthew's genealogy and its connection with the revealing history of Jesus is based on Chris Wright, *Knowing Jesus through the Old Testament* (Downers Grove, Ill.: InterVarsity Press, 1992), 9.

10. Ibid.

11. Ibid., 18.

12. Ibid., 28.

13. Ibid., 22–25.

14. Raymond Brown, *The Birth of the Messiah* (New York: Doubleday, 1977), 9.

15. Ben Witherington III, *The Jesus Quest: The Third Search for the Jew of Nazareth* (Downers Grove, Ill.: InterVarsity Press, 1995); and N. T. Wright, *Jesus and the Victory of God* (Minneapolis: Fortress, 1996).

16. It must be mentioned that not all writers associated with the third quest are as open to the contribution of the early church to the degree that Wright and Witherington are. See Wright's survey of third quest literature in *Jesus and the Victory of God*, 83–89.

17. Quoted in Vinoth Ramachandra, *The Recovery of Mission: Beyond the Pluralist Paradigm* (Grand Rapids: Eerdmans, 1996), 198.

18. C. S. Lewis, *Miracles* (New York: Macmillan, 1950), 132.

19. On this point, see the discussion in James Sire, *Why Should Anyone Believe Anything at All?* (Downers Grove, Ill.: InterVarsity Press, 1994), 143–45.

20. Ramachandra, *Recovery of Mission*, 202–3.

21. For a stimulating discussion of these points, see Sire, *Why Should Anyone Believe Anything at All?* 143–45.

22. Jürgen Moltmann, *The Way of Jesus Christ* (Minneapolis: Fortress, 1993), 137.

23. Alister McGrath, *A Passion for Truth* (Downers Grove, Ill.: InterVarsity Press, 1996), 41.

24. Patrick Johnstone, *The Church Is Bigger than You Think* (Ross-shire, U.K.: Christian Focus/WEC, 1998), 218–19.

25. John Frame, *Apologetics to the Glory of God* (Phillipsburg, N.J.: Presbyterian and Reformed), 134.

26. Lesslie Newbigin, "The Gospel according to the Religions," in *Missions Trends No. 5: Faith Meets Faith*, ed. Gerald H. Anderson and Thomas F. Stransky (New York: Paulist Fathers, 1981), 18.

27. Jonathan Edwards, *The Religious Affections* (1746; reprint, Grand Rapids: Sovereign Grace Publishers, 1971), 94.

28. Ibid., 94.

CHAPTER 4

1. Quoted in Steven Weinberg, "Five and a Half Utopias," *The Atlantic Monthly* (January 2000): 108.

2. Ibid.

3. Ibid., 109.

4. Ibid., 110.

5. Ibid., 112.

6. Ibid., 113.

7. Ibid., 114.

8. Quoted in ibid.

9. Quoted in Moltmann, *The Way of Jesus Christ*, 28.

10. Ibid., 28–29.

11. Wright, *Knowing Jesus through the Old Testament*, 104.

12. Wright, *Jesus and the Victory of God*, 485.

13. Wright, *Knowing Jesus through the Old Testament*, 106.

14. Ibid., 114.

15. Ibid., 450.

16. Wright, *Jesus and the Victory of God*, 450.

17. Sinclair Ferguson, *The Holy Spirit* (Leicester: Inter-Varsity Press, 1996), 48.

18. Moltmann, *The Way of Jesus Christ*, 93.

19. Ibid., 32.

CHAPTER 5

1. Scott, *Hollywood Dreams and Biblical Stories*, 104.

2. The eighteen references to the Father or sonship are as follows: Matthew 5:9—"sons of God"; 5:16—"praise your Father"; 5:45—"be sons of your Father in heaven"; 5:48—"be perfect . . . as your heavenly Father is perfect"; 6:1—"no reward from your Father in heaven"; 6:4—"your Father, who sees what is done in secret, will reward you"; 6:6—"pray to your Father"; 6:6—"your Father . . . will reward you"; 6:8—"your Father knows what you need"; 6:9—"our Father in heaven"; 6:14—"your heavenly Father will also forgive you"; 6:15—"your Father will not forgive your sins"; 6:18—"only to your Father"; 6:18—"your Father, who sees what is done in secret, will reward you"; 6:26—"your heavenly Father feeds them"; 6:32—"your heavenly Father knows that you need them"; 7:11—"how much more will your Father in heaven give good gifts

to those who ask him!"; 7:21—"not everyone who says to me, 'Lord, Lord,' will enter the kingdom of heaven, but only he who does the will of my Father who is in heaven."

3. Willard, *The Divine Conspiracy,* 117.

4. John Stott, *Christian Counterculture: The Message of the Sermon on the Mount* (Downers Grove, Ill.: InterVarsity Press, 1978), 19.

5. Discussed in Willard, *Divine Conspiracy,* 150.

6. Gerd Theissen, *The Shadow of the Galilean* (Minneapolis: Fortress, 1987), 123–24.

7. Willard, *Divine Conspiracy,* 269.

8. Ibid., 241–43.

9. Quoted in ibid., 267.

10. Adrio König, *The Eclipse of Christ in Eschatology* (Grand Rapids: Eerdmans, 1989), 55.

11. Ibid., 56.

12. C. C. Caragounis, "The Kingdom of God/Heaven," in *Dictionary of Jesus and the Gospels,* ed. Joel B. Green, Scot McKnight, I. Howard Marshall (Downers Grove, Ill.: InterVarsity Press, 1992), 421.

13. Ibid., 422.

14. John Stott, *Authentic Christianity* (Leicester: Inter-Varsity Press, 1992), 382.

15. Donald Bloesch, *Jesus Christ: Savior and Lord* (Downers Grove, Ill.: InterVarsity Press, 1997), 222–23.

16. Marcus Bockmuehl, *This Jesus: Martyr, Lord, Messiah* (Downers Grove, Ill.: InterVarsity Press, 1994), 126.

17. Jonathan Kozol, *Amazing Grace* (San Francisco: HarperCollins, 1996), 84.

CHAPTER 6

1. Harold S. Kushner, *When Bad Things Happen to Good People* (New York: Schocken Books, 1981).

2. Deepak Chopra, *How to Know God* (New York: Harmony Books, 2000), 65.

3. Ibid., 64.

4. Ibid.

5. Ibid., 151.

6. Ibid., 153.

7. Wright, *Jesus and the Victory of God,* 543.

8. Compare ibid., 550.

9. Ibid., 434.

10. Adrio König, *Eclipse of Christ in Eschatology,* 88.

11. Bloesch, *Jesus Christ,* 158.

12. Frame, *Apologetics to the Glory of God,* 189–90.

13. Bloesch, *Jesus Christ,* 174.

14. Quoted in James Sire, *Discipleship of the Mind* (Downers Grove, Ill.: InterVarsity Press, 1990), 180.

15. Moltmann, *The Way of Jesus Christ,* 154.

16. *Expositor's Bible Commentary,* comments on Colossians 1:19–20.

17. John Flavel, *The Works of John Flavel* (Edinburgh: Banner of Truth Trust, 1988), 418; quoted in John Piper, *Future Grace* (Sisters, Ore.: Multnomah, 1995), 117.

18. Piper, *Future Grace,* 116.

19. Paul Tillich, *The Courage to Be* (New Haven, Conn.: Yale University Press, 1952).

20. John Stott, *Evangelical Truth* (Leicester: Inter-Varsity Press, 1999), 81–82.

21. Piper, *Future Grace*, 335.
22. Os Guinness, *The Call* (Waco: Word, 1998), 121.
23. Ibid.
24. Ibid., 123.

CHAPTER 7

1. Coupland, *Life after God*, 359.
2. Chopra, *The Path to Love*, 36.
3. Ibid., 33.
4. Ibid., 11.
5. Chopra, *How to Know God*, 243.
6. Walker Percy, *Lost in the Cosmos: The Last Self-Help Book* (New York: Washington Square Press, 1983), 283.
7. Pinchas Lapide, *The Resurrection of Jesus* (Minneapolis: Augsburg, 1983), 15.
8. Ibid., 16.
9. Gregory Boyd, *God at War: The Bible and Spiritual Conflict* (Downers Grove, Ill.: InterVarsity Press, 1997), 243.
10. James Dunn, *Jesus and the Spirit* (London: SCM Press, 1975), 67.
11. Gordon Fee, *God's Empowering Presence* (Peabody, Mass.: Hendriksen, 1994), 876.
12. Ibid., 877.
13. Ibid., 878.
14. Ibid., 879.
15. Ibid., 881.
16. Ferguson, *The Holy Spirit*, 183.
17. Ibid., 184–85.
18. Piper, *Future Grace*, 124.
19. John Owen, Works, vol. 1, 253; quoted in J. I. Packer, *A Quest for Godliness* (Wheaton: Crossway Books, 1990), 189.
20. Piper, *Future Grace*, 206.
21. J. H. Bavinck, *An Introduction to the Science of Missions* (Phillipsburg, N.J.: Presbyterian and Reformed, 1960), 112–17.
22. Ibid., 112.
23. Ibid., 179
24. Ibid., 35.
25. Ibid., 36.
26. Reference must be made to the importance for missiology of Samuel Huntington's thesis about the new civilizational world order. Since the cold war era, the world has been organized into eight or nine civilizations, large cultural groupings defined not by ideology or geography so much as by culture and religion. The implications of this new concept of the world order for the mission of the church are many. Compare Samuel Huntington, *The Clash of Civilizations and the Remaking of World Order* (New York: Simon and Schuster, 1996).
27. Chopra, *The Path to Love*, 11.
28. Percy, *Lost in the Cosmos*, 283.
29. John Calvin, *Institutes of the Christian Religion*, ed. J. McNeill, trans. F. Battles, 2 vols. (Philadelphia: Westminster Press, 1960), 3.3.8.
30. Ibid., 3.3.9.
31. Wilhelm Niesel, *The Theology of Calvin* (Grand Rapids: Baker, 1980), 128.
32. Calvin, *Institutes of the Christian Religion*, 3.2.7.

CHAPTER 8

1. Bertrand Russell, "A Free Man's Worship," in *Why I Am Not a Christian*, ed. Paul Edwards (New York: Simon and Schuster, 1957), 107; quoted in Frame, *Apologetics to the Glory of God*, 36.

2. Chopra, *How to Know God*, 151.

3. König, *Eclipse of Christ in Eschatology*, 201.

4. Ben Witherington III, *Jesus, Paul, and the End of the World* (Downers Grove, Ill.: InterVarsity Press, 1992), 155.

5. König, *Eclipse of Christ in Eschatology*, 206.

6. Bruce Milne, *Know the Truth* (Downers Grove, Ill.: InterVarsity Press, 1982), 256.

7. Mark Shaw, *Doing Theology with Huck and Jim* (Downers Grove, Ill.: InterVarsity Press, 1993), 185.

8. Piper, *Future Grace*, 371.

9. C. S. Lewis, *The Last Battle* (New York: Collier, 1956), 171.

10. Jonathan Edwards, *Charity and Its Fruits* (1852; reprint, Edinburgh: Banner of Truth Trust, 1969), 342.

11. Ibid., 340.

12. Piper, *Future Grace*, 377.

13. Willard, *The Divine Conspiracy*, 383.

14. Ibid., 395.

15. Edwards, *The Religious Affections*, 162.

16. Guinness, *The Call*, 4.

17. Ibid.

18. Willard, *The Divine Conspiracy*, 376.

19. Ibid.

20. Ibid.

21. Piper, *Future Grace*, 387.

22. Ibid., 369.

23. Quoted in Willard, *The Divine Conspiracy*, 400.

24. Ibid.

25. C. S. Lewis, *The Last Battle*, 184.

CHAPTER 9

1. John Calvin, *Institutes of the Christian Religion*, 3.7.1.

2. Ibid.

Mark Shaw is a missionary professor who has spent most of the last twenty years teaching theology and church history in the African context. He is currently lecturer in theology and church history at Nairobi Evangelical Graduate School of Theology in Kenya. He is the author of *The Kingdom of God in Africa* (Baker) and two books with Inter-Varsity Press: *Doing Theology with Huck and Jim: Parables for Understanding* and *Ten Great Ideas from Church History: A Decision Makers Guide to Shaping Your Church.*